Cultural Geography

Cultural Geography

A Critical Dictionary of Key Concepts

Edited by
David Atkinson
Peter Jackson
David Sibley
Neil Washbourne

Published in 2005 by I.B.Tauris & Co Ltd
6 Salem Road, London W2 4BU
175 Fifth Avenue, New York NY 10010
www.ibtauris.com

In the United States and Canada distributed by Palgrave Macmillan,
a division of St. Martin's Press, 175 Fifth Avenue, New York NY 10010

Copyright © David Atkinson, Peter Jackson, David Sibley and Neil Washbourne, 2005

The rights of David Atkinson, Peter Jackson, David Sibley and Neil Washbourne to be identified as the authors of this work has been asserted by them in accordance with the Copyright, Designs and Patents Act 1988.

All rights reserved. Except for brief quotations in a review, this book, or any part thereof, may not be reproduced, stored in or introduced into a retrieval system, or transmitted, in any form or by any means, electronic, mechanical, photocopying, recording or otherwise, without the prior written permission of the publisher.

International Library of Human Geography 3

ISBN Hardback 1 86064 703 0
Paperback 1 86064 702 2
EAN Hardback 978 1 86064 703 1
Paperback 978 1 86064 702 4

A full CIP record for this book is available from the British Library
A full CIP record for this book is available from the Library of Congress
Library of Congress catalog card: available

Typeset in Ehrhardt by Dexter Haven Associates Ltd, London
Printed and bound in Great Britain by TJ International Ltd, Padstow, Cornwall

Contents

— Editors' Preface —

On Cultural and Critical Geographies

Cultural geography is an exciting, lively and diverse field, the energy and vitality of which is indicated by our decision to pluralise the term in this editorial preface. Cultural geographies, as currently practised, are now much wider in scope than developments within a single branch of human geography. As the essays that follow make clear, cultural geographers now routinely engage with complex but important questions about social processes such as identity formation, the construction of cultural difference, citizenship and belonging. These processes also challenge our understanding of such core geographical categories as space and place, landscape and environment, public and private. But cultural geographies, we argue, also link such ideas and imaginations with our changing material world. They allow us to explore *how* these processes are affected by increased mobility, by changes in our socio-technical environment, and by other forces that are transforming the established notions of the relationships between nature and culture. As several of the following chapters reveal, cultural geographies are also engaging with political and economic ideas about governance and flexible accumulation as the boundaries between former sub-disciplines such as cultural and economic, social and political geography, are increasingly transcended. Indeed, through its engagement with social and cultural theory, the entire field of cultural geography has been transformed, and its recent developments have prompted the rethinking of many key concepts in human geography and beyond. In addition, there are now many other social scientists as well as geographers 'doing' cultural geography (as contributors to this book themselves confirm).

The diversity of cultural geography defies easy definition. For example, the recent *Handbook of Cultural Geography* elected not to define the field but, rather, described cultural geography as an unruly affair best understood as a 'style of thought', without clearly identifiable boundaries, characterised by the valid and urgent questions that it seeks to ask (Anderson et al. 2002, xiii–xiv). In more conventional terms, it suggests that cultural geography addresses issues of distribution (where things are and why); ways of life; systems of meaning; questions of practice; and notions of power. In this collection we take a similar approach: allowing the individual essays and their authors to define the field, since more formal definitions immediately lead to problems of closure and exclusion. We would rather think of the essays that make up this creative and fuzzily bounded collection of cultural geographies as open-ended and post-disciplinary. This is reflected in their authorship: although the contributors to this volume have disciplinary identities including social anthropology, sociology, cultural studies and human geography, they are all producing cultural geographies and, in the process, they demonstrate theoretical convergences as well as refreshing differences in perspective.

Yet one thing we did encourage from our contributors was a *critical* perspective on cultural geographies. By engaging with aspects of social relations, with connections between people and the material world, and between culture and nature, the authors raise questions that are central to human well-being, but that are also political. Since cultural geographies are embedded in the politics of our contemporary world, inevitably this collection is avowedly critical in places. Several essays deal with questions of cultural difference, for example, a characteristic of societies for which, as Joel Kahn (1995, 125) has argued, we now have 'a consuming and erotic passion'. But, while cultural difference is celebrated in some realms, we must also acknowledge that difference becomes politicised when providing grounds for genocide as well as for routine, everyday oppression (as the recent history of the former Yugoslavia and Rwanda demonstrates). The political is often inescapable, and our authors reflect upon a range of political issues, such as the changing relationships between public and private space, anxieties about surveillance and the intrusion of the state into private lives, the connections between culture and nature, and environmental crises. Given the ways that power is embedded throughout society, we suggest that, in their theoretical articulation and in their engagement with social relations and questions of human well-being, cultural geographies – above all else – must be *critical*.

Although the re-invigoration of cultural geography in the early 1980s bore a marked critical edge (Cosgrove 1983, 1984; Cosgrove and Jackson 1987; Daniels 1989), the relationship between cultural geographies and a politicised perspective has proved controversial more recently. Some argue that cultural geography has lost its original critical impetus and plead for a more politicised agenda (Mitchell 2000). For others, the intangible subject matter of some cultural geography has diminished the relevance of human geography more generally, particularly when addressing practical social issues (Hamnett 2003; Storper 2001). Sympathetic voices worry that certain strains of social and cultural geography lose sight of the material geographies that underpin social worlds (Philo 2000; Jackson 2000; cf. Anderson and Tolia-Kelly 2004), while, as several authors highlight, the politics of actually *doing* critical geography varies markedly around the world (Garcia-Ramon et al. 2004; Sundberg 2005). Although far from conclusive, this debate draws attention to the relations between cultural geographies, socio-political contexts, and the politics of the knowledge we produce, disseminate and consume. And, because the history of cultural geography, as we understand it, has a substantive and enduring strain of critique, this collection seeks to explore the *critical* concepts in cultural geography further. In this respect, the book's subtitle uses the term 'critical' in two ways. First, it addresses as 'critical concepts' those that are fundamentally important to the emergence and form of cultural geography, those that provide the foundation and building blocks of our contemporary work in this area. Second, it refers to the 'critical' in terms of critique. The book serves both these meanings, but, as the second is more contentious, the rest of this introduction explores the potential for 'critical' perspectives in relation to the production of cultural geographies.

IN WHAT SENSE 'CRITICAL' KNOWLEDGE?

The project of developing ways of thinking critically (and reflexively) about the production of knowledge has a long and contested history that draws upon various theoretical perspectives and political alignments, including Marxist, feminist, postcolonial and post-structural thinking. Some of these are relatively recent developments, some have histories stretching back at least to the nineteenth century. Thus, given the sometimes contradictory and overlapping nature of these areas of thought, no simple chronology or delineation of a discrete theoretical territory is possible. Consequently, from the start of this project we recognised the decentredness of knowledge in the human sciences and the 'blurred genres' that Clifford Geertz has identified as characteristic of social thought (Geertz 1980). In the intervening years, feminism in particular and post-structuralism more generally have opened up the humanities and social sciences by challenging masculinised knowledge and claims to universal 'truths' (in geography, see McDowell and Sharp 1999; Rose 1993). In fields such as social anthropology this process has been taken further. Laura Nader (1996, 1–2), for example, cites the writing of the Yupiaq Alaskan Oscar Kwagley, who recalls that 'his great grandparents forbade his grandmother from attending school, saying that she would become dumb'. They feared that 'Western knowledge', imparted in Native Alaskan settlement schools, would erase indigenous knowledge. In refusing to use the school, the parents were resisting (neo)colonialism and rejecting assumptions about the superiority of Western knowledge hierarchies. A similar scepticism towards knowledge hierarchies also informs this book.

This collection is offered more in the spirit of Raymond Williams' *Keywords* (1976) than in the style of orthodox dictionaries of 'key concepts'. We make no attempt to be comprehensive in terms of coverage, to be definitive, or to provide the last word on any issue. Rather, borrowing from Williams' concept of 'fields of meanings', we attempt to show how some of the words, phrases and concepts we use in our everyday communication and in our academic work are invested with complex meanings that change with different contexts of use and reception, and that reflect different geographical and historical circumstances. We also share Williams' commitment to debate, to plurality, and to the cut and thrust that characterise the contemporary social science that defines itself as 'critical'.

Though Williams is a crucial reference point for discussing interrelated critical vocabularies, we should note some divergences of our project from his. For him, five words were central: 'culture', 'art', 'class', 'industry' and 'democracy', forming 'a kind of structure' (11) for the whole enterprise. We have not prioritised any of our concepts, treating each in similarly critical terms. For Williams, the frame of reference provided 'the record of an inquiry into a *vocabulary*: a shared body of words and meanings in our most general discussions, in English, of the practices and institutions we group as *culture* and *society*' (13, italics in original). This depends upon assumptions about the singularity of 'English' identity (literature, society, culture) that today seem highly questionable. Nevertheless, Williams' project provides a helpful template, and this collection explores key 'fields of meanings' in cultural geography, but with a critical inflection. Therefore, before we go any further, we want to outline and contextualise what '*critical* geography' has come to mean within Anglo-American academia.

THE MAKING OF CRITICAL GEOGRAPHIES

Although the last few years have seen 'critical geography' increasingly embedded at the heart of Anglo-American human geography, this tradition draws upon an earlier generation of radical geographies that, while centred upon Marxism, also had a range of other inspirations, including anarchism, feminism and environmentalism. Radical geography in the 1970s was articulated in opposition to the dominance of spatial science in human geography, and in sympathy with wider political processes of the period (such as the American Civil Rights movement, the global student protests of 1968, the women's movement and other forms of radical politics). Amidst all this, and galvanised by books such as David Harvey's *Social Justice and the City* (1973), Richard Peet's *Radical Geography* (1977) and the journal *Antipode*, academic geographers began to question the workings of power and authority within society – exploring how capital and the state produced unequal development at various scales, and what roles geography played within these processes. What these initiatives shared was a keen sense of the politicisation of societies and everyday lives and, concomitantly, that the spatial and geographical constitution of social life gave geography and geographers an active, if not activist, role in interrogating social processes.

One of the first uses of the term 'critical human geography' was as the title of a series of geography textbooks in the 1980s, which included Doreen Massey's *Spatial Divisions of Labour* (1984) and Derek Gregory and John Urry's *Social Relations and Spatial Structures* (1985). Here 'critical' referred to the school of 'critical theory' associated with Jurgen Habermas. His work explored the connections between different forms of knowledge and the political interests they served. It tried to establish a link between positivist (empirical–analytic) science and the legitimation of various structures of domination; between historical–hermeneutic science and the improvement of human self-understanding; and between 'critical' social science and human emancipation. While it may have fallen short of these ambitious goals, the *Critical Human Geography* series did help to reconnect human geography with other humanities and social sciences, to bridge the gap between social theory and empirical research, and to address the political implications of geographical knowledge. It promoted an argumentative style, based on original research, rather than a bland synthesis of existing material. It also claimed to engage readers in the project of developing 'a genuinely human geography'. These innovative objectives foreshadowed agendas that remain central to 'critical geography' today.

The questions and intellectual frameworks of geographers changed appreciably through the 1980s and 1990s as the wider political context was transformed. The collapse of communism in Europe, the end of apartheid in South Africa and the emergence of new challenges to the West from so-called 'rogue states' all fractured earlier assumptions about the world order. Human geographers were forced to conceptualise the world anew – adapting an increasing range of theoretical perspectives in the process (Peet and Thrift 1989). Likewise, globalisation also prompted the shaping of a critical human geography. Popular resistance to the economic and environmental policies of the GATT nations (epitomised by the 2000 'Battle for Seattle'), and towards the corporate ethics and practices of contemporary flexible capitalism, fuelled critical research, as did continuing global inequalities, poverty and hunger (Smith 2000). The fraught politics of the Middle East, the traumatic events at the World Trade Center on 11 September 2001, and the 2003 invasion of Iraq also demanded analysis (Gregory 2004). For many, these are starkly geographical phenomena, and our contemporary world calls for geographers to engage with its changing structures and challenges (see Johnston et al. 2002). Throughout this period, human geography became more politicised through the articulation of a specifically *critical* agenda.

At the same time critical geography is also intensely embroiled in 'cultural politics'. Within the academy there is widespread recognition that cultural activity cannot be divorced from social, political and economic forces; that 'culture' is itself a site of struggle (cf. Mitchell 2000). The production of knowledge (including academic practices such as creating books – this one included) clearly involves access to material and intellectual resources. It has its own established hierarchies and conventions, centres of excellence and marginalised sites, often defined in terms of racialised, gendered and class-based exclusions (Sibley 1995). Despite some concerns that contemporary cultural geography might lose sight of key issues such as inequality, exclusion and universal citizenship, there is much to be said for geography's reflexive recognition of the cultural politics of everyday lives and labours. Acknowledging how social groups construct and negotiate their life-worlds has further de-centred traditional, masculinist geographical gazes (Rose 1993) and necessitated new ways of approaching the political and the critical. In turn, this has further influenced the development of cultural geography.

At a more parochial level, the interrelation of global events and the cultural politics of the academy are illustrated by a recent debate within British geography.

The proposed merger of the university-based Institute of British Geographers (IBG), with the more broadly based Royal Geographical Society (RGS) – seen by many academics as a conservative body still tainted by its connections to imperialism (Driver 2001) – raised broader questions about the politics of geographical knowledge. A fierce debate erupted in 1995 over one of the newly merged RGS–IBG's corporate sponsors. The multinational oil corporation Shell had affiliated itself with the RGS in the interests of promoting environmental awareness. Its critics perceived a strategy of deflecting attention from the company's own environmental record. In 1995 the corporation attracted intense international criticism for the damaging environmental impacts of its oil extraction on the Ogoni delta in southern Nigeria, and for its alleged collusion in the persecution of local resistance. In particular, Shell was accused of complicity with the sudden arrest, trial and execution in November 1995 of Ken Sara-Wiwo, a leading Ogoni writer and environmental activist (Watts 1997, 2001). Although Shell denied the charges, for academics committed to highlighting environmental damage and exposing the workings of power, Shell's corporate sponsorship of their professional organisation was untenable. Many resigned (Gilbert et al. 1999). Of course, geographers' corporate affiliations are of minor relevance amidst wider global events, but for many academics the 'Shell debate' crystallised the ethics of academic knowledge production and its uses, and further prompted a shift towards a *critical* geography.

Such disputes also helped define the project's central goal of interrogating the social world. As Trevor Barnes and Derek Gregory wrote (1996, 8):

> a truly critical human geography [exposes] the taken-for-grantedness of everyday life… how the worlds which we inhabit are the products of processes operating over varying timescales whose outcomes could have been different: thus there is nothing inevitable about the [world or its] processes operating over varying geographical scales which join our lives to those of countless others.

Developing critical theories is thus a key concern of this field – although this also demands reflexivity about our own positionality and pedagogies (Castree 2000), and a more internationalist outlook in our work (Painter 2000). For some, critical geography also entails more *practical* engagements with the world through the linking of ideas and practices, and through confronting 'the exercise of power at a range of scales, and well beyond academia' (Katz 1998, 257). It encompasses an opposition to unequal and oppressive power relations and a commitment to transformative politics and greater social justice. It promotes closer relationships between theory and practice, and to pursuing the links between politics inside and outside the academy (Desbiens and Smith 1999; Painter 2000). In this vein, critical geography pursues a political as well as an academic agenda, encouraging participation from, and communication between, local activists and campaign groups as well as from academics (Desbiens and Smith 1999). For Cindi Katz (1998), reflecting on the inaugural 1997 International Conference of Critical Geographers, this initiative was about an 'oppositional geography' producing theory and practice that cross borders to bring about greater social justice, equality and self-determination at all scales.

Productive debate about the meanings, extent and purpose of critical geography continues (Garcia-Ramon et al. 2004). Hopefully, the loose and inclusive nature of critical geography allows space for all these concerns – whether individuals interrogate the social world theoretically, focus upon academic practice and pedagogy, or engage with activism. Certainly, as we write, 'critical geography' has become a self-conscious label signifying a commitment to some or all of these elements.

CRITIQUING CRITICAL GEOGRAPHIES

While we find these developments refreshing and productive, there are, of course, potential problems. The label 'critical' in academic work (including this book) implies that other geographers, past or present, approach their work *uncritically* – and this potential arrogance runs counter to the moving spirit of 'critical geography'. Our use of (plural) geograph*ies* indicates our recognition of the many ways of being critical. The danger of over-privileging any perspective within 'critical geography' demands reflexivity in the term's use. At the same time, 'critical geography' has rapidly become one of the key identifying labels within contemporary human geography. Academic articles, books and university posts have all been positioned within the frames of 'critical geography', threatening to institutionalise and normatise it within established academic structures and, by extension, threatening to dilute its critique.

A related threat to critical geography's purposes is the emergence of a tightly defined *school* of critical geography. The 'Chicago school' in sociology, or the 'Vidalienne', 'Los Angeles' and 'Berkeley' schools in human geography, construct distinctive versions of their disciplines characterised by specific theoretical, methodological or national–linguistic traditions. These intellectual spaces are frequently reproduced, policed and defended. It is inevitable that individual thinkers will align themselves with groups and seek to develop and enhance particular approaches collectively within self-identified traditions of knowledge. But all too often the casual categorisations of particular 'schools' – with assumptions of collective, consensual effort by a community of scholars, of innovative thought emanating from specific institutions, and the privileging of such place-related knowledge – does violence to reality. Sheer chance plays a role in where many individuals work, and the common ground implied in the term 'school' may mask significant differences. Robert Park and Ernest Burgess both collaborated and differed in their interpretations of 1920s Chicago, for example; meanwhile, their 'Chicago school' found no space for the social and spatial perspectives of the women of Hull-House and the Chicago University School of Social Services Administration (Sibley 1995). Therefore, the production of knowledge and intellectual evolution seldom happen in ways suggested by idealised historical accounts. Most intellectual histories are more haphazard, ad hoc and compromising – with inevitable exclusions, contradictions, false starts and contestation. We should be wary of the idea of a discrete school of 'critical geography' but, rather, look to the potential contributions that a critical geographical perspective might make to established fields such as cultural geography.

By contrast, an encouraging aspect of critical geography has been its open flows of information. Above all, electronic communication has facilitated loose and fluid networks, virtual interactions and connections (see, for example, www.crit-geog-forum). Although yet to be realised fully, these technologies offer the potential to constitute knowledge in new ways, spreading across divisions of class, gender, 'race' and other markers of status and difference. Certainly, they erode the tendency for 'schools' of knowledge to be restricted to particular sites. They also promise that the future development of critical geography might better resist being subsumed within orthodox academic structures.

Having said all this, there is still much to do in order to create a genuinely accessible space for critical thinking and debate in geography and beyond. Any pretence of an international, critical geography continues to be undermined by the inequalities of global wealth between and within the North and South. This is manifest, for example, in access to electronic communications equipment; in the time, space and resources afforded to academics from different contexts; or in the unequal ability of critical geographers to attend non-virtual conferences scattered around the world. Although critical geography makes some efforts to engage with various linguistic traditions (Agnew et al. 2000; Desbiens 2002; Ramirez et al. 2000), the language of human geography is overwhelmingly English (Gutiérez and López-Nieva 2001). This poses further difficulties. Those not fluent in this language are disadvantaged, and are constantly forced to translate materials (cf. Garcia-Ramon 2003; Minca 2000; Samers and Sidaway 2000). They also have to deal with some of the unexamined assumptions and prejudices that shape Anglo-American debates.

Simultaneously, failure to engage with non-English literatures places Anglophone critical geography at a similar disadvantage with respect to work in other languages. Key elements of what we have outlined as 'critical geography' were developed much earlier by the international collective of radical geographers connected to the French journal *Hérodote* (Lacoste 1976). Although that initiative spread to Italy and beyond, few English language geographers noticed these precedents (cf. Atkinson 2000; Claval 2000; Hepple 2000). Critical thinking germane to geography but developed in non-English language traditions (such as that of Henri Lefebvre or Antonio Gramsci) received careful attention within the Anglophone world only when translated into English. Anglo-American geographers need to retain sight of the multiple geographies beyond the Anglophone world, and to avoid advocating insights long familiar in other languages.

TOWARDS A CRITICAL CULTURAL GEOGRAPHY

We outlined the development of critical geography in order to contextualise the critical spirit of some of the cultural geographies that follow. The excitement of cultural geography lies in the ways that meanings and social understandings are constructed, contested and negotiated, and in exploring the diverse ways these fuse and splinter around intersecting notions of culture, place and space. It lies in the challenging theoretical arguments that pervade the field and that throw new light on established ways of thinking geographically. This alone makes it an intriguing and relevant field. But it is much more that the study of discourses, texts and imaginations (as some critics allege). Cultural geography attracts widespread interest because it is a way of linking ideas and imaginations with the material world. It explores how social groups engage with their landscapes, how people construct and make sense of their places and spaces. To these ends, cultural geographies increasingly explore creative practices and the ways that people enact identity, belonging, pleasure and difference throughout society – from mundane, quotidian spaces to the celebratory and the spectacular. And, because 'culture' cannot be contained or separated from the social, the economic or the political, our studies also cross intellectual boundaries. Cultural geographies now draw upon an exhilarating range of sources and traditions, ranging from social theory through continental philosophies to psychoanalytical approaches, for example. These don't replace traditional geographical modes of analysis, but complement and extend their analytical potential in exciting new ways. In turn, the analysis that results can also challenge the traditional dualisms – such as mind–body, global–local, culture–nature, self–Other – that structure conventional knowledge. In response to a fluid, changing world, this supple and nuanced way of seeing and thinking allows us to study the new cultural configurations that emerge and develop as our social worlds transform. And, because we accept that our perspective and analysis is embedded within the worlds we analyse, cultural geographies must also address the power structures that saturate these worlds.

This book tries to follow these guidelines. We do not define cultural geography, nor sketch its contours definitively. For ease of organisation we have gathered the collection into three substantive sections to help readers see the more obvious synergies and connections between cognate topics. Each section covers significant areas of cultural geography, but it should be equally clear that there is overlap between some of the essays. Boundaries are transgressed and blurred, and readers should certainly not interpret our arbitrary divisions as fixed or prescriptive. Similarly, the virtues of interdisciplinarity are evidenced by our wide range of authors from subjects including anthropology, cultural studies and sociology as well as different branches of human geography. They draw upon a broad range of theories and literatures to explore how these coalesce around the key concepts of cultural geographies. The authors also share a critical perspective, and a concern to connect intellectual theories and ideas to their socio-political contexts and to the practices of communities and individuals. In addition to covering contemporary debates in cultural geography, many of the essays also contribute to these discussions. The complex and shifting relations of society, nature and technologies are addressed in Hinchliffe's, Eden's, Bingham's and Tsouvalis' chapters; the plurality and hybridity of contemporary identities concern Martin's, Bonnett's, Fortier's and Katharyne Mitchell's chapters; while, elsewhere, matters of embodiment, the more-than-human world, consumption, research practice and ethnicity are also covered. Finally, these essays are also reflexive, acknowledging the ethics of the research process and the situated nature of the perspective they produce.

CONCLUSIONS

We hope that the book does justice to a critical cultural geography, and provides a serious engagement with some of the key terms and debates in this emerging field. We hope that readers will follow references to pursue their own trans-disciplinary work, and continue the process of de-centring knowledge. Notwithstanding our post-disciplinary stance, we want the book to feed into wider discussions about what constitutes human geography, with the cultural being linked to other spheres in debates about nature–culture, culture–economy and the political–economic (Cook et al. 2000). These debates should be seen as responses to emerging global issues and the way the world is developing in the twenty-first century. This global context demands that we develop ever more *critical* cultural geographies; we trust that readers will engage critically with the essays that follow and use them to develop this new generation of cultural geographies. To that end, this collection aims to open up further debate and conversation. We hope it gets you thinking critically about cultural geography.

REFERENCES

Agnew, J., Atkinson, D., Bettoni, G., Giordano, B., Zanfrini, L. and Trabalzi, F. 2000. Italian books and *Society and Space*: a review section, *Environment and Planning D: Society and Space*, 18: 290–300.

Anderson, B. and Tolia-Kelly, D. 2004. Matter(s) in social and cultural geography, *Geoforum*, 35, 6: 669–674.

Anderson, K., Domosh, M., Pile, S. and Thrift, N. eds. 2003. *Handbook of Cultural Geography*. London, Sage.

Atkinson, D. 2000. Geopolitical imaginations in modern Italy, in K. Dodds and D. Atkinson, eds. *Geopolitical Traditions: A Century of Geopolitical Thought*. London, Routledge, 93–117.

Barnes, T. and Gregory, D. 1996. Introduction: the natures of reading in human geography, in T. Barnes and D. Gregory eds. *Reading Human Geography: The Poetics and Politics of Inquiry*. London, Arnold, 1–17.

Blomley, N. 1998. The poetic geography of gentrification, *Environment and Planning D: Society and Space*, 16: 279.

Castree, N. 2000. Professionalisation, activism and the university: whither 'critical geography?' *Environment and Planning A*, 32: 955–970

Claval, P. 2000. Hérodote and the French Left, in K. Dodds and D. Atkinson eds. *Geopolitical Traditions: A Century of Geopolitical Thought*. London, Routledge, 239–267.

Cook, I., Crouch, D., Naylor, S. and Ryan, J. eds. 2000. *Cultural Turns, Geographical Turns: Perspectives on Cultural Geography.* Harlow, Prentice-Hall.

Cosgrove, D. 1983. Towards a radical cultural geography, *Antipode*, 15: 1–11.

Cosgrove, D. 1984. *Social Formation and Symbolic Landscape*. London, Croom Helm.

Cosgrove, D. and Jackson, P. 1987. New directions in cultural geography, *Area*, 19: 95–101.

Daniels, S. 1989. Marxism, culture, and the duplicity of landscape, in R. Peet and N. Thrift eds. *New Models in Geography* (vol. 2). London, Unwin Hyman, 196–220.

Desbiens, C. 2002. Speaking in tongues, making geographies, *Environment and Planning D: Society and Space*, 20: 1–25.

Desbiens, C. and Smith, N. 1999. The International Critical Geography Group: forbidden optimism?, *Environment and Planning D: Society and Space*, 17: 379–382.

Driver, F. 2001. *Geography Militant: Cultures of Exploration and Empire*. Oxford, Blackwell.

Garcia-Ramon, M.-D. 2003. Globalization and international geography: the questions of languages and scholarly traditions, *Progress in Human Geography*, 27: 1–5.

Garcia-Ramon, M.-D., K. Simonsen, Vaiou, J. Tamár, S. Raju, B. Ramirez, S. Hones and L. Berg. 2004. The spaces of critical geography, *Geoforum*, 35, 5: 523–558 (special issue).

Geertz, C. 1980. Blurred genres: the reconfiguration of social thought, *American Scholar*, 49: 165–179.

Gilbert, D. et al.1999. Sponsorship, academic independence and critical engagement: a forum on Shell, the Ogoni dispute, and the Royal Geographical Society (with the Institute of British Geographers), *Ethics, Place and Environment*, 2: 14–29.

Gregory, D. 2004. *The Colonial Present*. Oxford, Blackwell.

Gregory, D. and Urry, J. eds. 1985. *Social Relations and Spatial Structures*. London, Macmillan.

Gutiérez, J. and López-Nieva, P. 2001. Are international journals of human geography really international?, *Progress in Human Geography*, 25: 53–69.

Hamnett, C. 2003. Contemporary human geography: fiddling while Rome burns?, *Geoforum*, 34, 1: 1–3.

Harvey, D. 1973. *Social Justice and the City*. Oxford, Blackwell.

Hepple, L. 2000. *Géopolitiques de gauche*: Yves Lacoste, *Hérodote* and French radical geopolitics, in K. Dodds and D. Atkinson eds. *Geopolitical Traditions: A Century of Geopolitical Thought*. London, Routledge, 268–301.

Jackson, P. 2000. Rematerialising social and cultural geography, *Social and Cultural Geography*, 1: 9–14.

Johnston, R.J., Taylor, P.J. and Watts, M.J. eds. 2002. *Geographies of Global Change: Remapping the World* (2nd ed.). Oxford, Blackwell.

Kahn, J. 1995. *Culture, Multiculture, Postculture*. London, Sage.

Katz, C. 1998. Lost and found in the posts: addressing critical human geography, *Environment and Planning D: Society and Space*, 16: 257–278.

Lacoste, Y. 1976. *La Géographie, ça sert, d'abord, à faire la guerre*. Paris, Maspero.

Massey, D. 1984. *Spatial Divisions of Labour*. London, Macmillan.

McDowell, L. and Sharp, J.P. eds. 1999. *A Feminist Glossary of Human Geography*. London, Arnold.

Minca, C. 2000. Venetian geographical praxis, *Environment and Planning D: Society and Space*, 18: 285–289.

Mitchell, D. 2000. *Cultural Geography: A Critical Introduction*. Oxford, Blackwell.

Nader, L. 1996. *Naked Science*. London, Routledge.

Osborn, B. 1998. Raise shit, *Environment and Planning D: Society and Space*, 16: 280–288.

Painter, J. 2000. Critical human geography, in R.J. Johnston, D. Gregory, G. Pratt and M.J. Watts eds. *The Dictionary of Human Geography* (4th ed.). Oxford, Blackwell, 126–128.

Peet, R. 1977. *Radical Geography: Alternative Viewpoints on Contemporary Social Issues*. Chicago, Maaroufa Press.

Peet, R. and Thrift, N.J. eds. 1989. *New Models in Geography* (vols. 1 & 2). London, Unwin Hyman.

Philo, C. 2000. More words, more worlds: reflections on the cultural turn and human geography, in I. Cook, D. Crouch, S. Naylor and J. Ryan eds. *Cultural Turns / Geographical Turns: Perspectives on Cultural Geography*. Harlow, Pearson, 26–53.

Ramirez, B. et al. 2000. Spanish and Portuguese literature: some reviews, *Environment and Planning D: Society and Space*, 18: 557–558.

Rose, G. 1993. *Feminism and Geography: The Limits of Geographical Knowledge*. Cambridge, Polity.

Rose, G. 1997. Situated knowledges: positionality, reflexivities and other tactics, *Progress in Human Geography*, 21: 305–320.

Samers, M. and Sidaway, J. 2000. Exclusions, inclusions, and occlusions in 'Anglo-American geography': reflections on Minca's 'Venetian geographical praxis', *Environment and Planning D: Society and Space*, 18: 663–666.

Sibley, D. 1995. *Geographies of Exclusion: Society and Difference in the West*. London, Routledge.

Smith, N. 2000. Global Seattle, *Environment and Planning D: Society and Space*, 18: 1–5.

Storper, M. 2001. The poverty of radical theory today: from the false promises of Marxism to the mirage of the cultural turn, *International Journal of Urban and Regional Research*, 25: 155–179.

Sundberg, J. 2005. Looking for the critical geographer, or why bodies and geographies matter to the emergence of critical geographies of Latin America, *Geoforum*, 36, 1: 17–28.

Watts, M. 1997. Black gold, white heat: state violence, local resistance and the national question in Nigeria, in S. Pile and M. Keith eds. *Geographies of Resistance*. London, Routledge, 33–67.

Watts, M. 2001. Petro-violence: nation, identity and extraction in Nigeria and Ecuador, in N. Peluso and M. Watts eds. *Violent Environments*. Ithaca, Cornell University Press, 189–212.

Williams, R. 1976. *Keywords: A Vocabulary of Culture and Society*. London, Fontana.

— PART I —

SPACE, KNOWLEDGE AND POWER

— Introduction —

Space, Knowledge and Power

In recent years problematising the intersections of knowledge and power has preoccupied critical thinkers across academic disciplines. Post-structural initiatives – especially inspired by the suggestive work of Michel Foucault – have informed thinking about the ways that knowledge is power-laden and implicated in the exercise of authority in different contexts. Critical geographers and specialists from other disciplines realised that space was enmeshed in this relationship too – as partially constitutive of the differing negotiations of power/knowledge that shape our world. Thus, the trinity of space, knowledge and power sit at the heart of the ways that contemporary cultural geographers make sense of society.

At the same time, the focus on knowledge has also prompted reflection upon the ways that geographical imaginations produce social worlds: how individuals and communities understand themselves and their relations with each other across space. Thus, the essays in this section problematise some of the ways that collective knowledges shape society in material and imaginative ways. This post-structural awareness has also led geographers to interrogate their *own* production of knowledge and its various political applications. This has further discredited ideas of 'neutral', 'objective' science, and encouraged the recognition of our roles in the construction, representation and legitimation of the structures constituting our world. Hence, our articulations of geographical 'science', our epistemologies, and the ways we produce and sustain intellectual categories are also assessed in this section.

Our ways of thinking and representing, our positionalities as researchers, and the politics of these processes are addressed by the first three essays. Ulf Strohmayer tackles a problematic that runs throughout the book by considering the nature of post-structural analysis in the aftermath of deconstruction. He raises the issue of how we can retain scepticism towards all truth claims while finding something useful to say to society. The next two essays attend to related questions. Ola Söderström tackles the fundamental issue of representation and its problematisation in recent years. He outlines the key critical questions of who wields the power to represent and which objects are selected for representation. But he augments these with an expanded conceptualisation of representation that encompasses other aspects of 'the broader flows of knowledging', including practices and presentation. Ian Cook et al. likewise discusses the hard-wired power relations endemic to orthodox academic knowledge. He considers how these might be undermined by reflexive strategies that eschew over-arching claims and acknowledge our positionalities and partiality in the research process.

Denis Cosgrove applies these themes to mapping and cartography – perhaps the most distinctive and iconic form of geographical knowledge. We now acknowledge these representations as being saturated with power, but Cosgrove also explores the metaphor of mapping in contemporary, fluid cultures, and its reworking as a means of engaging with different spatialities and geographical imaginations. Mike Crang then introduces travel and tourism as spatial practices: equally implicated in geo-graphical ways of knowing and representing, and in the experience and consumption of place. The challenge for critical analysis is to encompass the complexity of these processes without reproducing the dualisms of existing conceptual structures.

The next three chapters address key concepts in geographical thought. Phil Hubbard and Don Mitchell examine how power is etched into, and mediated through, space/place and landscape, respectively. Both trace the evolution of these categories and complicate them in the light of recent thought. Mitchell focuses particularly on the social relations, alienation and exclusion reproduced through landscapes. Hubbard also calls for the recognition of the 'texture' of space and place as experienced by individuals, but also emphasises the practices, languages and representations that are continually remaking space/place. In turn, Sally Eden traces how amorphous and changing understandings of 'environment' have been adopted in a series of debates. Again, the moral, cultural and political contours of the continual remaking of this concept are outlined.

The final chapters deal with three further concepts at a series of scales. First, Gearóid Ó Tuathail/Gerard Toal considers 'geopolitics' as a gathering point for ideas about geography and its relationship with the political. Given the continuing potential for the appropriation of this knowledge by state power, he dissects and problematises these 'spatial grids of intelligibility for world politics' and suggests ways of interrogating wider geopolitical cultures. At the scale of the state, Andrew Jonas and Aidan While think about 'governance' as another set of ideas through which power is articulated. They too trace the development of this debate, but emphasise how its problematic engagement with ideas of the state can be brought into focus by the recognition of the importance of space and geography. Finally, Suzanne Reimer explores enduring ideas about 'flexibility' that are directed at the individual in modern society and the workplace. She critiques the obsession with the term in contemporary capitalism and broadens the discussion to debates on citizenship and consumer cultures. But, in so doing, she warns against oversimplification in any analysis of the power relations embedded in these phenomena.

All the chapters deal with questions of space, knowledge and power, and their realisation in social, economic and political realms. They also address the ways our geographical epistemologies conceptualise and interrogate these matters. While there are common themes holding these essays together, the arguments resonate with writing elsewhere in the book and we encourage readers to pursue these connections.

— Post-structuralism —

Ulf Strohmayer

As the twentieth century came to a close it was perhaps telling that the intellectual landscape became littered with a series of 'post'-isms, all claiming in their own way to capture the sense of closure that permeated the hearts and minds of many. Something or another had come to an end: modernism, Marxism, feminism and Fordism all acquired their particular conclusive affix, but the gestures lacked the verve of old. Intellectual debate, it seemed, no longer led to the formulation of alternative visions. On the contrary, the very notion of 'alternatives' was now seen to be highly problematic and questionable. The following chapter traces some of the key elements of this disillusionment. Through the lens provided by the term 'post-structuralism', it asks questions about the genealogy of the present state of intellectual affairs and seeks to contextualise the practices generated within geography during the last two decades.

The context required to understand the recent pessimistic transformation of intellectual positions across the board of the human sciences clearly extends beyond the immediate confines of the last turn of the century. While some skilfully trace the roots of the malaise as far back as the betrayed promises of the humanist Renaissance (Toulmin 1990), it is perhaps the nineteenth century that holds more direct explanatory poise to readers of this book. The invocation of 'pessimism' earlier in this paragraph has as its correlate the widespread optimism so characteristic of the nineteenth century. Embodied in the notion of 'progress', optimism permeated everything: science, medicine, social and technological progress were all part and parcel to its construction. If today many commentators see nineteenth-century 'optimism' as deeply tarnished by its implication in imperialist practices, masculinism and nationalist posturing, we can and should attribute these insights not simply to the benefit of hindsight but to the same impulse that motivated the age of the 'post': a sceptical rereading of past accomplishments and a growing awareness of the blind spots that accompany the postulation of desirable developments.

Rather than being fostered by intellectual meanderings, this particular scepticism grew out of disillusionment pure and simple: if the long nineteenth century can best be characterised as the century of confidence and endlessly prolonged horizons of expectation, the short twentieth century witnessed the demise of many a dream into the man-made hells of Flanders and Auschwitz, My Lai and Biafra. Rescued from an overdue re-appraisal after World War II only by the political and cultural stasis of the Cold War – basically a lease on the life of nineteenth-century certainties full of reformist élan (e.g. the events surrounding 1968) and conservative desires (the 1950s virtually everywhere in Western Europe) – 'optimism' finally gave way in the years of glasnost, only paradoxically to collapse during the fall of the Berlin Wall. Like no other event, 9 November 1989 neatly encapsulated a caesura in history that still defined the intellectual agenda when this chapter was written. It is no coincidence that the barrage of 'post'-isms alluded to above coincided with this break: closure there was, but the 'beyond' remained elusive and largely framed by what preceded it. In other words: while many appeared eager to create a distance between the certainties, dreams and frames of reference of old, few were willing to risk their necks in an attempt to redefine the intellectual agenda. 'Post-structuralism' should be seen as an attempt to create the ultimate distance from the unfulfilled longings of the nineteenth century and their often catastrophic consequences during the twentieth century. It questions the key underlying notion of any postulation of 'progress' and 'optimism': the assertion of stability embodied in the concept of 'structure'. The concrete shapes embodying 'stability' were many: from the notion of 'democracy' and its incorporation of a 'general will' to the identification of 'classes', from the powerful rhetorics of any 'plan' to the seemingly straightforward context provided by different technologies, 'structures' provided the ultimate recourse for any coherent attempt at rationalising a present state of affairs.

In other words, any science interested in social and cultural realities, any cultural interpretation of the modern world, could anchor its efforts in timeless instruments in its pursuit of intellectual illumination. Centrally implicated in this 'structural quest' was the realm of 'social and cultural theory', arguably the twentieth-century heir to the philosophical pretensions of the nineteenth century. Grateful for the structuralist impulse emanating from the work of Claude Lévi-Strauss, Jean Piaget and others, social and cultural theorists had laboured for the better part of the twentieth century to develop coherent explanatory models that captured central aspects of the world surrounding them. Key to this endeavour were the boundaries surrounding the concepts used: they had to be crystal clear, unambiguous and general enough to allow for comparative analyses. The success of this epistemological strategy, however, came at a price: the 'clarity' and 'generality' of concepts not only effectively masked the situatedness of knowledge production discussed elsewhere in this volume but rendered invisible a constitutive 'other' that 'shadowed' many emerging concepts. Take, for instance, a key concept in the history of nineteenth-century ideas: 'the citizen'. Developed in the aftermath of the French Revolution, the concept of 'the citizen' quickly became an important touchstone of political inclusivity and modernity. At the same time, however, it was implicated in the rise of nationalism, defined the realm of 'normality' in an increasingly narrow manner and served to justify the exclusion of a large percentage of the population from the public arena (Butler and Scott 1992; Fitzsimmons 1994; McCrone and Kiely 2000).

In their attempt to acknowledge and address this predicament, post-structuralist philosophers, social and cultural theorists and intellectuals posited the lack of recognisable structures or the 'shifting' character of concepts as a key and non-negotiable characteristic of any production of knowledge. Following the lead set by authors such as Jacques Derrida, Gilles Deleuze, Félix Guattari and Jacques Lacan and the early work of Jean Baudrillard, post-structuralism thus expanded upon the realisation that, for every postulated structure, there exists an unacknowledged, but necessary, 'negative' context. Against this backdrop, the fixation of early post-structuralist texts and debates with Hegelian philosophy comes as no great surprise; the departure from the Hegelian, idealist 'thesis–antithesis–synthesis' triad, however, was to lay out the space for the development of post-structuralist thinking ever since. Crucially, or so especially Derrida argued, the relationship between 'positive' concept ('presence') and 'negative' context ('absence') could itself be categorised – i.e. fully understood – if only its own inherent instability was overlooked; categorical identity, in other words, was always purchased at the expense of an arbitrary – and thus irrational – 'freezing' of precisely *the* process that breathed life into categories in the first place. Not coincidentally, this was also the mechanism, according to Baudrillard, that transformed 'insights' into commodities (a highly relevant point in today's world of increasingly commercialised scientific practices).

In the majority of post-structuralist writings, the departure from stable structures was rationalised within the realm of language: critically building upon the theories of early linguist Ferdinand de Saussure, the shifting character of categories was often theorised in terms of the arbitrary and fleeing relationship between 'signifier' and 'signified', the two constitutive elements of any sign. Arguably, it is in this linguistic form and through the door opened up by the 'postmodern' crisis of representation that post-structuralist ideas received their first airing in geography. Written as early as 1983, Nigel Thrift's highly influential assault on the central pillar of 'structuralism' broadly conceived, although firmly implanted in a structurationist framework, had the unintended consequence of opening the floodgates towards the recognition that not all was well in the wonderlands emanating from structurally guaranteed knowledge (Thrift 1983). From here it was but a small step towards the acknowledgement of representational practices as being centrally implicated in the production and re-production of power relations – one of the key points mooted in postmodern discourses.

The practice that most readers will associate with post-structuralist manners of thinking is directly implicated in this context. Derived from the Derridaen lexicon, the term 'deconstruction' signals the act of destabilisation ('uprooting' might be a more fitting term) that has become a central matter of concern for post-structuralist practices. At the same time, and in marked contrast to earlier, idealist – and inherently Hegelian – pretences at epistemological transcendence (viz. 'revolution'), 'deconstruction' acknowledges that no new elements will serve to replace existing structures. 'Bricolage' would seem to be a fitting description for the ensuing set of practices, would not this term ultimately be implicated in structuralist manners of thinking. Within geography, the ensuing developments thus had little in common with the 'possibilism' of old even where the structure of many critiques was not dissimilar from, say, Paul Vidal de la Blanche's assault on the bastions of environmental determinism (viz. structuralism) one *fin de siècle* earlier. In contrast to the regionalist insistence on 'scale' as the principal geographical 'deconstruction' of all-too-general forms of knowledge, post-structuralist approaches were decidedly more interested in disturbing concrete existing geometries of power than in re-erecting scaled-down forms of regional or local identity.

One underlying question, however, remains largely unanswered: is the postulation of a lack of structures rationally tenable? Given that any approach to social and cultural realities can escape neither from its constructed nature nor from the desire to communicate (in a post-structuralist context: the ever-shifting nature of reality), readers may well wonder whether the search for boundedness is (1) avoidable and (2) suspect per se. At the very least, post-structuralist-inspired research has arguably produced some of the more inspiring insights in recent geographic writings. From Brian Harley's early and extremely influential deconstruction of cartographic practices (Harley 1989) and Gunnar Olsson's relentless invocations of difference in post-structural thought-pieces and provocations (Olsson 1991) to the more recent development of 'non-representational theoretical practices' (Thrift 1996), from the invocation of 'body', 'hybridity' and 'performance' as metaphors for the inherent instability of concepts (Lewis and Pile 1996; MacLeod 1998; Nash 1996; Proudfoot 2000; Crewe 2001) to the often baroque meanderings around the spaces opened up by post-structuralist forms of abstraction (Doel 1999), complexity has never before been presented as lucidly in a non-numerical kind of language.

However, the danger inherent in such positions should not be glossed over in conclusion. This danger is less to do with the reification of concrete existing structures through a lack of alternative visions, nor principally what Thrift calls the glossing 'over shared practices situated in time-space' (1996, 56), but centres around problems already unearthed by the undoubted great grandfather of post-structuralism, Friedrich Nietzsche. Where context is everything and flux the norm, where 'mobility' is celebrated and 'roots' become demonised, the spectre of social Darwinism looms larger than ever: the subjugation of identities here threatens to be systemic and thus impossible to avoid. Surely the task of any form of geographic knowledge is not to affirm that which oppresses?

KEY REFERENCES

Doel, M. 1999. *Poststructuralist Geographies*. Edinburgh, University of Edinburgh Press.

Harley, B. 1989. Deconstructing the map, *Cartographica*, 26: 1–20.

Natter, W. and Jones, J.P. III 1993. Signposts toward a poststructuralist geography, in J.P. Jones III, W. Natter and T.R. Schatzki eds. *Postmodern Contentions: Epochs, Politics, Space*. New York, Guilford, 165–203.

Pred, A. 1990. *Lost Words and Lost Worlds: Modernity and the Language of Everyday Life in Late Nineteenth-century Stockholm*. Cambridge, Cambridge University Press.

Toulmin, S. 1990. *Cosmopolis: The Hidden Agenda of Modernity*. New York, Macmillan.

OTHER REFERENCES

Butler, J. and Scott, J. eds. 1992. *Feminists Theorize the Political*. London, Routledge.

Crewe, L. 2001. The besieged body: geographies of retailing and consumption, *Progress in Human Geography*, 25, 4: 629–640.

Fitzsimmons, M. 1994. *The Remaking of France: the National Assembly and the Constitution of 1791*. Cambridge, Cambridge University Press.

Gregory, D. 1997. Lacan and geography: *The Production of Space* revisited, in G. Benko and U. Strohmayer eds. *Space and Social Theory. Interpreting Modernity and Postmodernity*. Oxford, Blackwell, 203–234.

Hannah, M. 1999: Sceptical realism: from either/or to both–and, *Environment and Planning D: Society and Space*, 17: 17–34.

Hetherington, K. 1998: *Expressions of Identity: Space, Performance, Politics*. London, Sage.

Lewis, C. and Pile, S. 1996. Woman, body, space: Rio Carnival and the politics of performance, *Gender, Place and Culture*, 3, 1: 23–42.

McCrone, D. and Kiely, R. 2000. Nationalism and Citizenship, *Sociology*, 34, 1: 19–35.

MacLeod, G. 1998. In what sense a region? Place hybridity, symbolic shape, and institutional formation in (post-)modern Scotland, *Political Geography*, 17, 7: 833–865.

Nash, C. 1996. Reclaiming vision: looking at landscape and the body, *Gender, Place and Culture*, 3, 2: 149–170.

Olsson, G. 1991. *Lines of Power, Limits of a Language*. Minneapolis, University of Minnesota Press.

Proudfoot, L. 2000. Hybrid space? Self and Other in narratives of landownership in nineteenth-century Ireland, *Journal of Historical Geography*, 26, 2: 203–221.

Sidaway, J.D. 2000. Postcolonial geographies: an exploratory essay, *Progress in Human Geography*, 24, 4: 591–612.

Soja, E.W. 1996. *Thirdspace: Journeys to Los Angeles and Other Real-and-imagined Places*. Oxford, Blackwell.

Strohmayer, U. 1997. Forget the delivery, or, what post are we talking about?, in G. Benko and U. Strohmayer eds. *Space and Social Theory: Interpreting Modernity and Postmodernity*. Oxford, Blackwell, 383–393.

Thrift, N. 1983. On the determination of social action in space and time, *Environment and Planning D: Society and Space*, 1: 23–57.

Thrift, N. 1996. *Spatial Formations*. London, Sage.

— Representation —

Ola Söderström

> The picture which holds traditional philosophy captive is that of the mind as a great mirror, containing various representations – some accurate and some not – and capable of being studied by pure, non-empirical methods.
>
> Richard Rorty, *Philosophy and the Mirror of Nature*

Representation, to rephrase Raymond Williams' famous observation on 'culture', is certainly one of the most complex words in the human sciences. It is used in nearly every social field: art, culture, politics, science, law. Its semantic richness and complexity is due to the cross-fertilisation in history of its meanings in these different worlds. It is, in other words, a 'boundary notion', and therein lies still today, as we will see, its innovative potential.

A corollary to this introductory remark is that any discussion of the notion of representation is bound to be partial and incomplete. This contribution is no exception to the rule. It starts with some observations on the notion of representation in science, philosophy and the social sciences before considering recent debates in human geography, and, finally, identifies some possible future developments.

Representation is at the core of scientific practice. It is even often seen as summarising the whole process of knowledge production. The critique of this equation (science/knowledge = representation) has been a central issue in modern philosophy. The works of Martin Heidegger, Michel Foucault and Richard Rorty are among the most important landmarks in this philosophical discussion.

Considering truth as the exactitude of representation is for Heidegger the basic flaw of Western philosophy. To put it in simple words: with this centrality of representation, the world becomes, for Heidegger, a conceived image (*Bild* in German) and Man [*sic*] an individual seeking to control and possess the world in its totality (Heidegger 1962, 69–100). As a result, the essence of Man changes (he becomes a subject, centre of reference of the world), the world is kept at bay, and human reason is reduced to an instrumental reason. Cartesian epistemology is central to this process – with Descartes, writes Heidegger, 'thinking means representing' (96) – but, he argues, its roots are much deeper. They are to be found in the passage between the philosophy of Parmenides and Plato in Ancient Greece. For Parmenides, Man is taken in the flow of the world, s/he is primarily a 'hearer' of the world, and this is why the world cannot be an image. For Plato, on the contrary, the world is primarily seen, put in front of us, and can thus become an object of representation.

Like Heidegger, Foucault also historicises the relation between representation and knowledge, but he uses other time-frames. Representation characterises for him one of the major phases of Western episteme: the Classical Age (1600–1800) (Foucault 1976). Resemblances – i.e. imprints of a divine order in the world out there – and the activity of recognising analogies or sympathies between them, deciphering and comparing signs, traces, marks, is what characterises forms of knowledge in the preceding period: the Renaissance. In the Classical Age, exact representations of the world, located by Descartes in the mind of the subject, will be the way out of this endless play of resemblances. Between 1775 and 1825, however, 'words, classes and wealth acquire a mode of being which is no longer compatible with representation' (Foucault 1976, 233). With the reference in natural history, economy and grammar to underlying, non-visible structures, the 'being of what is represented falls outside representation' (252). In other words, for Foucault, if representation remains an epistemological *model* in the Modern Age after 1800, representations as *products* of knowledge touch their limits as practical cognitive tools at the beginning of the nineteenth century.

In his seminal work on the representational model in philosophy, Richard Rorty articulates these two accepted uses of the term (as tool and model) differentiated by Foucault by identifying new modes of knowing opened up by the critique of that model (Rorty 1979). According to Rorty, three authors – Heidegger, Ludwig Wittgenstein and John Dewey – launched at the beginning of the twentieth century the most effective attacks on philosophy considered 'as a "general theory of representation". A theory which will divide culture up into areas which represent reality well, those which represent it less well, and those which do not represent it at all (despite their pretense of doing so)' (3). Despite their differences, these three authors agree, according to Rorty, on the fact 'that the notion of knowledge as accurate representation made possible by special mental processes and intelligible through a general theory of representation, needs to be abandoned' (6). Rorty's conclusion is that, after the charges of his three heroes against representationalism, we should draw the conclusion that 'the notion of knowledge as the assemblage of accurate representation is optional – that it may be replaced by a pragmatist conception of knowledge which eliminates the Greek contrast between contemplation and action, between representing the world and coping with it' (11). Early twentieth-century philosophy has thus paved the way for a critique of representation in different disciplines and for the subsequent development of non-representational scientific practice.

To avoid producing too much of a philosophico-centred discussion, it is worth mentioning here that this critique of representation is anticipated (or 'paralleled':

this doesn't really matter) in the arts. Paul Cézanne is classically considered as the first deconstructor of traditional forms of representation in painting. The long naturalist age – starting with Leon Battista Alberti's theory of linear perspective – fades away with Cézanne's fragmented visions of the Montagne Sainte-Victoire and explodes dramatically with cubism and abstractionism in the first decades of the twentieth century.

This vast critique of representation in philosophy and in the arts is thematised in the human sciences of the 1960s and 1970s as the 'crisis of representation'. The success of semiotics in particular will popularise Ferdinand de Saussure's position on the arbitrary relation between signifier and signified. With modern semiotics a gap is opened between words and things, which will never be closed again. In the process, representation becomes in the human sciences a questionable and active fabrication instead of a source of certainty. Interestingly enough, this crisis of scientific representation is paralleled by a crisis of political representation. Civil movements all over the world, and May 1968 in France in particular, will question the legitimacy of representational democracy either in favour of a revolution or, in its milder version, participative democracy. What these crises – in science, arts and politics – have in common is an attack against authority and established forms of discursive power.

The shockwave of this general phenomenon begins to be felt in geography in the early 1970s. Since then there have, schematically speaking, been two distinct moments: the first is characterised by a critique of representation, the second by the development of non-representational geographies.

During the 1970s so-called 'radical geography' proposes alternative representations of the city. William Bunge, for instance, unveils and maps urban realities not represented by mainstream human geography: spaces of death or spaces dominated by the machines (Bunge 1971). David Harvey spectacularly points to the existence of alternative theories and representations of social justice in the city (Harvey 1973). Both insist on the ideological character of geographical representations. The movement is amplified in the 1980s and 1990s with the development of feminism, gender and queer studies in human geography. These fields of inquiry valorise formerly devalorised conceptions and practices of space. Feminism questions representation at its roots as a gendered epistemological position (Rose 1993) and criticises, more specifically, the claims of certain geographers to identify a privileged representation of spatial realities (Deutsche 1991). Geographers from non-anglophone research communities, and especially from the 'South', make their voices heard, for example during the Inaugural International Conference of Critical Geographers in Vancouver in 1997, expressing their unease concerning their (under-) representation on the main stages of contemporary human geography. The basic question here, which is also central more broadly to the field of cultural studies, is that of the politics of representation, i.e. who has the power to produce authorised representations of the world and what/who are the legitimate objects/subjects of scientific representation?

During the same period, Brian Harley patiently deconstructs geography's tool of representation 'par excellence': cartography (Harley 2001). Maps, he argues, are sites of power knowledge. In the aftermath of the work of Harley, and also that of Christian Jacob in France (Jacob 1992), Franco Farinelli (Farinelli 1992, 2003), in Italy and Denis Cosgrove in Great Britain (Cosgrove 1999), mapping appears as imbued with power, product and source of a reductionist reason, embedded in action rather than being a passive, transparent carrier of geographical knowledge. At the same time, authors active in the field of science studies publish their work on representation in the natural sciences, describing it as a practical and social process, central to the production of scientific facts (Lynch and Woolgar 1990). This body of work participates in a rather spectacular 'visual turn' in the human and social sciences through which vision, visualisations and visual methodologies (Rose 2001) are given new prominence.

The second half of the 1990s and the first years of this century witness the continuation of this critique of representation and of work on politics of representation but also the rise of non-representational research strategies in which practice, presentations, operations become more central than *re-presentations*. The expression 'non-representational', as a cover term to sum up these new lines of thought in geography, is introduced in the discipline by the British geographer Nigel Thrift. The sources of these new geographies are, according to Thrift, to be found in different theories of practice 'denying the efficacy of representational models of the world, whose main focus is the "internal", and whose basic terms or objects are symbolic representations, and are instead committed to non-representational models of the world, in which the focus is "external", and in which basic terms and objects are forged in the manifold of actions and interactions' (Thrift 1996, 6). These geographies do not deny the importance of representations – as Rorty does not deny their role in the process of knowledge acquisition – but try to situate them in the flow of a broader process of knowledging including crucial pragmatic dimensions. Non-representational thinking has led geographers to downplay in their approaches the (formerly dominant) role of mental processes, language and vision and to introduce instead, on the stage of their research and publications, new figures such as: the body, emotions, spatial practice, interaction, performance, 'things', technology.

Does this mean that the era of representation in geography has come to an end? Certainly not. Once the Cartesian mirror conception of knowledge has been shattered, two ways are left open. The first is a 'business as usual' attitude, leading geographers to continue with contemporary means (Geographical Information Systems – GIS, for instance) the task of producing 'truthful' and univocal images of the (geographical) world. The second consists in tracing links between the dispersed fragments of the mirror. Representations are not rejected here altogether but profoundly revisited by action-oriented perspectives. No longer more or less correct mental images, they are seen as one of the elements in a network of human and non-human distributed intelligence, which constantly transforms the world we inhabit. This means that geographers are (and, probably increasingly, will be) analysing the interplay between different forms of representations of space – in maps, photographs, cinema, etc. – and fields of practice, such as patterns of behaviour in the urban environment or urban planning. They study, in other words, 'representations in the wild' (i.e. having escaped from the prison house of the *cogito*). In this second perspective, lies the possibility of responding to the limitations of classical representationalism but also of rescuing the important idea that geographers are inescapably (and should remain) representatives of certain (generally spatial) phenomena. As such, they are always giving voice or muting certain things and actions, giving importance and visibility to certain processes and not to others, and thus contributing to the transformation of the world (which they thought for too long they were only 'representing').

KEY REFERENCES

Foucault, M. 1976. *Les mots et les choses.* Paris, Gallimard.

Heidegger, M. 1962. Les temps des conceptions du monde, in *Les Chemins qui ne mènent nulle part*. Paris, Gallimard, 69-100 (French translation of Die Zeit des Weltbilds, conference given in Freiburg, 1938).

Rorty, R. 1979. *Philosophy and the Mirror of Nature*. Princeton, Princeton University Press.

Thrift, N. 1996. *Spatial Formations*. London, Sage.

OTHER REFERENCES

Bunge, W. 1971. *Fitzgerald: Geography of a Revolution.* London, Schenkman.

Callon, M. 1995. *Representing Nature, Representing Culture*, conference for the inauguration of the Centre for Social Theory and Technology, University of Keele, 24 March.

Cosgrove, D. ed. 1999. *Mappings.* London, Reaktion.

Deutsche, R. 1991. Boys' town, *Society and Space*, 9: 5–30.

Farinelli, F. 1992. *I segni del mondo: Immagine cartografica e discorso geografico in età moderna.* Scandicci, Nuova Italia.

Farinelli, F. 2003. *Geografia. Un Introduzione ai modelli del mondo*. Torino, Einaudi.

Harley, J.B. 2001. *The New Nature of Maps: Essays in the History of Cartography.* Baltimore, Johns Hopkins University Press.

Harvey, D. 1973. *Social Justice and the City.* London, Arnold.

Jacob, C. 1992. *L'empire des cartes.* Paris, Albin Michel.

Lynch, M. and Woolgar, S. eds. 1990. *Representation in Scientific Practice.* Cambridge, MA, MIT Press.

Rose, G. 1993. *Feminism and Geography: the Limits of Geographical Knowledge.* Cambridge, Polity.

Rose, G. 2001. *Visual Methodologies*, London, Sage.

— Positionality/Situated Knowledge —

Ian Cook et al.

INTRODUCTION

For many, most, perhaps all researchers, one of the most difficult tasks is to turn the experience of research into respectable academic writing. Research can be a tricky, fascinating, awkward, tedious, annoying, hilarious, confusing, disturbing, mechanical, sociable, isolating, surprising, sweaty, messy, systematic, costly, draining, iterative, contradictory, open-ended process.[i] But you wouldn't necessarily be able to tell that from the way that it often has to be written up in theses, book chapters, journal articles and other official outlets for academic work. Good arguments are rational, linear, ordered, dispassionate, confident, objective, universal. Aren't they? Well, not necessarily. That's the answer you might get from the reflexive anthropologists, sociologists of science and feminist writers who, since the mid-1980s, have produced some key readings for geographers taking a cultural turn.[ii] The main point they make is that academic and other knowledges are always *situated*, always produced by *positioned* actors working in/between all kinds of locations, working up/on/through all kinds of research relations(hips). All these make a huge difference to what exactly gets done by whom, how and where it's done, how it's turned into a finished product, for whom. Thus, so the argument goes, writing about academic knowledge as a *relational process* rather than a straightforward thing might highlight the politics of knowledge in academic research, produce more modest, embodied, partial, locatable and convincing arguments and, in the process, make it possible for researchers (and their audiences) to see and make all kinds of, often unexpected, politically progressive connections.

Writing about these two key terms is a tricky business. They're often used interchangeably, but aren't the same. Advocates argue that they make sense in principle, can vividly be seen at work in studies of other people's academic practices, but cause confusion and discomfort when they're used nearer to home.[iii] Critics might argue that writing in this area can, itself, be inadequately positioned and/or un-situated. And purists could argue that it's inappropriate to *step back* and offer an *overview* of an approach that criticises those who claim to be able to step back and offer an overview! But, I've been asked to write 2,000 words explaining these terms. They're important. And I'm going to try to do it. In five easy steps.

1. THE RESULTS OF RESEARCH: TWO SNAPSHOTS

Figure 1 illustrates the latest writing to come from my Ph.D. research. In the early 1990s I tried to connect the sale of fresh papayas in British supermarkets to the work that went into producing them on two Jamaican farms. Recently, I was asked to draw upon this to write 1,000 words on trade by the editors of a book very much like this one. I sent a draft in September 2001. It's December now. I'm waiting for comments. Some advice on revisions to make it better. Perhaps.

Figure 2 is a still from a TV documentary called *Lions – Spy in the Den*, made by John Downer Productions and first aired on the BBC in the autumn of 2001.

draft for S. Harrison, S Pile & N Thrift (eds) *Patterned Ground: Ecologies of Culture & Nature*

Trade:

Ian Cook

"a seed contains inside its coat the history of practices such as collecting, breeding, marketing, taxonimising, patenting, biochemically analysing, advertising, eating, cultivating, harvesting, celebrating, and starving" (Haraway 1999 p.47).

Once they're picked, they start to die. Twisted off the stem. Just as they've 'turned'. From fully green, to green with a yellow streak. By farm workers. On a platform made from scaffolding. Welded to a trailer. Pulled slowly along avenues of trees. By a tractor. Jerked about. As the wheels follow undulating tracks in the baked mud. Under the hot sun. Shaded by leaves splaying out from the treetop. Leaves that shade the fruit growing around that stem. In a column. 'Turning' fruits at the bottom and flowers at the top. These 18 month old trees will soon be felled. The leaves have finally succumbed to 'bunchy top'. The sprayer can't reach them. 30 feet up. Where eight 'pickers' are leaning precariously off that platform. Four a side. Jerked around. Slowly moving. Looking for those colour changes. Cupping the bottom of 'turning' fruits. Carefully twisting them off. Each a good handful. Placing them in crates for the packing house. Trying not to let the white latex oozing from their peduncles drip onto their skin. It's nasty. We're on a papaya farm. Picking fruit for the export trade. To the USA and Europe. 'Fresh'. Sold in mainstream supermarkets. 'Product of Jamaica'.

1992. On a 50 acre farm. Where sugar cane used to be grown. Great House, sugar factory, rum distillery, and slave hospital ruins at the centre of the farm. Equipment rusting away inside. The farm manager's house built in the ruins of the overseer's. Traces of the agricultural, export-oriented, plantation society which Jamaica was set up to be. When world trade was in its infancy. In the 1500s. Much has changed since then. But this land is still devoted to export agriculture. Jamaica is still an impoverished country. The farm workers are descendants of enslaved African people. The farm's owners and managers aren't. But at least they're not still farming cane. That's a horrible business.

1

Figure 1: Page 1 of a draft copy of Cook (2004).

Figure 2: A still from John Downer Productions (2001).[iv]

A more or less standard wildlife documentary, it details how lion cubs grow into adult lions in the grasslands of East Africa. But they're not the only stars of the film. The 'Bouldercam' – a piece of remote-controlled audio-visual equipment specially developed to make it – is represented both behind and within the scenes. That's interesting.

2. 'TEXTS' REPRESENTING RESEARCH?

Both of these are (extracts from) 'texts': texts that represent the results of research into the international papaya trade and the private lives of lions. This trade and these lives can be called Cook's and Downer's 'objects of study'. Here, we need to get into arguments about how such 'texts' (appear to) represent such 'objects of study'.

Figure 3 illustrates the 'God trick' (Haraway 1988), which many feel that they have to pull off to make those 'good' arguments we began with. It's a one-way relation in which the 'text' – a spreadsheet, a map, a journal article – simply represents the 'object of study'. That 'object' is out there. It's waiting to be discovered, collected, processed as 'data'. By researchers using established methods. In a

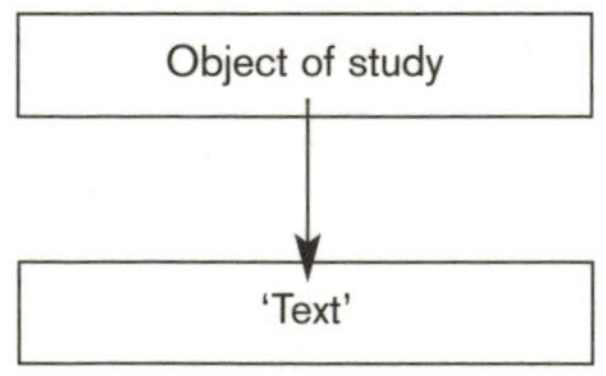

Figure 3: The view from nowhere and/or everywhere.

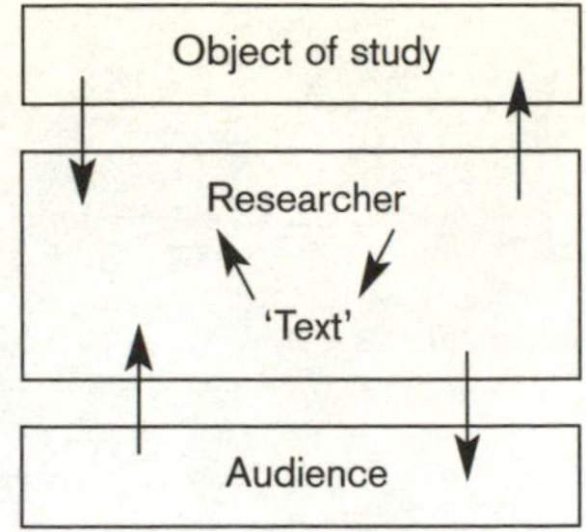

Figure 4: The view from somewhere (source: Keith 1992).

systematic manner. You don't need to know anything about them. They're not people. Like you and me. They're operating as standardised conduits. Their 'texts' are matters of fact. There's no doubt about that.[v]

Figure 4 illustrates critiques of this 'trick' that highlight the role of *positionality* and the *situated* nature of all (academic) knowledge. These complicate the picture: first, giving the 'researcher' and the 'audience' an active role in the relations between the 'text' and the 'object of study' and, second, making the relations more than one-way traffic. 'Texts' are suspended in, and constructed out of, these relations. And the researcher is in the thick of this. A person. Like you or me. Working with the materials and technologies of their trade. Moving in/between contexts. Initiating relations(hips) and/or building upon established ones. Struggling to make things happen. To make sense of them. Fit them together. In some kind of order. That's acceptable. To them. To others. Working hard to separate things out. Because the 'object of study' can't simply be re-presented. The researcher's knowledge about it is negotiated. Made. His/her 'text' is far from a matter of fact. There's no doubt about that.[vi]

So, research is more of a relational process than many would admit. In print, at least. Debates about *positionality* and *situated knowledge* are debates about these relations. But one is more about social, and the other about material–semiotic, relations. This is where they differ. And this makes a difference. Now, let's go back to those snapshots. What went on behind the scenes?

3. SOCIAL RELATIONS, PAPAYA RESEARCH

1992. In the second year of my Ph.D. Spending six months in Jamaica doing interviews and participant observation research with women working in a papaya farm's packing house. Research that produced detailed insights into how this trade affected their lives. By a researcher (Figure 5) who couldn't be sure what he'd understood. His first language: Standard English. Theirs: Jamaican english (Cassidy and Le Page 1980). The Jamaican linguist who transcribed the tapes found the misunderstandings hilarious. Here's a researcher gaining a *feeling* that his understanding of this trade is gradually becoming clearer. But he can't *trust*

Figure 5: Cook the researcher.

that feeling. Research encounters were often ambiguous. What could be learned from them? What could be read into them? Who knows? The participant observation research should have provided another perspective. It did, but not one that made things much clearer. Research was being done on a farm where observation was central to the disciplining of labour. This was a place where a tall, white, middle-class, English male researcher washing, wrapping and packing fruit alongside a largely black, working-class, Jamaican female workforce could by no means go unnoticed. Every day, at least some of the farm workers saw that person talking with their boss. He wondered why someone would spend so much time talking to his employees. He knew that researcher had talked to his business rivals, as well as to people he shipped to in the United Kingdom. Many were curious about the way that researcher asked the women, one by one, to leave the packing house to have a chat with him in the shade of a tree, out of earshot but in full view of her colleagues. He was tacking between people who might not want others to know

Figure 6: The Bouldercam.[vii]

what they were up to. So, what was he up to? Could he be trusted? Could fun be had at his expense? Where was his girlfriend? Was he looking for one? What were his politics? How did people in England dance? Comments. Questions. Answers. (Mis)understandings. Watching. Being watched. Speculation. Paranoia. Changing behaviour. But clinging to the research plan. Keeping focused. Noting. Taping. Photographing. Getting data. To write a Ph.D. that examiners would pass. And accounts that others would accept for publication. Maybe. Things he could put on a CV. Use in the classroom. Lecturing. His career. A lot of people have played a part in that.[viii]

4. MATERIAL–SEMIOTIC RELATIONS, *SPY IN THE DEN*

Wildlife documentary film-making is in crisis. It's hit the BBC's Natural History Unit hard. This public service broadcaster has been forced to be more commercial. Cutting costs. Contracting out. Chasing bigger audience figures. Entertaining more and informing less. Making films about the animals that are the most charismatic: the big cats, whales, polar bears, for example. But there's not much more that can be filmed or said about them. Unless there's a new angle. From some new audio-visual equipment, perhaps. Like a camera disguised as a boulder (Figure 6). Lion-proof. Operated remotely. At a safe distance. Trundling into the midst of a pride of lions. Rotating through 360°. To see and hear things. In amazing intimacy. A cub's eye view. With cub's ears. Stereo microphones. Up close. Recording pictures and sound to complement conventional shots. From remote cameras with telephoto lenses. High-quality film cameras and/or lightweight digital camcorders. On moving cranes. In moving vehicles. Operated by people used to working with both scientists and animals. A skilled film-maker tracks animals, knows when what s/he wants to film is about to happen, and knows her/his equipment. Intimately. To get shots from what might be once-in-a-lifetime opportunities. Shots that will fit into the film's storyline. Written before the filming takes place. Scripts with dodgy gender relations. Active, aggressive males. Passive, nurturing females. Often. Illustrated rather than discovered during the filming. Of how a lion cub grows into an adult lion. Perhaps. And East Africa makes for a great location. It's been used plenty of times before. Copious audio and film footage is already in the BBC archive. It has managed 'natural' habitats. Local scientists and rangers who know what's happening where. Lions used to being filmed. By amateurs and professionals. Grasslands that are relatively flat, dry and free from the kind of vegetation animals could disappear behind. Mid-shot. Or that could throw dark shadows across the action. A place where vehicles won't get stuck in the mud. Where they won't shake so much on the move that camera vibration ruins a shot. Where it's not so wet that film stock and equipment could get damaged. Where you're not so remote that charging camera batteries would be a headache. Like in West Africa. Yes, East African grasslands make an excellent outside studio. A studio where Downer and crew could spend 3,000 hours watching lions. 100 hours filming them. For a one-hour film.

Which may also include old footage from BBC archives. All quickly edited together, to support that storyline. Narrated by David Attenborough. Each shot no more than a few seconds long. Nearly half from the Bouldercam. Made to look like a real cub's-eye view. Clever editing.[ix]

5. CONCLUSIONS

So, researchers' identities and practices make a big difference. They can't hover above the nitty-gritty power relations of everyday life. Research can only emerge out of them. Tainted by them. Reproducing them. Perhaps. Wealth. 'Race'. Nationality. Class. Gender. Sexuality. Age. (Dis)ability. Attitudes to nature. More besides. Key questions. Who does research? Who/what is researched? Who decides what's important? How is research funded and why? Who's it for? Who gains from it? Relatively well-off, white, Western, middle-class, heterosexual non-disabled men? Who are supposed to behave in a cool, detached, objective, dispassionate, authoritative way, anyway? Maybe. That's got to be more than a coincidence. Be them or act like them, if you want to be a successful academic! It's about the way that we think, too. Those of us entertaining Enlightenment thoughts. Categorising things. As this/that. As 'self/Other, mind/body, culture/nature, male/female, civilised/primitive, reality/appearance, whole/part, agent/resource, maker/made, active/passive, right/wrong, truth/illusion, total/partial, God/man' (Haraway 1991, 177)? To which geographers might add global/local, here/there. The categorisations that 'have all been systematic to the logics of domination of women, people of colour, nature, workers, animals – in short, domination of all constituted as others, whose task is to mirror the (dominant) self'. Do you really want to help maintain such domination? If you believe the arguments?[x]

There are politics and ethics to be considered here. So, why not be more reflexive? At least make a stab at explaining where you're coming from. Your *position* in all of this. Talk about your research as partial, in both senses of the word. It's not the whole story and it's impossible to be 'impartial'. Give your reader something to think with. Include other voices. Position but de-centre your own. No single, straightforward conclusions. But provide materials to think with and about. Materials full of ideas, energy, doubt, learning, life. Materials that might destabilise those oppositions. Make connections. Make a difference. Understand how difference works. Channel this in 'politically progressive' ways. Re-interpret some rules. Don't write as if you're one of those Cartesian individuals. Those 'atomistic, presocial vessel(s) of abstract reason and will' (Whatmore 1997, 38). Or the kind of individual who knows exactly who s/he is and how this makes a difference (Rose 1997). Please! You're a collective. Like 'Ian Cook et al.'. Or 'John Downer Productions'. Other people help you to know. Not just your research subjects. But those you mention in acknowledgements, bibliographies, film credits. And more besides. In/between particular institutional contexts (Sidaway 1997). [*This is where debates about positionality and situated knowledge usually diverge. In the latter, research is not done only by 'people' but by socio-technical hybrids, cyborgs and actor networks. More than just people. Bouldercams. Tape recorders. Passports. Paper. Other 'co-agents'. Collectively. More thoroughly entangling the lives of selves and countless others. In fleshy ways.*] Nobody and nothing is outside. Connections must be seen and made on/from the ground. New responsibilities recognised and tackled. These hybrids can imagine and do things differently. Work with/around/against those separations and binaries. Change some geographies.[xi]

NOTES

i see Amit 2001; Bell et al. 1993; Moss 2001; Okely and Callaway 1992.
ii e.g. Clifford and Marcus 1986; Haraway 1988; Hartsock 1987.
iii see Ashmore 1988; Cook 1998, 2001; Rose 1997.
iv source: www.jdp.co.uk/images/programmes/lion.jpg (accessed 30/12/01).
v see Barnes 2000a; Harley 1996; Rabinowitz 1993.
vi see Clifford 1997; Latour 1993, 1996; Katz 1992, 1994.
vii source: cover of John Downer Productions 2001.
viii see Cook 1997, 1998, 2001.
ix see Anon n.d.a,b, 2001; Burgess and Unwin 1984; Clarke 2001a, 2001b; Crang 1997; Crowther 1997; G. Davies 1999, 2000a, 2000b; G.H. Davies 2000; MacDougall 1992; Whatmore 1999.
x see Cloke 1999; Crang 1992; Jackson 1993, 2000; Madge 1993; McDowell 1992; Oliver 1992; Parr 1998, 2000; Sidaway 1992; Women and Geography Study Group 1997.
xi see Angus et al. 2001; Barnes 2000b; Burgess 2000; Castree 1999; Cook 1998, 2000, 2001; Cook et al. 2000; Haraway 1988, 1991, 2000; Henwood et al. 2001; Kunzru 1997; Merrifield 1995; Willemen 1992.

KEY REFERENCES

Haraway, D. 1988. Situated knowledges: the science question in feminism and the privilege of partial perspective, *Feminist Studies*, 14: 575–599.

Hartsock, N. 1987. The feminist standpoint, in S. Harding ed. *Feminism and Methodology*. Milton Keynes, Open University Press, 157–180.

Katz, C. 1992. All the world is staged: intellectuals and the projects of ethnography, *Environment and Planning D: Society and Space*, 10: 495–510.

Merrifield, A. 1995. Situated knowledge through exploration: reflections on Bunge's Geographical Expeditions, *Antipode*, 27: 49–70.

Okely, J. and Callaway, H. eds. 1992. *Anthropology and Autobiography*. London, Routledge.

Oliver, M. 1992. Changing the social relations of research production?, *Disability, Handicap and Society*, 7, 2: 101–114.

OTHER REFERENCES

Amit, V. ed. 2001. *Constructing the Field*. London, Routledge.

Angus, T., Cook, I. and Evans, J. 2001. A manifesto for cyborg pedagogy?, *International Research in Geographical and Environmental Education*, 10, 2: 195–201.

Anon n.d.a. *Bouldercam with Century Lens*. www.global-dvc.org/detail.asp?item=58 (accessed 10/12/01).

Anon n.d.b. *A Boulder to Spy on: An Interview with Lions – Spy in the Den Producer John Downer*. www.amazon.co.uk/exec/obidos/tg/feature/-/151263/026-8922830-3045232 (accessed 17/8/01).

Anon 2001. *News Talk: 13/1 London*, UK. www.tvnewsweb.com /briefing/newstalk/2001/01/13london.shtml (accessed 17/8/01).

Ashmore, M. 1988. *The Reflexive Thesis: Wrighting Sociology of Scientific Knowledge*. London, Chicago University Press.

Barnes, T. 2000a. Objectivity, in D. Gregory, R. Johnston, G. Pratt and M. Watts eds. *The Dictionary of Human Geography* (4th ed.). Oxford, Blackwell, 560–561.

Barnes, T. 2000b. Situated knowledge, in D. Gregory, R. Johnston, G. Pratt and M. Watts eds. *The Dictionary of Human Geography* (4th ed.). Oxford, Blackwell, 742–743.

Bell, D., Caplan, P. and Jahan Karim, W. eds. 1993. *Gendered Fields: Women, Men and Ethnography*. London, Routledge.

Burgess, J. 2000. Situating knowledges, sharing values and reaching collective decisions: the cultural turn in environmental decision making, in I. Cook, D. Crouch, S. Naylor and J. Ryan eds. *Cultural Turns/Geographical Turns: Perspectives on Cultural Geography*. Harlow, Prentice-Hall, 273–287.

Burgess, J. and Unwin, D. 1984. Exploring the Living Planet with David Attenborough, *Journal of Geography in Higher Education*, 8, 2: 93–113.

Cassidy, F. and Le Page, R. 1980. *Dictionary of Jamaican English* (2nd ed.). Cambridge, Cambridge University Press.

Castree, N. 1999. Out there? In here? Domesticating critical geography, *Area*, 31: 81–86.

Clarke, S. 2001a. *Wild Kingdom…?* www.realscreen.com/ magazine/20010801/uktrends.html (accessed 10/12/01).

Clarke, S. 2001b. Life in the old iguana yet, *The Independent*, 27 February, millennium-debate.org/ind27febru8.htm (accessed 10/12/01).

Clifford, J. 1997. Spatial practices: fieldwork, travel, and the disciplining of anthropology, in J. Clifford ed. *Routes: Travel and Translation in the Late Twentieth Century*. London, Harvard University Press, 52–91.

Clifford, J. and Marcus, G. eds. 1986. *Writing Culture: the Poetics and Politics of Ethnography*. Los Angeles and Berkeley, University of California Press.

Cloke, P. 1999. Self–other, in P. Cloke, P. Crang and M. Goodwin eds. *Introducing Human Geographies*. London, Arnold, 43–53.

Cook, I. 1997. *A Grumpy Thesis: Geography, Autobiography, Pedagogy*. Unpublished Ph.D. thesis, University of Bristol.

Cook, I. 1998. *'You Want to be Careful You Don't End up like Ian. He's all Over the Place': Autobiography in/of an Expanded Field (the Director's Cut)*. Falmer, Research Paper in Geography No. 34. University of Sussex.

Cook, I. 2000. 'Nothing can ever be a case of us and them again': exploring the politics of difference through border pedagogy and student journal writing, *Journal of Geography in Higher Education*, 24, 1: 13–27.

Cook, I. 2001. 'You want to be careful you don't end up like Ian. He's all over the place': autobiography in/of an expanded field, in P. Moss ed. *Placing Autobiography in Geography*. Syracuse, Syracuse University Press, 99–120.

Cook, I. 2004. Trade, in S. Harrison, S. Pile, N. Thrift eds. *Patterned Ground: Ecologies of Culture and Nature*. London, Routledge, 124–126.

Cook, I. et al. 2000. Social sculpture and connective aesthetics: Shelley Sacks' 'Exchange Values', *Ecumene*, 7, 3: 338–344.

Crang, M. 1997. Picturing practices: research through the tourist gaze, *Progress in Human Geography*, 21, 3: 359–373.

Crang, P. 1992. The politics of polyphony: on reconfiguration in geographical authority, *Environment and planning D: Society and Space*, 10: 527–549.

Crowther, B. 1997. Viewing what comes naturally: a feminist approach to television natural history. *Women's Studies International Forum*, 20, 2: 289–3000.

Davies, G. 1999. Exploiting the archive: and the animals came in two by two, 16mm, CD-ROM and BetaSp, *Area*, 31, 1: 49–58.

Davies, G. 2000a. Narrating the Natural History Unit: institutional orderings and spatial practices, *Geoforum*, 31: 539–551.

Davies, G. 2000b. Science, observation and entertainment: competing visions of postwar British natural history television, 1946–1967, *Ecumene*, 7, 4: 432–460.

Davies, G.H. 2000. *Life with the Lions.* www.tvcameramen.com /lounge/tvnature01.htm (accessed 17/8/01).

Lions: Spy in the Den (video recording) 2001. London, BBC Worldwide Ltd, produced by John Downer Productions.

Haraway, D. 1991. A cyborg manifesto: science, technology and socialist feminism in the late twentieth century, in D. Haraway ed. *Simians, Cyborgs & Women: The Reinvention of Nature*. New York, Routledge, 149–181.

Haraway, D. 2000. *How Like a Leaf: An Interview with Thyrza Nichols Goodeve*. New York, Routledge.

Harley, J.B. 1996. Deconstructing the map, in J. Agnew, D. Livingstone and A. Rogers eds. *Human Geography: An Essential Anthology*. Oxford, Blackwell, 422–443.

Henwood, F., Kennedy, H. and Miller, N. eds. 2001. *Cyborg Lives? Women's Technobiographies*. York, Raw Nerve.

Jackson, P. 1993. Changing ourselves: a geography of position, in R. Johnston ed. *The Challenge for Geography: A Changing World, a Changing Discipline*. Oxford, Blackwell, 198–214.

Jackson, P. 2000. Positionality, in D. Gregory, R. Johnston, G. Pratt and M. Watts eds. *The Dictionary of Human Geography* (4th ed.). Oxford, Blackwell, 604–605.

Katz, C. 1994. Playing the field: questions of fieldwork in geography, *Professional geographer*, 46, 1: 67–72.

Keith, M. 1992. Angry writing: (re)presenting the unethical world of the ethnographer, *Environment and Planning D: Society and Space,* 10: 551–568.

Kunzru, H. 1997. You are cyborg, *Wired*, 5.02 http://www.wired.com/wired/archive/5.02/ffharaway.pr.html (accessed 5/6/01).

Latour, B. 1993. *We have Never been Modern*. Brighton, Harvester Wheatsheaf.

Latour, B. 1996. *Aramis or the Love of Technology*. London, Harvard University Press.

MacDougall, D. 1992. When less is less: the long take in documentary, *Film Quarterly*, 46, 2: 36–46.

Madge, C. 1993. Boundary disputes: comments on Sidaway (1992), *Area*, 25, 3: 294–299.

McDowell, L. 1992. Doing gender: feminism, feminists and research methods in human geography, *Transactions, Institute of British Geographers*, 17: 399–416.

Moss, P. ed. 2001. *Placing Autobiography in Geography*. Syracuse, Syracuse University Press.

Parr, H. 1998. Mental health, ethnography and the body, *Area*, 30, 1: 28–37.

Parr, H. 2000. Interpreting the 'hidden social geographies' of mental health: ethnographies of inclusion and exclusion in semi-institutional places, *Health and Place*, 6, 3: 225–237.

Rabinowitz, P. 1993. Wreckage upon wreckage: history, documentary and the ruins of memory, *History and Theory*, 32: 119–137.

Rose, G. 1997. Situating knowledges: positionality, reflexivities and other tactics, *Progress in Human Geography*, 21, 3: 305–320.

Sidaway, J. 1992. In other worlds: on the politics of research by 'First World' geographers in the 'Third World', *Area*, 24, 4: 403–408.

Sidaway, J. 1997. The production of British Geography, *Transactions, Institute of British Geographers*, 22, 4: 488–504.

Whatmore, S. 1997. Dissecting the autonomous self: hybrid cartographies for a relational ethics, *Environment and planning D: Society and Space*, 15: 37–53.

Whatmore, S. 1999. Culture–nature, in P. Cloke, P. Crang and M. Goodwin eds. *Introducing Human Geographies*. London, Arnold, 4–11.

Willemen, P. 1992. *Bangkok–Bahrain* to *Berlin–Jerusalem*: Amos Gitai's editing, *Screen*, 33, 1: 14–26.

Women and Geography Study Group 1997. *Feminist Geographies: Explorations in Diversity and Difference*. Harlow, Longman.

— Mapping/Cartography —

Denis Cosgrove

Conventionally, the geographer was represented with compasses in hand, in the act of consulting a map or globe. Mapping is popularly considered a geographical task, and the map regarded as the principal tool of geography. The spatial relationships revealed on maps generate geographical hypotheses, while the results of geographical research are characteristically illustrated in cartographic form. Such time-honoured formulations have been radically altered in recent decades as the concepts of map and mapping have been expanded, as traditional claims for cartographic representation have been subjected to critical interrogation, and as the use and significance of mapping within geography and beyond have been transformed. These changes are in large measure a function of the 'cultural turn' within the discipline, and thus bear heavily on theory and practice in cultural geography.

Geographers have long treated mapping and cartography as scientific endeavours, dividing maps into geographic and thematic types. The former, the history of which in the West goes back to the ancient world, seeks to give a visual impression of features over a part of the earth's surface, reduced to a measured and manageable scale. Using a combination of 'natural' and conventional signs, including colour and shading, contours, graphic symbols and lettering, such mapping produces a strongly 'pictorial' image. Thematic mapping, which developed alongside empirical and – especially – statistical science over the past three centuries, also uses graphic means but with the intention of revealing the spatial pattern, distribution or relations of classes of phenomena, not necessarily visible in reality, such as population, agricultural production, migration, language or other cultural traits. In both cases, scale is a critical determinant of the meaning and use of the map. In map work, geographers have paid specific attention to scale, as well as to other technical matters such as projection, orientation and date of production. As a scientific instrument, therefore, a map is to be judged by its accuracy and objectivity when measured against the real world that it claims to represent. Scientific cartography remains an adjunct technique to geographical research and teaching. Thus, university and college geography departments generally employ specifically trained cartographers. The techniques and methods used by these specialists have been revolutionised by satellite and remote-sensed technologies and by the capacities of the computer to manipulate and represent geo-referenced data with unprecedented speed, accuracy and graphic sophistication.

Thematic maps have played a central role in cultural geography's examination and representation of the distributions of cultural artefacts and patterns of cultural activity. From its mid-nineteenth-century European origins, especially in Germany, where mapping the distribution of such cultural traits as language and settlement form was fundamental to the project of national unification, cultural geography used maps to illustrate ecological connections between a physical environment and the human community that occupied it. With the decline of environmental determinism, landscape geographers, interested in defining and delimiting culture areas, continued to use the map as a principal tool for revealing the visible expressions of human agency in transforming physical regions and creating distinctive patterns of human occupance. A survey text such as William Norton's *Cultural Geography* (2000) contains maps on virtually every page, indicating spatial expressions for every type of cultural form and process. They include the distribution of world religions and of vernacular house types within the United States, the changing pattern of Mormon religious adherence, the spatial diffusion of neolithic plant domesticates and the patterns of racial segregation in apartheid Cape Town. Because culture, like every physical and social activity, is both spatially structured and geographically expressed, the map remains a powerful mode of visualising and representing the spatial aspects of how cultures form, interact and change. Mapping thus remains a vital tool of analysis and a significant mode of representation in the study of interconnections between culture and space.

But mapping and cartography play a much richer and more complex role within contemporary cultural geography. One of the foundational texts of the 'new' cultural geography of the 1980s and 1990s was titled *Maps of Meaning* (Jackson 1989), yet it contains very few maps and no discussion of mapping as a geographical technique. The author is using the terms 'map' and 'mapping' metaphorically, as his connection of maps to 'meaning' indicates. He calls on the representational significance of the map to draw attention to the significance of representation itself, to the idea that the world is only ever known through signs and symbols, and to the impossibility of guaranteeing, or indeed claiming, transparent or objective connections between these signs and symbols (the map) and what they claim to represent. From this perspective, the mapping process involves both a 'complex architecture of signs' – graphic elements with internal forms and logics capable of theoretical disconnection from any geographical reference – and a 'visual architecture' through which the worlds they construct are selected, translated, organised and shaped (Jacob 1996, 195). The mapping metaphor is therefore extended to include all graphic representations of knowledge. Thus, it is common today to refer to 'mapping' the human genome or a management system.

Peter Jackson's metaphorical use of mapping coincided closely with a radical reassessment within cartography itself of map makers' conventional claims to obtain ever greater accuracy and objectivity in their representations. In a series of essays, the historian of cartography Brian Harley (2001) drew upon the critical theories of writers such as Michel Foucault to argue that there was a structural connection between cartography and power. Cartographers had long been aware of the opportunities provided by the visual authority of mapped images to shape what is taken as truth. American map makers classified and castigated a whole category of 'propaganda maps', such as the geopolitical images developed by Italian and German map makers in the mid-twentieth century to support nationalistic ambitions and strategic goals. These maps used selected graphic techniques such as exaggerated scale, selected centring, framing and cropping of regions, sharp colour contrast and the aggressive symbolisation of military campaign plans to dramatise ideological claims. 'Scientific' cartographers sought to establish strict boundaries between such intentionally mendacious images and their own cartography. Their belief in the objectivity of their work led to similar criticism of the pictorial cartographic images developed by Richard Edes Harrison to illustrate for a popular readership the progress of the Pacific and European conflicts in World War II, because their basis was the photograph rather than the mathematical projection (Schulten 2001). But Harley and others argued that all maps are cultural artefacts and, as tools of those with wealth and authority, are inescapably bound as ideological instruments into the nexus of power–knowledge.

With his fellow historian of cartography David Woodward, Harley initiated a multi-volume project, *The History of Cartography*. Still in progress, this work has radically extended the scope of mapping history, first by extending the definition of the map to encompass 'graphic representations that facilitate a spatial understanding of things, concepts, conditions, processes, or events in the human world', and second by initiating serious study of the mapping histories of diverse cultures, both literate and non-literate, in time and space. The *History* thus treats mapping as a cultural activity that is present in some form in all societies as the expression of their concern to record, represent and communicate spatial knowledge. The Western mapping tradition, with its focus on rational, geometrically based spatial scaling, classification and allocation is thus revealed as merely one, culturally specific, mode of geographical representation rather than a timeless and universal technique of graphic communication.

A consequence of this recognition is to complicate Harley's initial claims concerning maps and power. The intimate connections between Western mapping, knowledge and power derive from their unique theoretical relations and historically specific circumstances. Theoretically, the rationalist and mathematical foundations of Western mapping entail a distanciation between the observer and the space observed. That distanciation is both intellectual in its objectivity and actual in presenting in the two-dimensional, scaled space of the geographic or topographic map, an image of actual space as seen from a measurable linear distance above it. Historically, from the mid-fifteenth century, the Western mapping tradition resurrected techniques of cartographic representation originally developed in Imperial Rome, and recorded by Claudius Ptolemy. It did so in the context both of developing new modes of property and land exploitation at home and of conquering and exploiting vast territories overseas. In both contexts, the map acted as a crucial agent of social imposition and spatial regulation, so that the cultural landscapes of colonised regions such as the American Midwest or Spanish South America actually reflect in their grids of farm boundaries, rural roads and administrative partition the cartographic structures that authorised their current forms of occupance. In this example, or in the colonial mapping of British India co-ordinated by the great meridian from Delhi to Bangalore, cartographic knowledge certainly has been intimately bound to the exploitative exercise of colonial power. We should be cautious, however, in attributing too simple a connection between the mastering European gaze, its inscription on the map, and the exercise of dominion over subject spaces and peoples. Graham Burnett's (2001) detailed reconstruction of Britain's imperial mapping of interior Guiana in the nineteenth century reveals a complex and fractured story of myths inherited from Renaissance exploration, picturesque attraction to spectacular topography, crucial contributions of native knowledge and appeals to the rhetoric as much as the practice of scientific survey, all of which together yielded a fluid, arbitrary and unstable geographic representation rather than an authoritative and authorising map. And, while connections between cartography and territorial authority are apparent beyond the West, for example in Chinese imperial mapping, other mapping traditions are not so easily subordinated to such a simple formula. The three-dimensional constructions of stick and yarn that Pacific Islanders use to represent knowledge of winds, currents and sea surface patterns, the Hindu cosmological mandalas illustrating Mount Meru rising from the Ocean of Milk, the narrated songlines of Australian native peoples, and Korean or Japanese charcoal sketches of geomantic lines all represent complex and culturally specific forms of spatial cognition and connection between people and place. Maps are sophisticated artefacts, to be read as much for what they reveal of the cultures that produce them as of the geographical information they represent.

If mapping conventions are culturally specific in the anthropological sense, they also vary socially within individual cultures. The idea of mental or cognitive mapping, that we carry spatial images in our heads that serve to guide spatial behaviour such as way finding or place recognition, was pioneered by the urbanist Kevin Lynch (1960), drawing upon psychological theories of images. Behavioural geographers have generated maps of how individuals and groups, defined by age, education, gender and so on, perceive familiar or new spaces. While such work may be criticised for failing to take sufficient account of the learned elements of mapping as a mode of graphic communication, it has produced a broader interest in the cognitive aspects of map making and meaning. Maps may be treated as cultural negotiations between cognitive subjects and material spaces. Further, 'maps' or spatial representations produced by ordinary subjects, and therefore not subject to the conventions of scientific cartography, allow insights not only into human perceptions and affective relations with space and place but also into the imaginative and aesthetic aspects of human spatiality. Even scientific mapping, despite attempts to regulate style and reduce the 'artistic' content of its images (such as the 'plain style' adopted by eighteenth-century map makers in order to distinguish their science from the symbolism and allegory of baroque cartography), cannot fully eliminate these imaginative and aesthetic aspects. In part because of this recognition, in the past decade mapping has witnessed a resurgence of critical interest within cultural studies and imaginative exploration among artists.

Feminist and postcolonial criticism of the 'master-narratives' of Western humanism has emphasised the 'situatedness' of knowledge, and thus focused attention on aspects of space and location. Cognitive and affective dimensions of space and place have been the principal subjects of attention rather than objective, material geographies. This has led not only to historical, literary and anthropological studies of maps as cultural texts, and thus of their selections, omissions, additions and inescapable contextual influences, but also to critical reflection on mapping *spatialities* rather than simply spaces. Western cartography's emphasis on the 'view from nowhere', its selection of material objects or empirical, statistical data to be mapped by regular spatial co-ordinates and its insistence on mathematical scaling renders it a 'masculinist' practice in the eyes of some feminist critics. Challenging this, the artist Kathy Prendergast has developed an 'Atlas of Emotions', revealing the presence of such terms as 'Lost' in the toponymy of colonised North America, thus disrupting the confident assertion of authority represented by the conventional topographic map (Nash 1998). In a similar vein, the artist Pat Naldi has reproduced a school geography exercise – colouring the British Empire red on a world map – as a video installation of the revolving globe to under-line and challenge the colonialist assumptions of her Gibraltarian education (Cosgrove and Martins 2000).

The contemporary world is witnessing a general 're-territorialisation' of social phenomena as the horizontal, bounded and regulated spaces of modernity (materialised, for example, in Fordist production spaces or in the nation state) give way to spaces characterised by interactive nodes, fluid connections, networked linkages, cultural hybridity and altered marginality (apparent, for example, in post-industrial production spaces, virtual reality and the internet). Transgression of fixed, linear boundaries and hermetic categories, and the non-hierarchical spatial 'flows' that characterise so many aspects of the contemporary world, render obsolete conventional geographic and topographic mapping practices, dominated by the logic of fixed spatial co-ordinates. Simultaneously they stimulate new forms of cartographic representation, to express not only the liberating qualities of new spatial structures but also the altered divisions and hierarchies they generate. It is now possible to effect the continuous transformation of a geographic surface through a quasi-infinite number of mathematical projections on the computer screen by means of a single program.

Culturally, at every scale, connections between phenomena formerly considered distinct and relatively fixed, rooted in space or holding to stable patterns of distribution and identity, become contingent and unstable. These characteristics are emphasised by the interactive nature of much of the cartographic information (both visual images and geo-referenced data) on the web (Kraak and Brown 2001). The implications are potentially both liberating and constraining. Geographical

Information Systems, which manipulate and correlate vast amounts of spatially referenced data, can guide terrain-sensitive 'smart' weapons as effectively as they can help pinpoint 'hotspots' of ecological vulnerability for the purposes of species protection. Mapping's conventional claim to represent spatial stability, at times to act as a tool in achieving it, has radically altered. In a world of labile spaces and structures, it is unsurprising that the idea of mapping should require rethinking.

This rethinking has been pioneered as much in the creative arts as in academic geography or professional cartography. Since the situationist subversion of urban mapping in the 1960s and the emergence of conceptual and land art movements in the same years, maps and mapping have been the subject of diverse artistic expressions, given the imprimatur of an art movement by a 1994 exhibition at the New York Museum of Modern Art (Storr 1994). Artists have distorted conventional scientific maps in various ways to explore the limits of their meaning and form, and have extended the concept of mapping into three-dimensional installations, land art works and performance pieces. Two New York examples will indicate the range of this work. The artists Lilla LoCurto and Bill Outcault (2000) used sophisticated body scanners to create full-surface, digitised images of their bodies, applying computer-generated programs to the scans in order to create body maps that dramatised pictorially the distortions of cartographic projection while forcing the observer to view the human body in wholly new ways. Using more conventional techniques of tourist guide mapping, the artist Laura Kurgan produced a powerful fold-out map of 'Ground Zero' for free distribution to visitors seeking to make sense of the huge site of devastation and recovery in lower Manhattan following the attack on the World Trade Center in September 2001. The project placed in sharp focus the sensitive moral and political terrain that all mapping must negotiate but that is too easily obscured by the apparent naturalness of the map in cartographically hyper-literate societies such as our own.

Commercial art has also made imaginative and effective use of maps and mapping. The value of using a map to indicate where a product may be purchased or to stress the accessibility of a location, has long been recognised. But advertising today makes much more sophisticated use of map images to suggest connections between place and product. The Italian clothing company Benetton pioneered the use of cartographic images during the 1980s and 1990s to connect its products to political and moral questions raised by the very globalisation its activities promoted. Cultural geographers have been concerned to interrogate and expose the implications of such uses in mobilising geographical imaginations.

In some respects all spatial activities might be regarded as 'mappings', and all maps as metaphorical to some degree. Mapping is always a performative act, a spatial activity incorporated into the creation and communication of individual and group identity, leaving a trace or mark in the world.

KEY REFERENCES

Cosgrove, D. 1999. *Mappings*. London, Reaktion.

Cosgrove, D. 2001. *Apollo's Eye: A Cartographic Genealogy of the Earth in the Western Imagination*. Baltimore, Johns Hopkins University Press.

Kraak, M.J. and Brown, A. 2001. *Web Cartography: Developments and Prospects*. London and New York, Taylor and Francis.

Wood, D. 1993. *The Power of Maps*. London, Guildford.

OTHER REFERENCES

Burnett, G.D. 2001. *Masters of All They Surveyed: Exploration, Geography, and a British El Dorado*. Chicago, University of Chicago Press.

Cosgrove, D. and Martins, L. 2000. Millennial Geographics, *Annals: Association of American Geographers*, 90: 97–113.

Harley, J.B. 2001. *The New Nature of Maps: Essays in the History of Cartography*. Baltimore, Johns Hopkins University Press.

Harley, J.B. and Woodward, D. 1987– *The History of Cartography*. Chicago, University of Chicago Press.

Jackson, P. 1989. *Maps of Meaning*. London, Unwin Hyman.

Jacob, C. 1996. Towards a cultural history of cartography, *Imago Mundi*, 48: 191–198.

LoCurto, L. and Outcault, W. 2000. *Selfportrait*. Map: LoCurto/Outcault. Seattle and London, University of Washington Press.

Lynch, K. 1960. *The Image of the City*. Cambridge, MA, MIT Press.

Nash, C. 1998. Mapping emotion, *Environment and Planning D: Society and Space*, 16: 1–9.

Norton, W. 2000. *Cultural Geography: Themes, Concepts, Analyses*. Oxford, Oxford University Press.

Schulten, S. 2001. *The Geographical Imagination in America 1880–1950*. Chicago, University of Chicago Press.

Storr, M. 1994. *Mapping*. New York, Museum of Modern Art.

Thrower, N.J. 1999. *Maps and civilization*. Chicago, University of Chicago Press.

— Travel/Tourism —

Mike Crang

> For my part I travel, not to go anywhere, but to go. I travel for travel's sake. The great affair is to move.
>
> R.L. Stevenson, *Travels with a Donkey*

Travel is a spatial practice that has been at the heart of geography. In its earliest origins geography was the stuff of travellers' tales; mixing accounts of varying degrees of heroism and veracity, it long functioned to tell people 'back here' what was going on 'over there'. I want to take us through this, then, firstly in the ways in which travel has created and shaped geographical knowledge. Second, I want to use this to raise questions about the types of knowledge produced – to suggest that we need to think critically about this legacy. Third, I want to think through the experience of journeys. These will focus on the possible transformations of the traveller through 'rites of passage' of various types. Finally, we will look at the structure of contemporary tourist journeys and destinations, and how they relate to more celebrated kinds of journeys.

Travel in the form of exploration became one of the dominant tropes of geography as a discipline that was centrally concerned with producing information on 'other places'. As part of the mythology of the discipline, the heroic explorer looms large, driven by a seemingly insatiable urge to map, name and catalogue the planet. From what the novelist Joseph Conrad terms an age 'Geography Fabulous', where mythical beasts populated the imagined edges of the known world, through to a 'Geography Militant' with the age of European imperial conquest – where mapping and colonisation became entwined – to culminate in a 'Geography Triumphant', where Conrad opines that all the 'blank spaces' on the map of the world have been filled. My purpose here is not to explore all the linkages of geography and its institutions with imperialism (see Driver 2001) but, rather, to think what difference travel made to the practice of geography. Even though the age of exploration has long since passed, popular geography often retains the form of the travelogue – as in articles about faraway people and places in *Geographical* magazine and others like it. Likewise, the notions of 'expeditions' and field trips suggest a continuing lineage of practice atavistically replaying the notions of accumulating knowledge about a foreign world. We might think not just about the places visited but the way that knowledge shapes our notion of the traveller, not just the objects of knowledge but also the subject producing it. It firstly, then, tends to emphasise just that polarity by objectivising people and places encountered, as they form elements of an unfolding series of things to know, while, conversely, 'subjectivising' the traveller, making him or her the main protagonist. This latter move often means downplaying the many institutions and local helpers and knowledge, until geographical knowledge is seen as being produced by the traveller alone – in Mary Louise Pratt's phrase 'he whose eyes passively look out and possess' (Pratt 1992, 7). There is a strong sense here of travel as aesthetically distancing the traveller from the landscape, rendering it an object for visual consumption. Moreover, knowledge is given authority by the travel – when you claim to know something because you were there. Feats of endurance and moments of danger not only add zest to the story but also enhance the credibility of the travelling witness. It may be that geography is engaged with a culture of travel that is not just about a specific gaze on the world but also this embodied practice. So we might look at how a bodily engagement with the environment is promoted as a form of disciplinary practice to suggest that, from eating in remote villages to wading through peat bogs, the physicality of 'fieldwork' is a little-noted but pervasive element of the discipline.

Although there are still 'expeditions' nowadays, this aspect hardly dominates contemporary geography, and issues of travel and knowledge have correspondingly faded from the agenda. However, this waning prominence for academic voyages is partly due to the fact that more people than ever are travelling further than ever before around the globe. So, it would seem important to be able to think through this spatial practice as shaping everyday knowledge about the world for millions of people. We might use geography's history as a starting point to unpack what is going on in travel and tourism. First, we might address the relationship between travel and tourism, travellers and tourists, as cultures of travel. In popular, and many academic, accounts travel is seen as a superior process when contrasted with tourism. Travel is seen as an attempt to engage with the unknown and the different, to expose oneself to other ways of life and cultures, while tourism tends to be defined in terms of visiting places that are made familiar and similar to the place from whence you come – perhaps the epitome being the English breakfast or pub located in a Mediterranean resort.

We have, then, a hierarchy of explorer (charting the unknown), the traveller (encountering difference) and the tourist (following the well-worn trail and reproducing the familiar). Except that it is also clear that these divisions are difficult to sustain the moment you examine them in any detail. So the traveller may well have guidebooks or even be part of a group expedition as much as any tourist. If we look at independent travellers in South-East Asia we can quickly find specific guides, locales and sites that form key points of a fairly standard itinerary.

Paradoxically, the tourist industry has rapidly been able to incorporate those that sought to get off the beaten track into what we might call a standardised alternative tourist system. If we follow up the implications of this, we would see the distinctions between these cultures of travel as social ones that are about status as much as anything. To paraphrase, this tends to be a product of a middle-class value system where I am a traveller while *they* are tourists. Both, though in different ways, act to turn the landscape and people encountered into objects of aesthetic pleasure. And, we might argue, they often do this through visual possession. John Urry (1990) calls this the 'tourist gaze' and suggests two different forms of it: romantic and collective. The latter is that which celebrates togetherness in visiting, which focuses on enjoyment and activities among and between visitors rather than between visitors and the environment. The former is that of the traveller, who seeks an individual encounter with the place visited – one that allows direct contact with the locale. It defines itself in opposition to the collective gaze, and in doing so sows the seeds of its own self-destruction. For, once a site is found and becomes popular, is laid out in guidebooks, develops kiosks or stalls, then it loses its appeal. The result is an expanding structure always looking over the next hill or to the next island for the 'untouched' valley, 'pristine' beach or 'authentic' locals. Thus Alex Garland's popular novel *The Beach* (later made into a film) is the story of jaundiced backpackers searching for and finding the perfect beach and desperately trying to keep it secret from others. As the main protagonist succinctly put it: 'Set up in Bali, Ko Pha-Ngan, Ko Tao, Borocay, and the hordes are bound to follow. There's no way to keep it out of the *Lonely Planet* [guidebook] and once that happens it's countdown to doomsday' (Garland 1998, 139). We can look at these two tendencies reflected in types of tourist photography: where collective tourism produces the snapshot, the caught, unscripted moment of interaction focusing on people, those who define themselves as 'travellers' tend to use more expensive cameras for more formally composed, 'arty' shots. But, as Urry points out, wearing a camera is like a badge announcing that you are a tourist and separated from the locals. It is saying that they are providing a spectacle for visual capture and consumption. So it should come as no surprise that studies also find that those who define themselves as 'serious travellers' occasionally elect not to have a camera at all lest it get in the way of the experience (Redfoot 1984).

We might think about cultures of travel, then, as specific ways of structuring experience. The notion of the traveller escaping the beaten path led Dean MacCannell (1976) to suggest that tourism is a quest for the authentic – the 'real thing'. Certainly, an analysis of tourist brochures suggests this is often one of the things promised: to see the 'real Greece', visit 'hidden Tuscany', '100% Pure New Zealand' and so on. At one level this approach again suggests that less discerning travellers are bamboozled by what Daniel Boorstin has called 'pseudo-events' – shows and exhibits created especially for the tourist. This sets up romantic-style tourism or travel as a quest for the authentic. The authentic is judged in contrast to artificial displays – such as genuine local artefacts rather than souvenirs especially produced for tourists or festivals for local people rather than performances staged for tourists. Drawing on the work of the sociologist Irving Goffmann, we can separate staged activities in a 'front area' – that is, performances set up to manage appearances and expectations of the viewers – from 'back areas', where people are 'off duty' and act as their genuine selves. It is the latter that the questing traveller seeks. As we have seen with 'new' destinations, these back areas too can quickly become commercialised and managed till we have what we might label with the oxymoron 'staged authenticity', where people perform their 'normal lives'. The very presence of visitors destroys the sense of unmediated authenticity. And so, in response, a new, really real backstage can be promised to other travellers. This questing thus continues ad infinitum.

There are other sides and organising principles to the tourist experience, and one such that anthropologists have pointed to is the links with traditions and practices of pilgrimage. Pilgrims would, for instance, set out from home to visit sites associated with, say, the life of a saint, or shrines consecrated to a deity. Pilgrimage in this form still continues, and involves millions of people. But tourists can look like secular pilgrims say, as Northern Europeans travel south as 'sun worshippers', or where devotees take tours of locations used in an author's books, in films of their books and the places they lived. In terms of the experience the common element is the structuring of space and time into the sacred and the profane. The profane is the space of everyday life while the sacred is the 'extra-ordinary' or elevated state. This can be seen to have two related implications – first for the traveller, and second for the places travelled to and through.

Nelson Graburn (1977) suggests that this structure can be interpreted as a 'sacred journey' that is about transforming the self, or gaining knowledge and status through contact with the non-ordinary or sacred, and that is a parallel process in formal pilgrimage and in tourism. If we return to our example of the South-East Asian independent traveller, it may be a cliché but let us imagine an eighteen-year-old perhaps spending some time before starting university. The young traveller is here setting out to gain experience. At one extreme we might look at the aim as one of transforming the self – learning about yourself, as well as others, by confronting different cultures, or by bonding with a peer group of fellow travellers. This process is a classic 'rite of passage'; that is, a social 'ritual' performed at a specific age and designed to change the social status of the individual concerned. The conventions on this may be more or less formal. Formal rites of passage, such as the Jewish bar mitzvah or Christian confirmation, tend to be related to a specific cultural background. We might look, then, at the way different types of travel and tourism act as informal rites of passage for people of different cultural backgrounds; so we might ask if the 'gap year' is related to a particular class or cultural background. Having been on a 'backpacking' holiday in, say, South-East Asia may then signal belonging to a specific cultural group – excluding those who have not been through this experience. The process may be one of transformation, or we might look at it as a process of accumulating what the French sociologist Pierre Bourdieu (1984) calls 'cultural capital'. This term denotes the stockpile of our knowledge, possibly in our heads, possibly shown through a collection of cultural artefacts (such as souvenirs).

So, for instance, where travellers tell each other they have 'done' Thailand or Phuket, or seem to be 'ticking off' 'must-see' sites on an itinerary, it may be that we can interpret this precisely as collecting items with cultural capital back home. We might connect this with practices such as collecting souvenirs or taking pictures: as evidence of the accomplishment of a successful holiday. So different sorts of people have different expectations and criteria for what makes a 'good' holiday, and they also involve specific material cultures – objects given special meaning in the process.

The second implication, from the point of view of travel and tourism, is that rites of passage often involve not only set periods of transition but transitional time-spaces. That is, these rites do not just occur 'at home' but, rather, the ritual is marked by a time apart from the normal routine, and here we might point out very often a time-space apart, as defined period and place of transition. So we need also to think about the effects on the places visited. The simplest take on this is to carry the 'sacred journey' metaphor through and think of the relationship of destinations with shrines. We might then suggest that modern secular tourism works through the 'sacralisation' (the making sacred) of sites, marking them out as different from the everyday spaces the visitors inhabit, and thus literally 'extra-ordinary'. This sacralisation can occur through official processes – for instance, the designation of 'national park' or 'world heritage site' – or it may be less formal but instead be developed through influential institutions, such as in the promotion of tourist sites in the Western United States by rail companies where they have developed a discourse of 'national tourism' and landscape, so that visiting sites such as the Grand Canyon or Yosemite could be seen as an expression of patriotism. Sacralisation is perhaps most common through these latter kind of institution, and is developed through discourses in guidebooks, brochures, TV programmes, newspaper reviews and many other media. These serve to inscribe various meanings (for instance, of how exotic a place is, how remarkable the culture of the locals is, how beautiful, how adventurous and so on) onto the landscape. This we might call an exercise in practical geography – writing the earth, labelling it and filling it with meanings. One of the ways we might approach this is to examine or deconstruct the language of tourism (Dann 1996) and look at how various media shape destinations (see Selwyn 1996). The process can develop its own momentum, whereby the very popularity of a site can make it 'sacred', such that people feel compelled to include it in their itinerary; or it can go the other way, as suggested above, with the cachet of a site perhaps depending upon its exclusivity, and thus its popularity may diminish the aura of sacrality for some visitors.

However, this is to focus a little too much on the prescriptions, and to suggest that things are a little too orderly. If we think about these sacralised spaces as extra-ordinary then we can see them as places where the normal rules either do not apply or perhaps shift or loosen. Following the work of Victor Turner, people have suggested that tourist destinations are 'liminal' or 'liminoid' zones (Shields 1991). The term derives from the Latin for beach – between sea and land, yet part of neither. So the term is used to suggest places between different sets of cultural rules, such that may be occupied by possibly transitory inhabitants for only a short period of time which put together, what is suggested is a place of an unstable, temporary order. So, for instance, when in these liminal zones of tourism, we are often required to be more sociable or outgoing in new and flexible arrangements in order to make friends with strangers. The 'liminal' status of these friendships is perhaps exemplified by how few times they are sustained after the travels – and indeed doubly emphasised by the sense of social awkwardness when one side does try and retain contact when the other saw their relationship as a temporary connection. We might then think about the way holiday resorts sanction – indeed, demand – behaviour that is not the same as norms at home. Behaviour that breaches or transgresses the norms of home is often very much part of travel culture. Thus holiday resorts have long been associated with sexual licence and relaxed social mores – from the 'kiss me quick' hats and 'saucy' seaside postcards of post-war British resorts to the hedonism promoted by Club 18–30 or the club culture of Ibiza or Aya Napa.

Tourism can thus be seen as a spatial practice that re-animates many of the structures in more 'classical' forms of travel – with 'sacred' sites, rites of passage, liminal experiences and the accumulation of cultural capital being involved in both tourism and traditional travel. It is also the case that tourism and travel can be about transgression, breaking free of everyday constraints and developing new experiences and attitudes, and that these freedoms are 'real' and appreciated. However, for all the emphasis in promotional material about personal freedom, the very notion – and market dominance – of package holidays speaks of a standardised product and set of practices. A strong tendency among academic commentators is to draw distinctions between 'mass tourists' and 'travellers'. Mass tourists are frequently treated as a homogeneous mass, who are often metaphorically described like animals as hordes, herds or flocks, making them sound almost like a separate species. But, as discussed above, this division is not really tenable. For a start, these 'typologies' of types of tourists miss the fluidity and dynamism of the practices of doing tourism. That is, when travelling our roles are complex and multifaceted, with us being – say – child or parent, cook, driver, tourist, party-goer and cultural tourist, all in the same twenty-four hours. Furthermore, there are similarities between even 'academic' travels (say to a field site, to bring back knowledge to make into a dissertation to get a degree) and 'tourist' travels (say to a holiday zone, to get a tan, to compare stories with your friends). So we need to think carefully about two implications. First, academic work may not be in a fundamentally different category from tourism, and thus we need to think through what this means about how we regard academic work and tourists. Second, if we can see the legacies of imperial travel and exploration in our forms of knowledge, we need to think carefully what that says about how tourists experience the world. For instance, we might reflect on how often the 'impacts' of tourism upon a local community are studied. Yet, if we think about this, it tends to position tourism as a mobile, global, powerful subject doing things to fixed, local objectivised inhabitants – exactly in the way that we have seen travel writing tends to portray locals. If we just think about this we can see that categories need to acknowledge, at least, how those who are tourists one day are the toured the next or how 'locals' often use global connections themselves.

So the challenge for a critical geography of tourism and travel is to come up with an approach (or approaches) that addresses the complex and powerful realities of tourism and travel, without replaying these divisions of traveller/host, local/outsider, authentic/inauthentic. It is perhaps a truism to say that, at the start of this century, more people are travelling further and more often than ever before. Geography is still working on a way of adequately making sense of where they go, why these places, what effects the travel has, and on whom.

KEY REFERENCES

MacCannell, D. 1976. *The Tourist: A New Theory of the Leisure Class*. New York, Schocken.

Selwyn, T. ed. 1996. *The Tourist Image: Myths and Myth Making in Modern Tourism*. Chichester, Wiley.

Shields, R. 1991. *Places on the Margin: Alternative Geographies of Modernity*. London, Routledge.

Urry, J. 1990. *The Tourist Gaze: Leisure and Travel in Contemporary Societies*. Beverly Hills, Sage.

OTHER REFERENCES

Bourdieu, P. 1984. *Distinction: A Social Critique of the Judgement of Taste*. London, Routledge.

Dann, G. 1996. *The Language of Tourism: A Sociolinguistic Interpretation*. Wallingford, Oxfordshire, CAB International.

Driver, F. 2001. *Geography Militant*. Oxford, Blackwell.

Garland, A. 1998. *The Beach*. East Rutherford, NJ, Riverhead Books.

Graburn, N. 1977. Tourism: the sacred journey, in V. Smith. *Hosts and Guests: The Anthropology of Tourism*. Philadelphia, University of Pennsylvania Press, 17–31.

Pratt, M.L. 1992. *Imperial Eyes: Travel Writing and Transculturation*. London, Routledge.

Redfoot, D. 1984. Touristic authenticity, touristic angst and modern reality, *Qualitative Sociology*, 7, 4: 291–309.

Stevenson, R.L. 2002. *Travels With a Donkey in the Cevennes*. Utah, Quiet Vision Publishing.

— Space/Place —

Phil Hubbard

Though the concepts of space and place may appear self-explanatory, they have been (and remain) two of the most diffuse, ill-defined and inchoate concepts in the social sciences and humanities. Hence, when asked to reflect on their significance, one is faced with a number of difficulties (difficulties that are multiplied if one stops to ponder the significance of the slash in space/place). Certainly, in their 'everyday' use, the two are often used synonymously with terms such as environment, region, location, area and landscape. In contrast, most human geographers have sought to differentiate between them, suggesting that they are related but distinct concepts. Crucial here is the legacy of two very different strands of geographic inquiry: on the one hand, those humanistic accounts that emphasise the 'sense of place' immanent in different settings, and, on the other, those Marxist and materialist accounts that explore the relations of domination and resistance played out across different spaces (Mitchell 2000). While the former tend to focus on place – typically understood as a distinctive (and bounded) location defined by the lived experiences of people – the latter emphasise the importance of space as socially produced and consumed. But, even if such traditions offer a basis for differentiating between space and place, the imbrication of these two streams of thought in the 'new' cultural geography has further problematised their definition, to the extent that there is little agreement among cultural geographers as to what these terms connote. In some cases, this means that the terms are used interchangeably, with Rob Shields (1991), for example, referring to both 'place myths' and 'space myths' and seemingly making no distinction between them. Given this ill-definition, it is tempting to conclude that space and place are classic 'fuzzy concepts', obscuring more than they reveal (Markusen 1999). But to dismiss these concepts lightly is to discard two terms that remain fundamental to the geographical imagination, providing the basis for a discipline that insists on grounding analyses of social and cultural life in appropriate geographic contexts.

In this sense, it is perhaps useful to return to the humanistic and Marxist geographies that became indelibly associated with the concepts of place and space respectively. Broadly speaking, both had their heyday in the 1970s, emerging as reactions to the absolute or 'empirico-physical' conception of spatiality that informed most geographical inquiry at that time. This suggested that the world was essentially a blank canvas, and, rather than playing an active role in shaping social life, formed a surface on which social relations were played out. Hence, the analysis of spatial patterns was deemed an appropriate and sophisticated way of examining the relationships between people and their surroundings. Rejecting this form of 'spatial science', the historical and geographical materialism that emerged in the 1970s ushered in a rather different interpretation of spatiality, whereby space was deemed to be implicated in social relations, both socially produced and consumed. Perhaps the most convincing articulation of these ideas (though certainly not the clearest) can be found in the work of the Marxist theorist Henri Lefebvre. A self-proclaimed 'philosopher of the everyday', Lefebvre (1991) infers that absolute space cannot exist because, at the moment it is colonised through social activity, it becomes relativised and historicised space. Insisting that every mode of production produces its own space, he further distinguishes between the 'abstract' spaces of capitalism, the 'sacred' spaces of the religious societies that preceded it and the 'differential' spaces yet to come. In outlining this history of space, Lefebvre implies that conceiving and representing space as absolute (as had been common in geography) reinforces the production of relativised abstract space (i.e. the space of capitalism). Rejecting this, he proposes a trialectics of spatiality that explores the entwining of cultural practices, representations and imaginations. Moving away from an analysis of the location of spatial phenomena, this is an account that sees space as 'made up' through a three-way dialectic between perceived, conceived and lived space. Here, place emerges as a particular form of space, one that is created through acts of naming as well as through the distinctive activities and imaginings associated with particular social spaces (see also Soja 1996).

In contrast, humanistic perspectives shifted the analytical focus of human geography from social space to lived-in place, seeking to supplant the 'people-less' geographies of positivist spatial science with an approach that fed off alternative philosophies – notably existentialism and phenomenology (Holloway and Hubbard 2001). Focusing on the experiential properties of space, it is Yi-Fu Tuan who is often credited with introducing humanistic notions of place to geographical studies, though his poetic writings have had much wider resonance in social and cultural geography. Particularly influential here was *Space and Place* (Tuan 1977), which suggests that place does not have any particular scale associated with it, but is created and maintained through the 'fields of care' that result from people's emotional attachment. Using the notions of *topophilia* and *topophobia* to refer to the desires and fears that people associate with specific places, his work alerted geographers to the sensual, aesthetic and emotional dimensions of space. Likewise, Edward Relph (1976) was one the first geographers to clarify the value of a phenomenological perspective in the understanding of people–place relations, suggesting that it is important to move beyond the idealisation of an objective analysis of space to strive for a more human-centred and empathetic understanding of the lived experience of place.

His book *Place and Placelessness* seeks to explore the various ways that places manifest themselves in the consciousness of the lived-in world, describing the distinctive and essential components of place and placelessness as they are expressed in the landscape. A major concern in Relph's writing is to suggest that certain places are more authentic than others, and that community, belonging and a 'sense of place' can only emerge in places where the bond between people and place is deep-rooted. His arguments combine insights into the way people imbue their surroundings with often highly idiosyncratic meanings along with his own obvious nostalgia for those places seemingly untouched by trends of modernisation and 'progress'. In this sense, he writes of how Modern planning and architecture, exemplified in the International-style tower blocks inspired by Le Corbusier, created placeless urban environments where there was no authentic connection between people and place. However, in so doing, he implies that there can only be one true or authentic relationship with place, ignoring the idea that place is polysemous (and laying his work vulnerable to the accusation that it rests on a number of gendered assumptions).

Suggesting that (bounded) places are fundamental in providing a sense of belonging for those who live in them, humanistic perspectives propose a definite but complex relationship between the character of specific places and the cultural identities of those who inhabit them. Against this, materialist perspectives propose that cultural battles create explicit inequalities in the way that space is occupied and used by members of different groups. On the surface, these different traditions present place and space as fundamentally opposed concepts – the former implying 'an indication of stability', the latter denoting 'a lack of univocality' (de Certeau 1984, 117). As such, place is often equated with security and enclosure, whereas space is associated with freedom and mobility (Tuan 1977). Taken to its logical conclusion, it seems one can have one, but not both: spaces are not places, but neither can places be spaces (Taylor 1999). This dualistic take on space and place is well illustrated in the work of Manuel Castells on the social consequences of globalisation and informational capitalism. In his acclaimed treatise on the information age, Castells describes contemporary society as a network society that operates in a global 'space of flows' transformed by electronic and communication innovations (see Castells 1996). Claiming that this 'space of flows' is increasingly responsible for disseminating a standardised repertoire of consumer goods, images and lifestyles worldwide, the implication is that 'local' ways of life and place identities are being undermined by the logic of global capital accumulation as place is annihilated by space. In Castell's summation, this means that the world of places – consisting of bounded and meaningful places, such as the home, city, region or nation state – has been superseded by spaces characterised by velocity, heterogeneity and flow. This, then, is a world of 'non-places', a term coined by anthropologist Marc Augé (1996) to describe the supermarkets, shopping malls, airports, highways and multiplex cinemas that are symptoms of a supermodern and accelerated global society. Drawing obvious parallels with Relph's work (1976) on placelessness, Augé argues that there are now many 'non-places' solely associated with the accelerated flow of people and goods around the world that do not act as localised sites for the celebration of 'real' cultures. Zygmunt Bauman (2000) similarly writes of these as 'places without place', making an explicit link to the spatial strategies of purification and exclusion at the heart of the consumer society (and simultaneously condemning the shallow and banal sociality evident in many sites of consumption).

Superficially, there is much evidence to support the idea that a space of flows is supplanting the world of places: take any city pivotal to the articulation of global financial flow, and one can find many sites that match Augé's (1996) description of a 'non-place'. For example, the public esplanade at the heart of the La Défense district in Paris (Figure 1) can be read as a quintessential space of flow, as Bauman (2000, no pagination) describes:

> What strikes the visitor to Défense is first and foremost the inhospitality of the place: everything within sight inspires awe yet discourages staying. Fantastically shaped buildings which encircle the huge and empty square are meant to be looked at, not in: wrapped from the top to bottom in reflexive glass, they seem to have neither windows nor entry doors opening towards the square; ingeniously, they manage to turn their backs to the square they face. They are imperious and impervious to the eye – imperious because impenetrable, these two qualities complementing and reinforcing each other. These hermetically sealed fortresses/hermitages are in, but not of the place – and they suggest to everyone lost in the flat vastness of the square to follow their example and feel likewise. Nothing interrupts, let alone punctuates

Figure 1: La Défense esplanade.

> the uniform and monotonous emptiness of the square. There are no benches to rest, no trees to hide from scorching sun and to cool off in the shades. As a matter of fact, there is a group of geometrically arranged benches in the far side of the expanse; they are set on a flat platform raised a few feet above the flatness of the square – a platform declaring itself to be a stage which would make the act of sitting down and resting into a spectacle for those who have business to be here. Time and again, with dull regularity of the Metro timetable, ant-like files of pedestrians emerge from beneath the ground, stretch over the stony pavement separating the Metro exit from one of the shining monsters around and disappear from view. And then the place is empty again – until next train arrives.

Unlike the *quartiers* of 'old' Paris, mythologised by Baudelaire, Colette, Hugo, Aragon, Debord et al., there is apparently little here that is characteristically Parisian, with La Défense virtually indistinguishable from monumental office developments in New York (Battery Park) or London (Docklands). As a consequence, tourists instead throng the streets of Montmartre in search of a more authentic Paris, buying into a place identity immortalised in the paintings sold by the artists who jostle for attention in the Place du Tertre.

But, inevitably, the relationship between space and place is much more complex than such superficial readings imply. La Défense may well be a space dedicated to flow, movement and international capitalism, but it is, as architect Doina Petrescu (2002) points out, also a place for the transnational migrants who squat in the abandoned housing on the edge of La Défense. For these Romanian migrants, the promenade is dubbed the 'vague field', and constitutes a space of social and cultural reproduction, where they rub shoulders with bankers during the week and play football on a Sunday. And nor does one have to be an anthropologist to note the diversity of different 'tribes' who routinely hang out on the promenade, skateboarding, posing, playing, and turning it into a meaningful place. Likewise, Montmartre may well be mythologised as an urban village, a place largely untouched by the passage of time (something caricatured in the film *Amélie à Montmartre*), but Louis Shurmer-Smith and Pamela Shurmer-Smith (2002) remind us that the hawkers in the Place de Tertre are not local artists but immigrants from *banlieues* on the outskirts of the city. Notions of authenticity are thus difficult to pin down, the distinction between space and place harder to sustain in practice than in theory.

But, if some commentators are guilty of deploying the concepts of space and place in a somewhat arbitrary and generalised manner, there are others who have worked with these concepts more profitably (and *critically*). Exemplary here is the work of David Harvey, whose discussion of the condition of postmodernity (rather than supermodernity) offers a rather more nuanced account of place making under conditions of globalisation. Drawing on the ideas of Lefebvre, Harvey (1989) explores how places are constructed and experienced as material artefacts, how they are represented in discourse and how they are used as representations in themselves, relating these changing cultural identities to processes of time-space compression that encourage homogenisation *and* differentiation. In doing so, he points out the contradictory manner in which notions of place are becoming more, rather than less, important in the period of globalisation, stressing that the alleged specificity of place (in terms of its history, culture, environment and so on) is crucial in perpetuating spatial processes of capital accumulation. Such arguments have also been addressed by geographers in the context of locality studies, where the attempt by Doreen Massey (1991) to interrogate a 'progressive sense of place' has been hugely influential for those seeking to clarify the relationship between space and place. Invoking notions of hybridity and diaspora, Massey's assertion that places represent a coming together of flows has challenged the idea that they are bounded spaces. Such notions are echoed in the work of John Urry (1995), who has considered the commodification of place in the light of the debates surrounding the changing experience of time-space. Through some intriguing case studies of place marketing and heritage-tourism, Urry shows that the meaning of place is vigorously contested as different cultural groups seek to have their interpretation of place territorialised in texts of all kinds (see also Johnson 2000). In the process, he suggests that a focus on cultures of consumption is crucial for understanding how places are invested with meanings that are the outcome of a complex, spatialised politics where 'insiders' and 'outsiders' are not easily discernible.

For some, this twin focus on relationships of power and the politics of representation is the defining characteristic of contemporary cultural geography (Baldwin et al. 1999). Such concerns with power and language were certainly writ large in the texts most significant in marking out the contours of the 'new' cultural geography. Peter Jackson's (1989) *Maps of Meaning*, for instance, offers a distinctive take on cultural politics by emphasising the discursive construction of space and place via language, with Antonio Gramsci's notion of hegemony used to stress that spatial languages are crucial in the making of social and cultural orders. Drawing on similar theoretical materials, Tim Cresswell's (1996) engaging *In Place/Out of Place* also demonstrates that close attention to the discursive workings of power can be used to illuminate the 'struggle' for place. This continuing preoccupation with the representation of place and space is testimony to geographers' willingness to engage with postmodern and post-structural theories that emphasise the slipperiness and instability of language. Rejecting universal definitions of 'place' or 'space', such notions stress that both are real-and-imagined assemblages constituted via language (Hubbard et al. 2002). As such, the boundaries of place and space are deemed contingent, their seeming solidity, authenticity or permanence a (temporary) achievement of cultural systems of signification that are open to multiple interpretations and readings. This attention to the contingent nature of space and place has also problematised the taken-for-granted (binary) distinctions that often structure cultural understandings of the world – e.g. the distinction of self and Other, near and far, black and white, nature and culture, etc. On occasion, this has shifted the attention of cultural geographers from the making of social and cultural identities to the making of subjectivities, though an obvious tension remains between those accounts that focus on the role of spatialised language in the construction of self (via Foucault, Butler, Derrida et al.) and those that borrow from psychoanalytical theories (e.g. the work of Kristeva, Winnicott and Benjamin) to explore the projection of the self into worlds that are part real, part fantasy (see Sibley 1995).

Summarising the impacts of this 'new' cultural geography, Elaine Baldwin et al. (1999) suggest that there is now a widespread agreement that both space and place are cultural artefacts the meaning of which is constantly fought over in the realms of language. Yet, until very recently, there has been a tendency for cultural geographers to prioritise 'readings' over 'experiences' of the world, distancing them from ongoing debates in anthropology, architecture and cultural studies concerning the *texture* of space and place rather than its textual representation (see, for example, Borden 2001; Highmore 2002 and MacKay 1997). To an extent, this is changing as the impact of non-representational theories makes itself felt (Crouch 2000), and geographers (re)turn to consider the tension between space and place in relation to concepts of embodiment and performance (as well as images, symbols and metaphors). Jackson's work (1999) offers some useful signposts in this regard, suggesting that the meaning (and hence value) of different artefacts is created and negotiated by consumers in everyday places, with the 'traffic in things' across space implicated in the making of wider social relations. In many ways, this echoes work in anthropology concerning the meaning of material artefacts, but adds a distinctive geographic focus by deploying notions of displacement, movement and speed. Far from asserting the redundancy of concepts of space/place, this points the way to a cultural geography that explores the mutually engaging relation between the two, implying that both space and place are made and remade through networks that involve people, practices, languages and representations. Hence, we might usefully conceive of both space and place as constantly becoming, in process and unavoidably caught up in power relations (see Bingham 1996). Ultimately, the fact that place and space cannot be conceived of outside the realms of culture should make us wary of making any simple definition of space or place. Perhaps, then, the key question about space and place is not what they are, but what they do.

KEY REFERENCES

Augé, M. 1996. *Non-places: Introduction to an Anthropology of Supermodernity.* London, Verso.

Castells, M. 1996. *The Rise of the Network Society, The Information Age: (vol. 1) Economy, Society, and Culture.* Oxford, Blackwell.

Holloway, L. and Hubbard, P. 2001. *People and Place: The Extraordinary Geographies of Everyday Life*. Harlow, Prentice-Hall.

Jackson, P. 1999. Commodity cultures: the traffic in things, *Transactions of the Institute of British Geographers*, 24: 95–108.

Lefebvre, H. 1991. *The Production of Space* (trans. by D. Nicholson-Smith). Oxford, Blackwell.

Taylor, P. 1999. Places, spaces and Macy's: place–space tensions in the political geography of modernities, *Progress in Human Geography*, 23: 7–26.

OTHER REFERENCES

Baldwin, E., Longhurst, B., McCracken, S., Ogborn, M. and Smith, G. 1999. *Introducing Cultural Studies.* Harlow, Prentice-Hall.

Bauman, Z. 2000. Urban battlefields of time/space wars, *Politologiske Studier*, 7 September. www.politologiske.dk/artikle01-ps7.htm accessed 25/11/02.

Bingham, N. 1996. Object-ions: from technological determinism towards geographies of relations, *Environment and Planning D: Society and Space*, 14: 635–657.

Borden, I. 2001. *Skateboarding, Space and the City: Architecture and the Body.* London, Berg.

Cresswell, T. 1996. *In Place/Out of Place: Geography, Ideology and Transgression.* Minneapolis, University of Minnesota Press.

Crouch, D. 2000. Places around us: embodied lay geographies in leisure and tourism, *Leisure Studies*, 19: 63–76.

de Certeau, M. 1984. *The Practice of Everyday Life.* Berkeley, University of California Press.

Harvey, D. 1989. *The Condition of Post-modernity.* Oxford, Blackwell.

Highmore, B. 2002. *Everyday Life and Cultural Theory.* London, Routledge.

Hubbard, P., Kitchin, R., Bartley, B. and Fuller, D. 2002. *Thinking Geographically: Space, Theory and Contemporary Human Geography.* London, Continuum.

Jackson, P. 1989. *Maps of Meaning.* London, Unwin Hyman.

Johnson, N. 2000. Historical geographies of the present, in B. Graham and C. Nash eds. *Modern Historical Geographies.* Harlow, Prentice-Hall, 251–272.

MacKay, G. 1997. *Consumption and Everyday Life.* London, Sage.

Markusen, A. 1999. Fuzzy concepts, scanty evidence and policy distance: the case for rigour and policy relevance in critical regional studies, *Regional Studies*, 33: 869–884.

Massey, D. 1991. The political place of locality studies, *Environment and Planning A*, 23: 267–281.

Mitchell, D. 2000. *Cultural Geography, A Critical Introduction.* Oxford, Blackwells.

Petrescu, D. 2002. Pl(a)ys of marginality: transmigrants in Paris, in N. Leach ed. *Hieroglyphics of Space: Reading and Writing the Modern Metropolis.* London, Routledge, 260–270.

Relph, E. 1976. *Place and Placelessness.* London, Pion.

Shields, R. 1991. *Places on the Margin.* London, Routledge.

Shurmer-Smith, L. and Shurmer-Smith, P. 2002. Looking at Paris, in P. Shurmer-Smith ed. *Doing Cultural Geography.* London, Sage, 165–175.

Sibley, D. 1995. *Geographies of Exclusion: Society and Difference in the West.* London, Routledge.

Soja, E. 1996. *Thirdspace.* Oxford, Blackwells.

Thrift, N. 1999. Steps to an ecology of place, in J. Allen, D. Massey and P. Sarre eds. *Human Geography Today*. Cambridge, Polity, 295-322.

Tuan, Y.F. 1977. *Space and Place: The Perspective of Experience.* Minneapolis, University of Minnesota Press.

Urry, J. 1995. *Consuming Places*. London, Routledge.

— Landscape —

Don Mitchell

In one of its everyday usages, the term 'landscape' signifies the specific arrangement or pattern of 'things on the land': trees, meadows, buildings, streets, factories, open spaces and so forth. A bit more technically, 'landscape' refers to the *look* or the *style* of the land: that is, it refers not just to house types, tree and meadow arrangements, or the order or make-up of a place (some of the traditional objects of cultural geographic research), but the social or cultural *significance* of this order or make-up (Meinig 1979). Even more technically, geographers have long understood the landscape to be a built *morphology* – the shape and structure of a place. Finally, 'landscape' refers to a form of *representation*, both as an art and as a complex system of meanings (see W. Mitchell 1994). The key issue for landscape research, in fact, is how these different meanings or senses of the term relate to each other and comprise something of a social totality (in the sense of the term outlined in Williams 1977).

The place to begin an analysis of the interrelationship of landscape as form, meaning and representation is with the understanding that any morphology, any patterns, arrangements and looks, any representational act, does not just arise spontaneously in place. At the most abstract level, all these are the result and reflection of the cultural imperatives of those who make and represent the landscape (Lewis 1979). Yet to say that does not really say much, since it leaves culture still to be specified, an all but impossible project (D. Mitchell 1995). A clearer analysis of the practices that make landscape, and the varying meanings that are attached to it, can be had by understanding that the landscape (as form, meaning and representation) actively incorporates the *social relations* that go into its making. The landscape (in all its senses) is both an outcome and the medium of social relations, both the result of and an input to specific relations of production and reproduction. In our world, those relations are capitalist, of course, and the landscape (again in all its senses) is a commodity. This is perhaps especially so in the case of landscape as a representational art and architecture; Denis Cosgrove (1985) traces landscape art explicitly to roots in both property's and art's commodification.

When understood as a built form, the landscape is, in David Harvey's (1982, 233) words, 'a geographically ordered, complex, composite commodity' that is 'fixed' in space and thus quite unlike many other commodities that circulate more freely. The fixed environment, Harvey continues, 'functions as a vast, humanly created resource system, comprising use values embedded in the physical landscape, which can be utilised for production, exchange, and consumption' (see also D. Mitchell 2003). In short, the built landscape consists in, and is reified out of, the social relations that make and use it – social relations that are defined by a capitalist, commodity economy (e.g. the means of satisfying needs and wants is through a system of commodity production, distribution and consumption predicated on the exploitation of labour).

But, as a representation, landscape is also ideology. It is a specific way of seeing; that is, while landscape signifies the look of the land, it also signifies a specific way of looking *at* the land. Landscape as an idea and ideology has its roots in Renaissance Italy (and, to some extent, Flanders). It developed as a means of representing a certain relationship between landowners and their land during the transition from feudalism to capitalism in Europe (Cosgrove 1984, 1985). Allied with the technology of perspective, landscape was a 'realist' depiction of properties estates. But, as Cosgrove (1984, 24) argues, this 'claim of realism is in fact ideological... Subjectivity is rendered the property of the artist and the viewer – those who control the landscape, not those who belong to it.' It would be impossible in a short essay to discuss in any detail *how* this rendering of subjectivity *as* property is accomplished through landscape representation (see, for this, Williams 1973). Suffice it to say, again quoting Cosgrove (1985, 55), that landscape developed as 'a way of seeing, a composition and structuring of the world so that it may be appropriated by a detached, individual spectator to whom an illusion of order and control is offered through the composition of space according to the certainties of geometry'. Landscape works ideologically to alienate 'those who belong to it': it is something outside them; it is property owned or controlled by someone else (Barrell 1980; Berger 1971; Blomley 1999; Helsinger 1994; Pugh 1990; Williams 1973). In this sense, the idea of landscape, like its morphology, is crucial to the development and functioning of capitalism.

Landscape works ideologically to establish the very conditions of what is 'natural' or 'right' in a particular place (D. Mitchell 1994). It is a representation of what *is* and what *can* be. But, importantly, it works normatively like this largely to the degree that it is a physical form, a concrete materialisation of social relations, and not 'merely' a representation, important as representations can be and are. As Henri Lefebvre (1991) argues, ideology gains force to the degree that it references material form. What is religion, he asks, without the church as a building? More broadly, the form of the land is enormously difficult to change. It is ossified in property lines (and laws) (Blomley 1999), in built structures, and it is deeply *invested* in. Capitalism may very well develop through what Joseph Schumpeter (1975) has called a constant process of creative destruction, but such destruction necessarily implies that some people will lose their fortunes and others will lose their lives (Harvey 1989; Marx and Engels 1998 [1848]; Smith 1990; Storper and

Walker 1989). People work very hard to maintain, to reproduce, the already existent landscape. The landscape – its very built form, in other words – has enormous inertia, an inertia made real not only in bricks and stone but also in people's livelihoods and homes (Harvey 1982).

In this sense, as Lefebvre (1991, 143) says of space more generally, landscapes are not produced 'in order to be read and grasped, but rather to be lived by people with bodies and lives in their own particular … context'. Nonetheless, landscapes certainly are read and grasped, and their varied meanings are struggled over (D. Mitchell 1996, 29; Duncan and Duncan 1988; Duncan 1990; Lewis 1979). They are read and struggled over because the meanings attached to landscapes, working together with the landscape's built form, establish the 'conditions of possibility' for how people live in place. The landscape 'tells' us – when we read it (or when others read it for us) – what is possible, what must be overcome, what is to be struggled for and against. Or, just as likely, it *masks* the relations that go into its making; as built form and representation, and especially as a capitalist commodity, the landscape fetishises (D. Mitchell 2001, 2003). It hides the work that makes it (Barrell 1980).

Kenneth Olwig has shown, however, that the *term* 'landscape' (as opposed to the *idea* of landscape, which Cosgrove explores) denotes communal, collective work. The English word 'landscape' derives from *landschap* (Dutch) or *landschaft* (German), and its various cognates. (Romance language terms that are functional equivalents of 'landscape' are quite different: the Italian *paesaggio*; the French *paysage*; or the Spanish *paisaje*.) The term in its early usage indicated 'an area carved out by axe and plough, which belongs to the people who have carved it out. It carries suggestions of being an area of cultural identity based, however loosely, on tribal and/or blood ties' (Olwig 1993, 311). It also carried with it legal or juridical connotations. If *landschaft* most clearly signals 'area' or 'region' (Sauer 1925 [1963]), then its Danish cognate *landskab* refers to a particular *kind* of region. In Jutland during the feudal period, 'a *landscab* was not just a region, it was a nexus of law and cultural identity' (Olwig 1996, 633), in which the people 'had a greater right to self-determination and to participate in the judicial process and in government' than elsewhere (Trap 1864, quoted in Olwig 1996, 631). The real power of the *idea* of landscape, and its association with property, therefore, derives from the fact that it has so successfully usurped and alienated (ideologically, legally and physically) the work that makes it. The history of the idea of landscape that Cosgrove details is a history of alienation and expropriation.

All this is to say that, while *grounded in* and *deriving from* work, landscape in the contemporary world functions as a source of alienation. Landscape both establishes the geography of production and works to naturalise that geography, to make it seem inevitable that those who build the landscape are not the same as those who own the landscape. This is a crucial move, because landscapes are necessarily not only the site of production (work) but also reproduction (leisure, rest, entertainment and the attendance of bodily needs). Feminist scholars (Anderson 1988; Bondi 1992; Carney and Watts 1990; Katz 1991; Mills 1988; Rose 1993) have shown that establishing the relations of reproduction – or, more accurately, *social* reproduction, since, like work, reproduction is a social process developed historically out of myriad social practices and shot through with the exercise of power (the site of one person's rest, leisure or attendance is, after all, the site of another person's labour, and the power relations of gender, race, class and so forth that structure this site are critical) – is an especially important function of the landscape. In the first place, if we remember, along with Marx (1987 [1867] 537), that 'the maintenance and reproduction of the working class is, and ever must be, a necessary condition of the reproduction of capital', then we can begin to understand how the landscape is a critical component in the setting of the value of labour-power as a commodity. 'In contradistinction to other commodities,' Marx (1987 [1867] 168) writes, there enters into the determination of the value of labour-power 'a historical and moral element'. The landscape, as a vast, humanly created but fixed and not easily destroyed reservoir of use-value, and as a physical and ideological representation of what is and is not possible at any given moment, of what is right, just and natural, is both an outcome of struggle and a mediator of it. The landscape is both a means of struggle and a means to staunch struggle (D. Mitchell 1994, 1996). Struggle in the streets, and in homes, parks, bars, grocery stores, churches, fields and so forth, is vital to the exact nature of surplus value extraction in any given place.

This is easy enough to understand when thinking historically, and when we understand the landscape in the sense in which it was imported into English-language geography – that is, as a term used to designate a bounded region or 'culture area' that was assumed to be relatively autonomous in culture and economy (Sauer 1925; Mikesell 1968). But, just as landscape under capitalism incorporates a history of alienation and expropriation, so too does it incorporate a history of the changing *scale* of social relations under capitalism. Seeing landscape as a delimited area or region, or even as the view from a single vantage point (a standard dictionary definition), is insufficient, because capitalism – with which the very idea and practice of landscape is so inextricably bound – has really never been localist, and so capitalist landscapes have never really been *incorporated* locally. Indeed, one of the functions of exchange is to define a set of equivalencies that tie disparate and often distant places together. These equivalencies are defined through the circulation of commodities, capital and, significantly, embodied labour power – that is, working people. But circulation does not just establish equivalencies across space; it also establishes the status of meaningful differences across landscapes. The circulation of capital, commodities and labour helps establish the calculus of similarity and difference that allows for economic development and change to occur. As theorists of geographically uneven development have shown (see especially Smith 1990), the development of some areas is made possible only through the creative destruction of other places.

In turn, such regional creative destruction – or, less spectacularly, local underdevelopment – sets people in motion, people often with little left to survive on but their own labour power. Given the centrality to circulation – and understanding that such circulation, historically structured and conditioned, is part and parcel of the social relations that landscape incorporates (see Henderson 1999) – landscape should be understood, in Richard Schein's (1997, 663) terms, 'as an articulated moment in networks that stretch across space'. These are networks defined by uneven development – indeed, made possible by uneven development; the sort of uneven development that requires that people move so as to sell their labour, so as to survive. Landscapes define, and are defined by, a geography of justice and injustice. But the very movement of people across already established landscapes – already produced and represented spaces that define the worlds people live in – throws up its own set of contradictions.

One of these contradictions resolves itself as a question of belonging, or 'insiderness'. Cosgrove (1984) has argued that landscape is an 'outsider's' way of knowing (since landscape is a mode of controlling a *view*), and that any affective relationship to the land based on existential insideness (see Relph 1981) is best indicated by some other term, such as 'place'. Important as that may be, there is another issue at work. If landscape is a node in a network of social relations (and is given form by those relations), then the bounding of landscapes, and with it a language of insideness and outsideness, makes no real sense, except as an exercise of power. This is what Western (1981) calls the 'power to define' – the power to define what a landscape is, what it means, who belongs to it and who belongs in it.

This 'power to define' is a complex dialectic since, despite Cosgrove's worries about the impossibility of existential insideness in a landscape, people do form affective identification with the landscapes they live in, and they often seek – sometimes violently – to defend 'their' landscapes against perceived threats and assaults from outside. Hence the contradiction: landscapes are incorporated through processes working at a myriad of scales, but are often perceived, defined and defended in localist terms. Consider, in these terms, the contested border landscape along the US–Mexico boundary. As neo-liberal economic restructuring has proceeded on both sides of the boundary, throwing into ever-quicker motion more and more commodities and people (some ripped unwillingly from long-time homes, others eagerly flocking to the border for the social and economic opportunities it presents), some residents on the American side of the boundary have reacted by calling up nativist, exclusionary images of the American nation (as represented in the contrast between its landscapes and those of the Mexican side of the boundary), and the American state has responded by hardening the boundary to slow the movement of people if not goods (Nevins 2001). The evolving border landscape, hoped by many to become a static representation of (a particular brand of) American nationalism, is nonetheless constantly being reconstituted by struggles over what the border means and how it is to work – and who has the power to define (and enforce) its meanings and its workings. In this regard, landscapes are defensive sites (Gold and Revill 2000).

They are also exclusionary (Cresswell 1996; Sibley 1995; Waldron 1991). As along the US–Mexico border, landscape is inextricably bound up in national identity (Daniels 1993; Matless 1998). Landscape is one means by which people come to know their 'home' (Morley and Robins 1995). But the question, of course, is always *which* people landscapes invite in and which people can find no place in them. To the degree that landscapes are sites of alienation (as well as affectation), it is not only working people (e.g. those whose labour makes the landscape) who are alienated from it. Rather, as Gillian Rose (1993) shows, landscapes are heavily gendered (property being, for so long, the provenance of men), and gender-based exclusionary practices in the landscape are rife (and complex: Nash 1996). And, as Phil Kinsman (1995) shows (by drawing on the photographs of Ingrid Pollard), visible minorities in a 'national' landscape (such as the Lake District in England) simply do not belong. This is a critical issue in an era of ratcheted-up 'globalisation', when new, diasporic patterns are emerging and older national identities seem threatened. But, as with the landscape itself, there is incredible inertia in nationalism, and the two in combination (the inertia of nationalism tied to the inertia of landscape) can be a potent force. It can, among other things, be a potent force in establishing, through the maintenance of inequalities as a natural function of regional and landscape difference, an exploitative labour condition. Again, the border landscape between the United States and Mexico is a primary example of this process.

While it is possible to define landscape as a morphology, or as an arrangement of things, or as a way of seeing, its *power* and *importance* derive from how each of these, working in combination, become the vehicle for all manner of exclusionary, alienating, expropriating and often racist and patriarchal social practices. Its importance as a critical concept in cultural geography derives from this social power and importance, certainly, but also from the fact that it is a reification and a fetishisation. Actually to *see* the power at work in the landscape requires attention not just to the landscape (as a form, representation or set of meanings) in and of itself, but to the social relations that give rise to and make possible the landscape's ability to do work – to function as a reification and a fetishisation – in capitalist societies.

KEY REFERENCES

Cosgrove, D. 1984. *Social Formation and Symbolic Landscape*. London, Croom Helm (2nd ed. Madison; University of Wisconsin Press, 1998).

Henderson, G. 1999. *California and the Fictions of Capital*. Oxford, Oxford University Press.

Matless, D. 1998. *Landscape and Englishness*. London, Reaktion Books.

Olwig, K. 1996. Recovering the substantive nature of landscape, *Annals of the Association of American Geographers*, 86: 630–653.

Rose, G. 1993. *Feminism and Geography: The Limits of Geographical Knowledge*. Minneapolis, University of Minnesota Press.

Williams, R. 1973. *The Country and the City*. New York, Oxford University Press.

OTHER REFERENCES

Anderson, K. 1988. Cultural hegemony and the race-definition process in Chinatown, Vancouver, 1880–1890, *Environment and Planning D: Society and Space*, 6: 127–149.

Barrell, J. 1980. *The Dark Side of Landscape: The Rural Poor in English Painting, 1730–1840*. Cambridge, Cambridge University Press.

Berger, J. 1971. *Ways of Seeing*. London, Penguin.

Blomley, N. 1999. Landscapes of property, *Law and Society Review*, 32: 567–612.

Bondi, L. 1992. Gender symbols and urban landscapes, *Progress in Human Geography*, 16: 157–172.

Carney, J. and Watts, M. 1990. Manufacturing dissent: work and the politics of meaning in a peasant society, *Africa*, 60: 207–241.

Cosgrove, D. 1985. Prospect, perspective, and the evolution of the landscape idea, *Transactions of the Institute of British Geographers*, 10: 45–62.

Cresswell, T. 1996. *In Place/Out of Place: Geography, Ideology and Transgression*. Minneapolis, University of Minnesota Press.

Daniels, S. 1993. *Fields of Vision: Landscape Imagery and National Identity in England and the United States*. Princeton, Princeton University Press.

Duncan, J. 1990. *The City as Text: The Politics of Landscape Representation in the Kandyan Kingdom*. Cambridge, Cambridge University Press.

Duncan, J. and Duncan, N. 1988. (Re)reading the landscape, *Environment and Planning D: Society and Space*, 6: 117–126.

Eagleton, T. 2000. *The Idea of Culture*. Oxford, Blackwell.

Gold, J. and Revill, G. eds. 2000. *Landscapes of Defence*. London, Prentice-Hall.

Harvey, D. 1982. *The Limits to Capital*. Chicago, University of Chicago Press.

Harvey, D. 1989. *The Urban Experience*. Oxford, Blackwell.

Helsinger, E. 1994. Turner and the representation of England, in W.J.T. Mitchell ed. *Power and Landscape*. Chicago, University of Chicago Press, 103–125.

Katz, C. 1991. Sow what you know: the struggle for social reproduction in rural Sudan, *Annals of the Association of American Geographers*, 81: 488–514.

Kinsman, P. 1995. Landscape, race, and national identity: the photography of Ingrid Pollard, *Area*, 27: 300–310.

Lefebvre, H. 1991. *The Production of Space* (trans. by D. Nicholson-Smith). Oxford, Blackwell.

Lewis, P. 1979. Axioms for reading the landscape: some guides to the American scene, in D. Meinig ed. *The Interpretation of Ordinary Landscapes: Geographical Essays*. New York, Oxford University Press, 11–32.

Marx, K. 1987 (1867). *Capital* (vol. 1). New York, International Publishers.

Marx, K. and Engels, F. 1998 (1848). *The Communist Manifesto*. London, Verso.

Meinig, D. ed. 1979. *The Interpretation of Ordinary Landscapes: Geographical Essays.* New York, Oxford University Press.

Mikesell, M. 1968. Landscape, in D. Sills ed. *International Encyclopedia of the Social Sciences*. New York, Crowell, Collier, and McMillan, 575–580.

Mills, C. 1988. 'Life on the upslope': the postmodern landscape of gentrification, *Environment and Planning D: Society and Space*, 6: 169–190.

Mitchell, D. 1994. Landscape and surplus value: the making of the ordinary in Brentwood, California, *Environment and Planning D: Society and Space*, 12: 7–30.

Mitchell, D. 1995. There's no such thing as culture: towards a reconceptualization of the idea of culture in geography, *Transactions of the Institute of British Geographers*, 20: 102–116.

Mitchell, D. 1996. *The Lie of the Land: Migrant Workers and the California Landscape*. Minneapolis, University of Minnesota Press.

Mitchell, D. 2000. *Cultural Geography: A Critical Introduction*. Oxford, Blackwell.

Mitchell, D. 2001. The devil's arm: points of passage, networks of violence, and the California agricultural landscape, *New Formations*, 43: 44–60.

Mitchell, D. 2003. California living, California dying: dead labour and the political economy of landscape, in K. Anderson, M. Domosh, S. Pile and N. Thrift eds. *Handbook of Cultural Geography*. London, Sage, 233–248.

Mitchell, W. 1994. Imperial landscape, in W.J.T. Mitchell ed. *Power and Landscape*. Chicago, University of Chicago Press, 5–34.

Morley, D. and Robins, K. 1995. *Spaces of Identity: Global Media, Electronic Landscapes and Cultural Boundaries*. London, Routledge.

Nash, C. 1996. Reclaiming vision: looking at landscape and the body, *Gender, Place and Culture*, 3: 149–169.

Nevins, J. 2001. *Operation Gatekeeper: The Rise of the 'Illegal Alien' and the Remaking of the U.S.–Mexico Boundary*. New York, Routledge.

Olwig, K. 1993. Sexual cosmology: nation and landscape at the conceptual interstices of nature and culture, or: what does landscape really mean?, in B. Bender ed. *Landscape: Politics and Perspectives*. Oxford, Berg, 307–343.

Pugh, S. ed. 1990. *Reading landscape: country-city-capital*. Manchester, Manchester University Press.

Relph, T. 1981. *Rational Landscapes and Humanistic Geography*. London, Croom Helm.

Sauer, C. 1925 (1963). The morphology of landscape, in J. Leighly ed. *Land and Life: A Selection of the Writings of Carl Ortwin Sauer*. Berkeley, University of California Press, 315–350.

Schein, R. 1997. The place of landscape: a conceptual framework for interpreting an American scene, *Annals of the Association of American Geographers*, 87: 660–680.

Schumpeter, J. 1975. *Capitalism, Socialism, and Democracy*. New York, Harper Torchbook.

Sibley, D. 1995. *Geographies of Exclusion*. London, Routledge.

Smith, N. 1990. *Uneven Development: Nature, Capital and the Production of Space* (2nd ed.). Oxford, Blackwell.

Storper, M. and Walker, R. 1989. *The Capitalist Imperative*. Oxford, Blackwell.

Trap, J. 1864. *Statistik-topographisk Berkskrivelse af Hertugdømmet Slesvig*. Copenhagen, Gad.

Waldron, J. 1991. Homelessness and the issue of freedom, *UCLA Law Review*, 39: 295–324.

Western, J. 1981. *Outcast Cape Town*. Minneapolis, University of Minnesota Press.

Williams, R. 1977. *Marxism and Literature*. New York, Oxford University Press.

— Environment —

Sally Eden

A while ago I bought a take-away pizza that came packaged in a disposable cardboard carton labelled 'totally environmentally friendly', with no detectable trace of postmodern irony. How could such a paradigmatic example of modern, throw-away consumption legitimately bear such a label and what meaning did it convey? What environment was my pizza box so friendly to and why bother mentioning it? This mundane phrase highlights the range of contested and contradictory meanings that we attach to the concept of 'the environment' today.

At one time we might have seen the environment unproblematically as that which surrounds human beings, the inanimate outside, that which human beings impact upon and manage (e.g. Thomas 1956). Although this notion persists today in concepts of 'the business environment' and 'the built environment', recent theoretical developments and policy interests have invoked the environment as a moral qualifier and a realm of contested meanings. Today 'the environment' is no longer an unproblematic concept but has become one for cultural geography, as well as physical geography, to argue over. Given geography's stereotypical preoccupation with the integration of the physical and the human sides of such arguments, the discipline's lack of conceptual leadership on this agenda has been disappointing so far (Coppock 1974; Cooke 1992; Turner 2002). More theoretical innovation has come from sociology, political science and philosophy, and even the 'dismal science' of economics has invented a new sub-discipline of environmental economics to suit the times. As ever, geographers have been borrowing concepts and theories from these and other disciplines to apply to 'the environment'. For cultural geography in particular, there are several areas of conceptual contestation that draw on work from sociology, philosophy and politics.

ENVIRONMENT

First, there is argument over the concept itself – and we immediately hit a contradiction. Academic research expends reams of paper and tonnes of ink on talking carefully about how we define 'nature', yet it often implicitly entwines the concept of nature with that of environment in a rather lazy manner, switching from 'nature' to 'environment' and back again between sentences (e.g. Macnaghten and Urry 1995; Harvey 1996) or subsuming 'environment' under concepts of 'nature' and 'landscape' (see chapters in this volume). These concepts are not simply synonymous. To distinguish more carefully between them, we could say that the environment is often (but implicitly) conceived as primarily *inorganic*, in contrast to the organicism of nature, and *functional*, in contrast to the visual or pictorial aestheticism of landscape. Hence we talk about 'environmental pollution' and 'environmental management', not natural pollution or management (which would be read as having the opposite meaning).

Second, there is argument over the environment as agent. There has always been debate within geography over how much the environment influences or determines human development and organisation. For centuries the environment was used to explain geographical differentiation, especially between races or nations – the original meaning of 'environmentalism' was precisely such 'environmental determinism' (Livingstone 1992). And such views persisted. In the early twentieth century geographers were still debating how far 'environmentalism' applied, although they were beginning to reject the crudest forms of environmental determinism in favour of a more complex idea of how environmental factors and human agency interrelated (e.g. Fleure 1947; Clark 1950; Taylor 1951). But, with the rising power of human technology and the dominant Enlightenment ideal of progress, more and more commentators questioned the environment's power to shape human destiny and instead argued that the power lay with humans to use the resources offered by the environment in fulfilling that destiny.

By the late twentieth century some researchers became concerned that the pendulum had swung too far, that academic work had moved so far away from the perils of environmental determinism that it was in danger of falling into the opposite trap of social determinism by denying any power to environmental processes. Sociologists in particular have been criticised for failing to appreciate nature's agency and seeing society as exclusively framed by human actors (e.g. Murphy 1994; see debates in Pickering 1992), and similar dangers face geographers (Gandy 1996; Demeritt 1994). The approach of social constructionism has been used to open the 'black box' that is 'environmental issues' and to explore how these issues are framed, communicated and argued, especially through the media and the input of environmental pressure groups (e.g. Downs 1972; Hansen 1993; Hannigan 1995).

But such approaches have been challenged for ignoring the influence on human development and organisation exerted by environmental forces, and for epitomising human arrogance. Environmental activists fear the implications for policy and action. If 'the environment' is merely a social construction, can there be any such thing as an 'environmental problem' that needs addressing? Does this take away the obligation to protect the environment by making the object of protection a chimera? In the wrong hands, it is argued, this undermines any attempt to protect lands seen as 'wild' or 'natural' because they become figments of the imagination. This is not the intention, and is instead rather like arguing that, if the idea of the family is socially constructed (which few would dispute), then parents and children do not exist or are worthy of protection. Showing how environmental 'problems' are constructed does not mean that they do not exist but does mean that they are named and framed so as to be identifiable and actionable by humans. As John Dryzek (1997, 10) notes, 'just because something is socially interpreted does not mean it is unreal'. Indeed, work on the social and cultural construction of the environment (e.g. Katz and Kirby 1991; Escobar 1996; Demeritt 2001; Cronon 1995) has shown us more clearly how we think about the environment, and may even tell us more about social processes than it does about environmental processes.

ENVIRONMENTAL

Third, a quite different conceptual argument revolves around using the environment not as a noun but as an adjective. This is quite different from the way in which we use nouns such as 'nature' or 'landscape', because the environment often does not serve as an essentialist category, as they do, but as a qualifier, an arbiter of degree rather than of essence. For example, what do we mean by environmental policy, environmental ethics, environmental perceptions, environmental values? To return to my pizza box, what does 'environment-friendly' mean? This has become increasingly difficult to define, as diverse ideologies, activities and groups have appropriated such 'environmental' labels since the 1970s. In consequence, analysing 'environmental' thinking, and specifically 'environmentalism', has become important. Analysts such as Timothy O'Riordan (1976) and Robyn Eckersley (1992) have classified environmental thinking based on commitment not only to environmental reform but also to challenging scientism and exclusionary technocracy. Andrew Dobson (1990) illustrates this nicely when he defines 'light' green policies and groups as 'environmentalism', to indicate how their reformist, incremental and ideologically insubstantial thinking fails to challenge the (environmentally damaging) status quo, and defines 'dark' green politics as 'ecologism', to indicate how their more radical thinking seeks to restructure our societies and economies in pursuit of environmentally sound arrangements. Such analyses attempt to reclaim the 'environmental' label and redefine it more clearly than the present free-for-all allows. The debate about whether green consumerism (sometimes called sustainable consumption) is a viable movement or an oxymoron again illustrates how the environmental label is stretched to cover all sorts of activities and in the process becomes highly contested itself (e.g. Luke 1997; Dobson 1990; Irvine 1989).

In effect, the slippery definition of 'environment' *enables* this appropriation of environmental labels. The ready identification of environmental quality as a public good makes environmental credentials morally and politically useful but not necessarily reliable. More and more groups, from fast-food companies to the World Bank, use 'environmental' concepts and terms in ways that can seem incongruous or simply false. In response, attention has been devoted recently to analysing and deconstructing 'green' discourses and metaphors (e.g. Hajer 1995; Dryzek 1997; Luke 1997; Harré et al. 1999). In the 1970s the concepts of 'limits to growth' and 'environmental crisis' were keenly contested: the finite 'spaceship Earth' and the 'global commons' of the neo-Malthusians were pitted against the limitless human imagination and innovation of the technocentrists (Harvey 1974; Sandbach 1980; O'Riordan 1976). Today other metaphors hold sway: the nuclear spectre, the 'global greenhouse' and the perils of genetically modified 'Frankenstein foods' carry powerful threats when deployed by environmental pressure groups. The contestation of environmental meanings is therefore shot through with political and economic contingency, and increasingly with fears about technology and control informed by Ulrich Beck's (1992) 'risk society' thesis.

Moreover, the early stages of environmentalism easily characterised business as the environmental enemy, but the growthist backlash has now taken shape (Rowell 1996). Environmentalism has been appropriated through the Wise Use movement in North America (Brick and Cawley 1996) and the debunking of the greenhouse effect (Beder 1999). Business and environmental non-governmental organisations (NGOs) battle over the framing of environmental and conservation issues – and both sides claim legitimacy (e.g. Eden 1999; Grolin 1998; Bridge and McManus 2000). The battle for environmental rhetoric is now tied in with anti-globalisation protests that seek to re-establish the connections between everyday consumption and its effects on distant farmers, labourers and environmental damage. Today we see that 'the environment' does not merely provide material resources but rhetorical and political resources for people to use in persuading others of their case.

ENVIRONMENTAL SCALES

Fourth, there is debate over the scale of environmental meanings. The 1980s saw the environment hit the agenda of international politics, especially through the UN World Commission on Environment and Development, which produced the 'Brundtland Report' in 1987, and the UN Conference on Environment Development in Rio de Janeiro in 1992, sometimes called the 'Earth Summit'. The post-Brundtland sustainable development agenda drove environmental ideas into national government policies and social science debates. The intangible sciences of atmospheric composition and climate change, as well as imagery of the Earth from space, contributed to a new conceptualisation of a singular 'global environment' (Buttel et al. 1990; Cosgrove 1994; Yearley 1996). This supranational construction is presented as worthy of international protection, as are other globally referential concepts such as 'free trade'. Indeed, some see parallels in these two global (and globalising) discourses (Yearley 1996). 'Modern environmentalism has accommodated itself surprisingly readily to the global free-market resurgence' (Taylor and Buttel 1992, 412), because both attend to the separation of consumption from production and borderless action beyond the nation state.

Sociologists such as Beck (1992) and Andrew Ross (1991) point to the distancing of people's ordinary perceptions from 'environmental issues' through the increasing scale of issues and the dominance of scientific construction. 'Instead of feeling the weather as we have felt it historically, as part of a shared local, or even national, culture, we are encouraged to think of it globally' (Ross 1991, 25). One quintessentially environmental issue in this new mould is the ozone layer: global, intangible, measurable only by science and its technological meters, its destruction the by-product of luxurious industrialisation, its consequences deleterious to human health and its protection the responsibility of ordinary producers and consumers. Yet the ordinary person cannot touch or measure the ozone layer because it lies beyond everyday experience.

The contested character of environmental meanings is thus geographically nuanced. At the same time as being constructed through global environmental rhetoric and agendas, the environment is differentiated locally (Gold and Burgess 1982). The familiar, the tangible and the immediate local environments that we know contrast with the detached global construct, as do the ethics and actions we associate with each. Driven by the humanistic approach and 'cultural turn', this has proved fertile ground for cultural geographers in the 1980s and 1990s. Explorations of the local and familiar, especially within environmental conflicts, illustrate how the environment is differently imagined and valued because of locality but also because of socio-political identification, gender, educational background and personality (e.g. Harrison and Burgess 1994; Harrison et al. 1996; Burningham and O'Brien 1994). We can see that, in this sense, there is not one 'environment' but multiple environments (Macnaghten and Urry 1998).

At the same time, the recent rise in academic attention to ethics has re-asserted the importance of linking ideas and action and in pursuing environmental justice, even in the face of postmodernist challenges to the possibility of judgement. Morally, the connection that each individual has with the (especially local) environment is argued to be useful for imbuing environmental citizenship in moves towards sustainability. Environmental awareness and education are seen as valuable projects for the new civil society, in the interests of democratically involving publics in environmental decision making, but also in the interests of implementing environmental policies through citizen action (Parker 1999). In this way, the environment is internalised in the individual, even as global constructions of environmental change dominate the media headlines.

But, in debates about policy programmes, practical developments and ethical dilemmas, the perils of relativism in accepting social constructionism arise again. If there are multiple environments, which one does policy accept or pursue? Are the environmental arguments of Exxon as good as those of Friends of the Earth? On what grounds can we justify our allegiance? The environment is highly contested as a concept and a meaning, often reflecting broader rationalities and ideologies into which specific environmental conflicts are drawn. The cultural politics of the environment become crucial to understanding not merely how policies are made and implemented but how groups draw on different conceptual resources to frame and promote their arguments (Burgess 1992, 1990). The arenas for contesting environmental meanings become not only the more obviously adversarial public inquiries but also local and national newspapers, community groups, local and national government committees, recreational events and everyday meetings and conversations.

CONCLUSION

Clearly, in the late twentieth century, the concept of 'environment' moved away from implying simply the surroundings that we seek to manage or that influence us. Associated also with notions of nature and landscape, the environment is contested and re-presented through moral, cultural and political debates. Geographers are finding that it is not enough to consider their discipline as *implicitly* environmental because it deals with the interface between environments and societies and with contemporary environmental issues. Instead, we need to engage *explicitly* with the theoretical and conceptual concerns raised by this new environmental agenda. The myriad appearance of 'the environment' has become its appeal: we can seemingly all be environmentalists now, as well as being growthists, Marxists, feminists, free marketers, neo-liberals and nationalists *at the same time*. In a postmodern lexicon, the environment can serve all, and now it leads both outwards to global constructions of the world and inwards to personal motivations and attitudes.

KEY REFERENCES

Burgess, J. 1990. The production and consumption of environmental meanings in the mass media: a research agenda for the 1990s, *Transactions of the Institute of British Geographers*, 15: 139–161.

Dobson, A. 1990. *Green Political Thought*. London, Unwin Hyman.

Macnaghten, P. and Urry, J. 1998. *Contested Natures*. London, Sage.

O'Riordan, T. 1976. *Environmentalism*. London, Pion.

OTHER REFERENCES

Beck, U. 1992. *Risk Society*. London, Sage.

Beder, S. 1999. Corporate hijacking of the greenhouse debate, *The Ecologist*, 29, 2: 119–122.

Brick, P. D. and Cawley, R.M. ed. 1996. *A Wolf in the Garden*. Albany, SUNY Press.

Bridge, G. and McManus, P. 2000. Sticks and stones: environmental narratives and discursive regulation in the forestry and mining sectors, *Antipode*, 32, 1: 10–47.

Burgess, J. 1992. The cultural politics of nature conservation and economic development, in K. Anderson and F. Gale eds. *Inventing Places*. Melbourne, Longman Cheshire, 235–251.

Burningham, K. and O'Brien, M. 1994. Global environmental values and local contexts of action, *Sociology*, 28, 4: 913–932.

Buttel, F. H., Hawkins, A.P. and Power, A. 1990. From limits to growth to global change: constraints and contradictions in the evolution of environmental science and ideology, *Global Environmental Change*, 1, 1: 57–66.

Clark, K.G. 1950. Certain underpinnings of our arguments in human geography, *Transactions and Papers of the Institute of British Geographers*, 16: 15–22.

Cooke, R. 1992. Common ground, shared inheritance: research imperatives for environmental geography, *Transactions of the Institute of British Geographers*, 17, 2: 131–151.

Coppock, J. 1974. Geography and public policy: challenges, opportunities and implications, *Transactions of the Institute of British Geographers*, 63: 1–16.

Cosgrove, D. 1994. Contested global visions: One-World, Whole-Earth and the Apollo space photographs, *Annals of the Association of American Geographers*, 84, 2: 270–294.

Cronon, W. ed. 1995. *Uncommon Ground*. New York, Norton.

Demeritt, D. 1994. The nature of metaphors in cultural geography and environmental history, *Progress in Human Geography*, 18, 2: 163–185.

Demeritt, D. 1998. Science, social constructivism and nature, in B. Braun and N. Castree eds. *Remaking Reality*. London, Routledge, 173–193.

Demeritt, D. 2001. The construction of global warming and the politics of science, *Annals of the Association of American Geographers*, 91, 2: 307–337.

Downs, A. 1972. Up and down with ecology – the 'issue-attention cycle', *The Public Interest*, 28: 38–50.

Dryzek, J. S. 1997. *The Politics of the Earth*. Oxford, Oxford University Press.

Eckersley, R. 1992. *Environmentalism and Political Theory*. London, UCL Press.

Eden, S. 1999. We have the facts – how business claims legitimacy in the environmental debate, *Environment and Planning A*, 31, 7: 1295–1309.

Escobar, A. 1996. Constructing nature: elements for a post-structural political ecology, in R. Peet and M. Watts eds. *Liberation Ecologies*. London, Routledge, 46–68.

Fleure, H. 1947. Some problems of society and environment, *Transactions of the Institute of British Geographers*, 12, 1–37.

Gandy, M. 1996. Crumbling land: the postmodernity debate and the analysis of environmental problems, *Progress in Human Geography*, 20, 1: 23–40.

Gold, J. R. and Burgess, J. eds. 1982. *Valued Environments*. London, Allen and Unwin.

Grolin, J. 1998. Corporate legitimacy in risk society: the case of Brent Spar, *Business Strategy and the Environment*, 7, 4: 213–222.

Hajer, M. 1995. *The Politics of Environmental Discourse*. Oxford, Blackwell.

Hannigan, J. 1995. *Environmental Sociology*, London, Routledge.

Hansen, A. ed. 1993. *The Mass Media and Environmental Issues*. Leicester, Leicester University Press.

Harré, R., Brockmeier, J. and Mühlhäuser, P. 1999. *Greenspeak*. London, Sage.

Harrison, C. M. and Burgess, J. 1994. Social constructions of nature: a case study of conflicts over the development of Rainham Marshes, *Transactions of the Institute of British Geographers*, 19, 3: 291–310.

Harrison, C. M., Burgess, J. and Filius, P. 1996. Rationalizing environmental responsibilities: a comparison of lay publics in the UK and the Netherlands, *Global Environmental Change*, 6, 3: 215–234.

Harvey, D. 1974. Population, resources, and the ideology of science, *Economic Geography*, 50, 3: 256–277.

Harvey, D. 1996. *Justice, Nature and the Geography of Difference*. Oxford, Blackwell.

Irvine, S. 1989. Consuming fashions: the limits of green consumerism, *The Ecologist*, 19, 13: 88–93.

Katz, C. and Kirby, A. 1991. In the nature of things: the environment and everyday life, *Transactions of the Institute of British Geographers*, 16, 3: 259–271.

Livingstone, D. 1992. *The Geographical Tradition*. Oxford, Blackwell.

Luke, T. 1997. *Ecocritique: Contesting the Politics of Nature, Economy, and Culture*. Minneapolis, University of Minnesota Press.

Macnaghten, P. and Urry, J. 1995. Towards a sociology of nature, *Sociology*, 29, 2: 203–220.

Murphy, R. 1994. *Rationality and Nature*. Boulder,Westview Press.

Parker, G. 1999. The role of the consumer–citizen in environmental protest in the 1990s, *Space and Polity*, 3, 1: 67–83.

Pickering, A. ed. 1992. *Science as Practice and Culture*. Chicago, University of Chicago Press.

Ross, A. 1991. Is global culture warming up?, *Social Text*, 28: 3–30.

Rowell, A. 1996. *Green Backlash*. London, Routledge.

Sandbach, F. 1980. *Environment, Ideology and Policy*. Oxford, Blackwell.

Taylor, G. ed. 1951. *Geography in the Twentieth Century*. New York, Philosophical Library.

Taylor, P. J. and Buttel, F.H. 1992. How do we know we have global environmental problems? Science and the globalization of environmental discourse, *Geoforum*, 23, 3: 405–416.

Thomas, W. L. Jr. ed. 1956. *Man's Role in Changing the Face of the Earth*. Chicago, University of Chicago Press.

Turner, B. 2002. Contested identities: human-environment geography and disciplinary implications in a restructuring academy, *Annals of the Association of American Geographers*, 92, 1: 52–74.

Yearley, S. 1996. *Sociology, Environmentalism, Globalization*. London, Sage.

— Geopolitics —

Gearóid Ó Tuathail/Gerard Toal

The term 'geopolitics' is a gathering point for a series of varied and distinctive discourses about 'geography' and its relationship to the 'political' (O'Loughlin 1994; Parker 1998). Geopolitics can be considered in the broadest manner as the relationship between objects and entities conventionally understood as 'geography' and the 'political'. For some, geopolitics is an objective relationship between geographical forms – rivers, mountains, soil, climate and location – and political structures, particularly states and national communities. This relationship is often conceptualised as one between fixed geographical forms that are permanent and unchanging – part of 'nature' – and human structures that are conditioned and even determined by the physical environment (Spykman 1942; Sprout and Sprout 1969). Certain objectivist narratives feature a geopolitical dialectic at their centre such as a 'timeless' opposition between landpower and seapower, maritime states and continental states, heartland and rimland, East and West, or the West and 'the rest' (Gray 1990; Huntington 1997). These narratives are unsatisfactory not only for their reductive reading of human history but also because they are premised on an unsustainable distinction between the 'geographic' and the 'political'. Put differently, their objectivism is an unreflexive social construction that leaves the power relationships operating in these various 'geopolitical gazes' invisible and unexamined. The recognition, identification and attribution of meaning to 'geography' is always already a social and political process (Ó Tuathail and Agnew 1992). Geography, in other words, is a geo-graphing, a form of 'writing the earth' that necessarily involves culture, discourse and power/knowledge. All geography is cultural geography and all geopolitics a cultural geopolitics (Agnew and Toal 2002).

'Critical geopolitics' is a discursive approach that has sought to rethink the meaning and analytical utility of the notion of 'geopolitics' over the last two decades (Ó Tuathail 1996; Ó Tuathail and Dalby 1998; Ó Tuathail et al. 1998). In doing so, it has contributed to the development of a comprehensive framework by which 'geopolitics' as a problematic, a conundrum of power/knowledge and seeing, can be understood (Agnew and Corbridge 1995). Critical geopolitics begins by asserting the open textual and socially constructed nature of geo-graphy. All geo-graphy is a form of power/knowledge and a form of geo-politics, the hyphen marking the openness of the meaning of 'geography' and the 'political'. Within the universe of possible geo-graphy/geo-politics is that domain of knowledge directly related to the state as a politico-territorial entity. This domain of knowledge can be described as 'geo-power', or the geo-graphing/geo-politics produced by the state as a functioning nexus of power, culture and territory. Thus the production of cartographic maps of the territory of the state is a form of geo-power, as is the creation of territorial surveys, administrative inventories and the demarcation of borders and frontiers. The everyday practices of border patrol, border management and territorial surveillance are forms of geo-power. Geo-power is geographical knowledge for and by the state.

The particular structure, form and functioning of geo-power depends on the nature of the state and interstate system. While many commentators have noted the operation of forms of geographical and geopolitical knowledge in classic and pre-modern states, little systematic study of this subject has been undertaken in contemporary geography. The transition from the pre-modern to the modern state system is taken to be a critical period in the development of modern geo-power and modern geopolitical thinking. Modern states began to organise themselves around the principles of state sovereignty, territorial integrity and national community. With this material transition developed a particular geopolitical ontology. The vision of world political space as a unitary whole divided into territorial units of sovereign statehood is the geopolitical ontology that John Agnew terms 'the modern geopolitical imagination' (Agnew 1997). He identifies four principles of the modern geopolitical imagination.

1. The development of a global vision that enabled the seeing of the world as a unitary whole and its subsequent division into a hierarchy of different places. This global vision displaced theological cosmologies but operated by means of an unproblematised 'view from nowhere' that, in practice, institutionalised ethnocentric ways of seeing and imagining world political space.

2. The turning of 'time into space' as the geopolitical ontology organised the world into 'backward' and 'modern' regions. Places are essentialised, exoticised and relative differences turned into absolute ones (Said 1979).

3. A state-centric ontology premised on assumptions that the world is made up of states exercising power over blocks of space, that the territorial state is a container of society and that there is a fundamental divide between 'foreign' and 'domestic' affairs' (Walker 1993). Agnew terms this specific principle the 'territorial trap' in thinking and acting about world politics.

4. The assumption that the interstate system is characterised by a 'condition of anarchy' and that dominant states accumulate power at different rates and struggle in a pursuit of primacy.

Agnew notes how the modern geopolitical imagination is a particularistic spatial ontology of world politics, one that began in the sixteenth century but did not become dominant until the nineteenth and twentieth centuries. It is Eurocentric in that the modern territorial nation state first developed in Europe, and this particularistic fusion of geography, identity and power came to be exported to the rest of the world through the history of European colonialism. In addition, this modern geopolitical imagination has always been contested by competing spatial ontologies. The ideology of liberalism, for example, envisions a world made up of trading relationships between different regions and economic actors. Socialist internationalism envisages a world of worker solidarity across different states. Contemporary transnational civil society is characterised by many alternative imaginations, from the ocean-centrism of Greenpeace to the planetary environmental consciousness of organisations such as the World Watch Institute or the Nature Conservancy (Luke 1997).

Agnew periodises the modern geopolitical imagination into 'three ages of geopolitics'.

1. Civilisational geopolitics, which he dates from the late eighteenth century through to the late nineteenth century. This was the geopolitical discourse of aristocratic and conservative bourgeois states concerned about the rising nationalism unleashed by the French Revolution and the emergent class consciousness developing as a result of the Industrial Revolution. Civilisational geopolitics envisaged the world as organised by a civilisational hierarchy, with the most advanced and superior states having a 'civilising mission' to rule over the more 'barbarous' and 'savage' parts of the world.

2. Naturalised geopolitics, which is associated with the period of inter-imperialist rivalry from 1875 to 1945. This epoch, according to Agnew, was characterised by the naturalisation of the practices of imperialism and territorial expansionism by rival states. 'Science', particularly biology but also geography and racialised ethnography, was evoked to justify imperial domination and aggressive militarism (Henrik Herb 1997; Murphy 1997).

3. Ideological geopolitics, which is associated with the epoch of the Cold War rivalry between the United States and the Soviet Union. In this schema the world is divided into antagonistic blocks, with a 'Third World' in between as a terrain of competition and proxy wars (Dalby 1990).

Agnew's 'three ages of geopolitics' encompass traditional understandings of geopolitics within a much larger history of geopolitical ontology and discourse. The term 'geopolitics' itself was first coined by the Swedish political scientist Rudolf Kjellen in 1899. It was later codified into a distinctive tradition of thinking by Karl Haushofer and those associated with the journal *Zeitschrift für Geopolitik* in Weimar and, later, Nazi Germany (Natter 2003). Although this tradition's relationship to Nazi foreign policy is complex, it did help naturalise the aggressive expansionist and racist policies of that regime. Repudiated as a term after World War II, the term returned to common parlance only as a consequence of its popularisation by the German émigré scholar-turned-diplomat Henry Kissinger from the late 1960s. Nominally fixated accounts of geopolitics are useful in tracing how the word has historically functioned as a 'floating signifier' for a vague yet apparently grounded, scientific and realist approach to world politics (Demko 1999). What these accounts lack, however, is any systematic critical reflection on geopolitics as a spatial grid of intelligibility for world politics. Put differently, these accounts reproduce rather than develop critical scholarly distance from the categories of the modern geopolitical imagination.

Complementing the systemic historical account offered by Agnew are other critical geopolitics conceptualisations that have sought to analyse the geopolitical problematic in particular states. Stressing the generalised rather than particularistic nature of geopolitics, critical geopolitics makes a distinction between three types of geopolitics.

1. Formal geopolitics, or the codified geopolitical reasoning of intellectuals of statecraft in civil society and various institutions of the states that seek to enframe world politics within a certain spatial logic of intelligibility (Dodds and Atkinson 2000).

2. Practical geopolitics, or the ad hoc geopolitical reasoning of political leaders and foreign policy decision makers engaged in the practical politics of foreign policy making (Ó Tuathail 2002).

3. Popular geopolitics, or the geopolitical logics of identity and difference that permeate the various manifestations of popular culture, from visual media to news magazines and novels (Dijkink 1996; GoGwilt 2000; Sharp 2000).

Contemporary critical geopolitics is also characterised by a series of other concepts, which have not been systematically elaborated. These can, however, be organised into a series of complementary concepts, each building upon the other in a pyramidal fashion, and representing an analytical elaboration of the previous.

1. At the base one has **geopolitical imagi-nations**, or the geopolitics of identity and difference that characterise particular states (Campbell 1992; Sparke 2003). The geopolitical imagi-nations of a state are the self-images that characterise that state and define it in relations of equivalence and antagonism to other actors in world affairs (Atkinson 2000; Newman 2000). Studying geopolitical imagi-nations requires consideration of the construction and maintenance of certain hegemonic notions of 'the nation': who is a citizen and how rights are delimited, what historical myths define the nation, how is it institutionalised in the bureaucratic workings of the state, etc. But it is also requires careful research into the everyday identity assemblage processes that define the life of the geopolitical imagi-nation as a social unconscious. Here contemporary feminist and psychoanalytic perspectives are valuable (Jeffords 1989; Weber 2001).

2. **Geopolitical culture** can be defined as the interpretative culture and traditions within which a state makes sense of its identity and its encounter with the world of states, and codifies a set of strategies for negotiating that encounter. Geopolitical culture is how a state's geographic location, historical experiences, institutional organisation and political culture interact to produce a distinctive mode of interpreting world politics. American geopolitical culture, for example, is shaped by the particular form of colonialism, racism, capitalism and modernity that has taken shape on the North American continent since the late eighteenth century. The

state's perceived historical separation from the world by two mighty oceans yet its close economic ties to Europe, Asia, Latin America and the Caribbean have contributed to a cultural conversation on foreign policy characterised by isolationism, internationalism and unilateralism. Tensions between Eurocentric and Asiacentric orientations abound (Agnew 1984). Geopolitical cultures are built upon and elaborations of geopolitical imagi-nations.

3. A **geopolitical tradition** is a particular foreign policy orientation within a larger geopolitical culture. Russian geopolitical culture, for example, is composed of a series of geopolitical traditions usually codified around the sometimes crude labels 'Westernisation' and 'Eurasianism' (Smith 1999). Walter Mead divides American geopolitical culture into four distinct geopolitical traditions: the missionary ethic of Wilsonianism, the self-sufficient isolationism of Jeffersonianism, the commercial orientation of Hamiltonianism, and the chauvinistic militarism of Jacksonianism (Mead 2002). Geopolitical traditions are established modes of antagonistic dialogue within geopolitical cultures.

4. **Geopolitical discourse** refers generally to the spatialisation of world politics by foreign policy elites (Ó Tuathail and Agnew 1992). Practical geopolitical reasoning, as we have noted, is the daily representation of world affairs and state interests by foreign policy leaders. A central concept within the study of practical geopolitical reasoning is a 'script' which is a regularised way of acting and talking when negotiating certain social situations, scenarios and challenges. A **performative geopolitical script** is what a foreign policy leader draws upon to articulate, explain and enunciate foreign policy. It often takes the form of a leader literally reading a script from a teleprompter when giving a major foreign policy speech. It is foreign policy in public articulation and practice.

5. Within geopolitical scripts are various geopolitical storylines. Unlike a script, storylines are argumentatively developed and relatively coherent narratives used to classify and particularise specific foreign policy problems and challenges. They can be broken down and studied as a **'grammar of geopolitics'**, with situation descriptions, location specifications, subject positioning, attributions of causality and blame, and interest annunciations (Ó Tuathail 2002).

6. **Geostrategic storylines** are those particular types of geopolitical discourse that seek to delimit and define that which is in the 'strategic national interest' of the state. Military planners and national security intellectuals tend to monopolise these discourses with appeals to 'expertise', 'professionalism' and 'hard-headed realism' (Gray and Sloan 1999).

Contemporary critical geopolitics is itself a form of geopolitics, and while it has long sought to deconstruct geopolitical knowledge it also, inevitably, engages in its production. The structures of geopolitical world orders (Taylor 1990), globalisation and 'borderlessness' (Newman 1998), techno-territorial complexes (Mattellart 2000; Sidaway 2001), tensions between geo-economics and geopolitics (Sparke

1998), environmental security (Dalby 2002), geopolitical regions (Dodds 1997) and the contemporary geopolitical condition (Ó Tuathail 2000) are some of the subjects it has engaged. In sum, while there is no stable and singular notion of 'geopolitics', it is a domain of foundational questions, nested plural problematics and pressing political challenges, which is now attracting considerable critical attention within geography and other social sciences.

KEY REFERENCES

Agnew, J. and Corbridge, S. 1995. *Mastering Space: Hegemony, Territory, and International Political Economy*. London, Routledge.

Campbell, D. 1992. *Writing Security: United States Foreign Policy and the Politics of Identity*. Minneapolis, University of Minnesota Press.

Dalby, S. 2002. *Environmental Security*. Minneapolis, University of Minnesota Press.

Dodds, K. and Atkinson, D. eds. 2000. *Geopolitical Traditions: A Century of Geopolitical Thought*. London, Routledge.

Ó Tuathail, G. 1996. *Critical Geopolitics*. Minneapolis, University of Minnesota.

Ó Tuathail, G. 2002. Theorizing practical geopolitical reasoning: the case of US–Bosnia Policy in 1992, *Political Geography*, 21, 3.

OTHER REFERENCES

Agnew, J. 1984. An excess of national exceptionalism: towards a political geography of American foreign policy, *Political Geography Quarterly*, 2: 151–166.

Agnew, J. 1997. *Geopolitics: Revisioning World Politics*. London, Routledge.

Agnew, J. and Toal, G. 2003. Cultural geopolitics, in K. Anderson, M. Domosh, S. Pile and N. Thrift eds. *Handbook of Cultural Geography*. London, Sage.

Atkinson, D. 2000. Geopolitical imaginations in modern Italy, in K. Dodds and D. Atkinson eds. *Geopolitical Traditions: A Century of Geopolitical Thought*. London, Routledge, 93–117.

Dalby, S. 1990. *Creating the Second Cold War*. London, Pinter.

Demko, G. 1999. *Reordering the World: Geopolitical Perspectives on the Twenty-First Century*. Boulder, Westview.

Dijkink, G. 1996. *National Identity and Geopolitical Visions: Maps of Pain and Pride*. London, Routledge.

Dodds, K. 1997. *Geopolitics in Antarctica*. Chichester, Wiley.

GoGwilt, C. 2000. *The Fiction of Geopolitics: Afterimages of Culture, from Wilkie Collins to Alfred Hitchcock*. Stanford, Stanford University Press.

Gray, C. 1990. *War, Peace and Victory: Strategy and Statecraft for the Next Century*. New York, Touchstone.

Gray, C. and Sloan, G. eds. 1999. *Geopolitics: Geography and Strategy*. London, Frank Cass.

Henrik Herb, G. 1997. *Under the Map of Germany: Nationalism and Propaganda, 1918–1945*. London, Routledge.

Huntington, S. 1997. *The Clash of Civilizations and the Remaking of World Order*. New York, Simon and Schuster.

Jeffords, S. 1989. *The Remasculinization of America: Gender and the Vietnam War*. Bloomington, Indiana University Press.

Luke, T. W. 1997. *Ecocritique: Contesting the Politics of Nature, Economy, and Culture*. Minneapolis, University of Minnesota Press.

Mattellart, A. 2000. *Networking the World, 1794–2000*. Minneapolis, University of Minnesota Press.

Mead, W. R. 2002. *Special Providence: American Foreign Policy and How it Changed the World*. New York, Routledge.

Murphy, D. 1997. *The Heroic Earth: Geopolitical Thought in Weimar Germany, 1918–1933*. Kent, OH, Kent State University Press.

Natter, W. 2003. Geopolitics in Germany, 1919–1945, in J. Agnew, K. Mitchell, G. Ó Tuathail eds. *A Companion to Political Geography*. Oxford, Blackwell, 187–203.

Newman, D. ed. 1998. *Boundaries, Territory and Postmodernity*. London, Frank Cass.

Newman, D. 2000. Citizenship, identity and location: the changing discourse of Israeli geopolitics, in K. Dodds and D. Atkinson eds. *Geopolitical Traditions: A Century of Geopolitical Thought*. London, Routledge, 302–331.

O'Loughlin, J. ed. 1994. *Dictionary of Geopolitics*. Westport, CT, Greenwood Press.

Ó Tuathail, G. 2000. The postmodern geopolitical condition: states, statecraft, and security at the millennium, *Annals of the Association of American Geographers*, 90 1: 166–178.

Ó Tuathail, G. and Agnew, J. 1992. Geopolitics and discourse: practical geopolitical reasoning and American foreign policy, *Political Geography*, 11: 190–204.

Ó Tuathail, G. and Dalby, S. 1998. *Rethinking Geopolitics*. London, Routledge.

Ó Tuathail, G., Dalby, S. and Routledge, P. 1998. *The Geopolitics Reader*. London, Routledge.

Parker, G. 1998. *Geopolitics: Past, Present and Future*. London, Pinter.

Said, E. 1979. *Orientalism*. New York, Vintage.

Sharp, J. P. 2000. *Condensing the Cold War: Reader's Digest and American Identity*. Minneapolis, University of Minnesota Press.

Sidaway, J. 2001. Rebuilding bridges: a critical geopolitics of Iberian transfrontier cooperation in a European context, *Environment and Planning D: Society and Space*, 19: 743–778.

Smith, G. 1999. The masks of Proteus: Russia, geopolitical shift and the new Eurasianism, *Transactions of the Institute of British Geographers*, 24: 481–500.

Sparke, M. 1998. From geopolitics to geoeconomics: transnational state effects in the borderlands, *Geopolitics*, 3, 2: 62–98.

Sparke, M. 2003. *Hyphen Nation-States*. Minneapolis, University of Minnesota.

Sprout, H. and Sprout, M. 1969. Environmental factors in the study of international politics, in J. Rosenau ed. *International Politics and Foreign Policy – A Reader in Research and Theory*. New York, Free Press, 41–56.

Spykman, N. 1942. *America's Strategy in World Politics: The United States and the Balance of Power*. New York, Harcourt Brace.

Taylor, P. J. 1990. *Britain and the Cold War: 1945 as Geopolitical Transition*. London, Pinter.

Walker, R. 1993. *Inside/Outside: International Relations as Political Theory*. Cambridge, Cambridge University Press.

Weber, C. 2001. *International Relations Theory: A Critical Introduction*. London, Routledge.

— Governance —

Andrew Jonas and Aidan While

THE CONUNDRUM

Within the last decade the term 'governance' has become widely used in the Western social sciences. Its popularity has risen along with a growing perception that the power of the national state has waned in relation to the growing political and strategic influence of non-state agencies (private corporations, religious organisations, community groups, non-profits and the like) and international and sub-national governmental and parastatal organisations. Why this situation has come about, and what its implications are for critical geographical perspectives on the state and governance, provide the immediate foci of this chapter.

FROM 'STATE' TO 'GOVERNANCE'

The ideological Right and some factions on the New Left have zealously embraced the principle that individuals, organisations and economies can be self-governing (or self-regulating). Indeed, the alleged 'retreat of the state' is often causally associated with the rise of neo-liberalism as a political ideology to replace Keynesianism. Even some groups on the Old Left appear to have accepted the principle that egalitarian forms of economic and political organisation do not necessarily presuppose a centralised interventionist state and that certain forms of state–collective provision are not necessarily 'democratic' or 'equitable'. It is not that the word 'state' has disappeared from academic and political discourse altogether (although one could be forgiven for thinking that social scientists have abandoned any attempts to develop a theory of the state). Rather, the current preoccupation with the language of governance signifies the extent to which modes of social, economic and cultural regulation in modern democracies have changed almost to the point where the term 'state' has become archaic – or so it seems.

The advance of the language of governance in relation to the retreat of discourses of the state poses a number of challenges for political and cultural geographers, for whom concepts such as the state, territories in states, nationalism and territoriality continue to have some theoretical purchase on the world (Cox 2002). Although there can be little doubt that new discourses of governance are inextricably linked to the emergence of new state forms in capitalism (if not to new territorialities and understandings thereof), the concept of governance carries with it no obvious connotation as a set of necessarily territorialised practices. It is perhaps not surprising, then, that research into geographies of governance abounds while corresponding studies of the territorial state or territories in states appear to be on the decline. It is as if geographers see the emergence of governance as another social science conspiracy to deny the causal efficacy of the spatial. Yet *is* governance non-territorial? Where does territoriality – the act of controlling, shaping or engaging with spatial structures to produce social and material outcomes – fit into understandings of the capacity to govern? Can there be a theory of governance without a theory of the state?

In the remainder of the chapter, we critically examine whether an interest in the geography of governance necessarily equates with abandoning concepts of state and territoriality. We seek to make two points. First, to the extent that governance inside the territorial state does not occur without steering by the state, there must be some critical attention paid to what Bob Jessop (1998) has called 'meta-governance'. Meta-governance can be defined as the 'government of governance': the strategies, policies, incentives and practices used by the state to co-ordinate and steer various governance projects in directions that are consistent with the wider interests (fiscal, political, etc.) of the state itself. Second, and by inference, all governance projects are territorial. Governance not only occurs inside the state but also can connect spatially non-contiguous local, regional and national territories. Contra the analytical trend from state to governance, we argue that theories of governance cannot ignore the state as a fundamental dimension of territoriality in contemporary capitalist democracies. Governance is territoriality.

WHAT IS GOVERNANCE?

Governance refers to any social mode of co-ordination in which the aim is to control, guide or facilitate economic and social activities distributed across the landscape, including activities involved in transforming nature. In general terms, social scientific research has focused on two issues (Jessop 1998): (a) *the performance of governance*, including the actions and actors involved in steering and co-ordinating activities; and (b) *the capacity to govern*, including the relationships between actors and institutions involved in performing governance, and the distribution of resources among actors and the construction of networks and coalitions. If (a) places the emphasis on the role of agency and strategy, then (b) requires a focus on the structures and power relations through which governance is performed. Together, (a) and (b) refer to the social structuration of the means and acts of social regulation and co-ordination.

Early work on governance tended to focus on the control and regulation of *individuals* by institutions, including the state. For example, Michel Foucault (1984) understands governance – or what he calls 'governmentality' – in terms of the systems through which the human subject is constituted in relation to wider power relations. Foucauldian interpretations of governmentality therefore tend to focus on the historical development of the relationship between the self qua citizen and state. Recent usage has emphasised the co-ordination or steering of the various interests and groups that together constitute a given system. The system could refer to a particular service, such as education, a group of industries or a territorial system (a regional economy or the state itself). It is the dynamic interaction (and conflict) between different constituencies – traditionally government and civil society actors – that form the basis of contemporary approaches to governance (Painter 2003). Key elements of such approaches include an interest in partnerships, co-operation and the articulation of interests. An important critical angle is that governance arrangements and processes embody interests in the distribution of power, responsibility and accountability among a range of participants in governing relationships.

Sometimes a conceptual distinction is drawn between government (the state) and governance (non-state agencies working alongside or apart from the state). Particular attention is given to the 'informal' venues in which governing decisions are made or power wielded. For example, in urban political theory there has been considerable interest in partnerships formed between the public and private sector agencies involved in urban regeneration. Since such arrangements tend to establish themselves outside the formal realm of electoral politics, urban political theory has abandoned its notions of elitism and pluralism in favour of the idea of an urban regime (Stone 1993). Urban regime theory recognises that the capacity to govern cities reflects a complex interplay between managing state interests, on the one hand, and enabling private sector access to, and control of, public resources on the other. Although regime theory is right to give causal emphasis to the management of private sector interests by the state, its tendency to persist with the formal (state)/informal (market) duality is less satisfactory in part because the kinds of powers sought by private interests are distributed unevenly through the different levels of the state apparatus. In other words, an interest in the character and content of urban regimes would seem to require some prior knowledge of the geography of the state.

What has motivated the rise of interest in governance? There can be little doubt that there has been a substantial and ongoing reconfiguration of functional, organisational and spatial boundaries between the state and civil society. Yet there seems no reason to presume that the rise of governance is simply a function of the rise of postmodernist thinking, post-Fordist forms of social regulation in capitalism or, for that matter, neo-liberalism. Feudal, autarkic and fascist states have all exhibited elements of what could be termed governance (e.g. forms of social control by the state). There is a danger that the term 'governance' refers to anything that is socially regulated or controlled and yet (since all social systems imply means of structuring and controlling individual behaviour within systemic relations) nothing in particular. A key question has to be whether there is something distinctive and different about contemporary state–society relations and struggles to warrant this critical interest.

It has been claimed that the use of the term governance represents a different way of seeing and describing power relations and political processes, exposing what was formerly hidden by 'government' (the state) and therefore neglected by, for example, Marxist state theory. Such theory tended to see the state as derivative of or functional to class relations and struggle. Indeed, criticisms of Marxist state theory have tended to emphasise this very point. This could also explain why conservative commentators and policy makers, to whom (especially in the United States) the notion of the state is an anathema, seem quite comfortable with the idea of governance and its banal expression in discourses of partnership. Belatedly, they (along with some Marxist theorists) have recognised that markets and economies cannot work without some form of extra-economic co-ordination. However, this does not explain why states continue to exist and play a major role in the delivery of services, warfare, economic development and so on. In other words, can there be a theory of governance without a concept of the state?

THEORISING GOVERNANCE

Since governance has only recently emerged as a standard critical concept in the Western social sciences, it might seem premature to talk in terms of a theory or theories of governance (see Rhodes 1997). What is perhaps more intriguing is the fact that its emergence as a critical term has coincided with its widespread use in policy and political discourses. As we have suggested, this can be traced to the search for new ways of conceptualising modes of social co-ordination amidst new challenges for societal management and new interactions between government and society (Kooiman 1993). Indeed, the rise of intellectual interest in governance has been encouraged and legitimated by the state, in part to conceal anti-democratic tendencies in emerging modes of social and cultural regulation. Many of the objects to which the term applies, such as quangos and partnerships, are far from socially inclusive or accountable to electorates. Discourses associated with governance, such as 'partnership', 'entrepreneurialism', 'citizenship' and 'leadership', are closely connected to the neo-liberalisation of economies, cities and territories. To some extent, the state is disguising its own failure to restore coherence to local and regional economies by placing responsibility on individuals, economies and places to be self-governing. Since these lack the resources to undertake governance through means that produce just ends, the shift from redistributional to entrepreneurial modes of governance is a serious threat to liberal notions of territorial justice.

If the relationship between governance and democracy is contingent, and yet governance discourse is so pervasive in contemporary states in capitalism, is it wise to talk of governance without thinking about the state? For Jessop (1998), the increasing use of the term marks the move away from the idea that political authority is vested solely in the territorial state (which in turn derives its authority from sovereignty). Governance does not prejudge the organisational form or territorial locus of decision making, as reflected in the emphasis on networks, associations, coalitions, regimes and other forms of interaction and interdependence among organisations, functional hierarchies and territories. Jessop believes that the rise of governance is a part of complex changes in political economy that favour heterarchical rather than hierarchical modes of economic, political and social co-ordination. Furthermore, it reflects changes in the ways that governance relations are shaped by ideologically motivated processes of state restructuring.

In his earlier work, Jessop places particular emphasis on seeing the state as a contested social formation – a site of competing and conflicting accumulation strategies (1990). In this context, governance discourse has been associated with fundamental changes in modes of capitalist organisation, not least in terms of a purported shift from Fordism to post-Fordism. Notions of governance have also flourished in areas where decision making was formerly controlled by hierarchical state processes (e.g. describing new patterns of interactions in Eastern Europe or developing countries following the collapse of authoritarian central planning: Hyden and Bratton 1992). Governance has been particularly strong in helping make sense of international relations, where new forms of geopolitical arrangements appear to transcend the territoriality of the modern state. Here the notion of global governance has emerged, which presupposes that there are sets of negotiations and organisational forms that occur 'above' the state. Interestingly, most research has focused on intergovernmental organisations such as the World Bank, the United Nations and trading blocs in which states continue to play a role. Such organisations remain highly politicised and continue to incorporate the strategic territorial interests of states. This brings us to the question of geography.

GEOGRAPHIES OF GOVERNANCE

It is not clear (at least to us) that interest in governance is a substitute for the need to examine the state, territoriality and geography. For example, Jessop (1998) refers to the need for meta-governance. As the number of extra-state interactions has multiplied, there is an ever-greater requirement for the state reflexively to monitor such interactions within and outside its territorial jurisdiction. This monitoring can be described as 'the government of governance'. Given that states are predisposed to secure their territories, it is impossible to think about meta-governance without at the same time invoking a concept of the state and territoriality. To be sure, the shift from government to governance marks the emergence of a *qualitatively different state*; but it is no less territorial than before. At most, meta-governance implies a softening or re-alignment of the division of labour between the state, civil society and economy, and perhaps a more porous definition of state territoriality (Figure 1).

One of the consequences of ignoring territoriality when thinking about governance is that questions of power and empowerment (whether understood in terms of class, 'race', gender, nature and so forth) lose their grounding in particular places, territories and spatial relations. While governance theorists such as Jessop cannot be accused of ignoring the spatial dimension, there is a tendency in social scientific work to see space as contingent rather than causal in terms of its role in the structuring of social, economic and political regulatory systems. The reasons for this are not clear but they may have to do with the deployment of a critical realist perspective. Insofar as the causal properties of social objects are concerned, critical realists have suggested that space makes a difference, but only in terms of the effects of social processes rather than their formative structures and preconditions (Sayer 1985). In terms of a complex system such as the state apparatus, this is a difficult position to sustain when one thinks that one of the necessary properties of the state *is* its territoriality. To be sure, this says very little about the spatial *content* of state policy. Nevertheless, as critical geographers, our concern must be with the ways in which governance projects take shape inside and beyond a territorial state, and in turn how the territoriality of the state enables or constrains governance projects as these take shape in the landscape.

Workplaces, social and ecological movements, economic development policies, labour markets and other strategic projects grounded in particular settings all require some level of time–space co-ordination. Insofar as territoriality is the

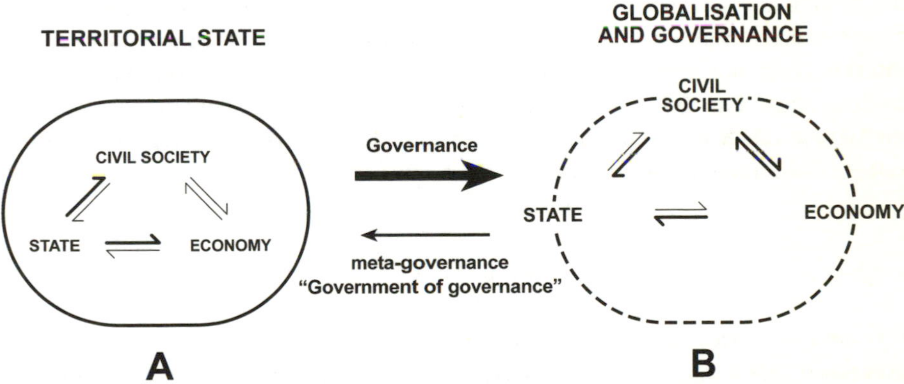

Figure 1: A conceptual model of the changing boundaries between state and governance.

Key: Diagram A represents the organisational and functional relationships between state, economy and civil society in the modern territorial state. Note that the state plays a strong co-ordinating role in relation to strategic economic and social projects within the state's territory. In Diagram B, the territorial boundaries of the state are porous and the capacity of the state to co-ordinate economic and social governance projects within its territory is attenuated. The shift from government to governance is directionally represented as A [arrow pointing right] B. Meta-governance is represented as A [left arrow] B.

performance of strategic acts in and through space that empower different groups and factions, then governance equates to the performance of territoriality. Although political geography has long been comfortable with the idea of the state as a territorial entity, political geographical writing about the state suffers from a tendency to fetishise the territorial as a fixed structure or a spatial container – i.e. a means of social control over objects and subjects in space. Thinking in terms of governance shifts the emphasis away from state territory as a fixed spatial container to the networks and relations that, when constituted spatially, enable and empower. Thinking in these terms also helps to place governance more centrally in the frame of understanding the state as a contested socio-territorial ensemble.

Pushing these arguments further, we can propose that the socio-territorial restructuring of the state is associated with the emergence of new spaces and scales of governance and new forms of state territoriality. For example, globalisation is enabled by the stretching out of territoriality through inter-local networks of co-ordination, many of which transcend national state boundaries but nevertheless amount to a profound re-territorialisation of the (global) economy (Herod et al. 1998). Geographical research has been particularly important in investigating the post-Fordist governance of local and regional economies and the embedding of transactional relations between firms and states. Here the earlier emphasis on the local state and spatial divisions of labour has given way to a more explicit recognition that uneven development *requires* state intervention in order to bring coherence to local modes of economic, social and cultural regulation (Peck and Tickell 1992).

This, in turn, brings us back to the idea of the government of governance. Spaces of governance represent arenas of conflict in which the state continues to play a strategic role, not simply as a territorial structure around which strategic interests are mobilised but also as a self-serving steering agent of spatial management and co-ordination. Just as the state cannot exist without territory, governance cannot cohere without an enabling or driving state.

CODA

Governance is necessarily territorial and therefore intrinsically geographical. Critical geography has a role to play in understanding and mapping the rise of governance by looking at, for example, the ways in which governance projects are situated in space, how such projects bring about coherence (or not) to society, economies and territories, and the role of the state and its different branches in strategically regulating struggles around the spaces of governance so produced.

KEY REFERENCE

Jessop, R. 1998. The rise of governance and the risks of failure, *International Social Science Journal*, 155: 29–45.

OTHER REFERENCES

Cox, K.R. 2002. *Political Geography: Territory, State and Society*. Oxford, Blackwell.

Foucault, M. 1984. *The Foucault Reader* (ed. P. Rabinow). Harmondsworth, Penguin.

Herod, A., Ó Tuathail, G. and Roberts, S. eds. 1998. *Unruly World: Globalization, Governance and Geography*. London: Routledge.

Hyden, F. and Bratton, M. 1992. *Governance and Politics in Africa*. Boulder, Lynne Reiner.

Jessop, R. 1990. *State Theory: Putting Capitalist States in Their Place*. Cambridge, Polity.

Kooiman, J. 1993. *Modern Governance: New Government–Society Interactions*. London, Sage.

Painter, J. 2003. State and governance, in E. Sheppard and T.J. Barnes eds. *A Companion to Economic Geography*. Oxford, Blackwell, 359–376.

Peck, J. and Tickell, A. 1992. Local modes of social regulation? Regulation theory, Thatcherism and uneven development, *Geoforum*, 23: 347–363.

Rhodes, R. 1997. *Understanding Governance*. Buckingham, Open University Press.

Sayer, A. 1985. The difference that space makes, in D. Gregory and J. Urry eds. *Social Relations and Spatial Structures*. London, Macmillan, 49–66.

Stone, C. 1993. Urban regimes and the capacity to govern: a political economy approach, *Journal of Urban Affairs*, 15: 1–28.

— Flexibility —

Suzanne Reimer

> Many analysts are very critical of the concept...arguing that it is a 'fetish' that dazzles our eyes and conceals from us the real processes of oppression that are going on.
>
> E. Martin, *Flexible Bodies: Tracking Immunity in American Culture*, p. 275 fn. 3

In a footnote to her account of flexibility within human resource management discourses (and its concomitant pervasiveness within debates about economic restructuring), Emily Martin raises an issue that strikes at the heart of the vast corpus of work that has taken flexibility as its central focus. Writers – especially those positioned broadly on the 'Left' – may have wished to decry the slipperiness and messiness of the term, and to emphasise that managerial strategies to develop flexibility within firms and organisations have had little to do with the possibilities for workers to manage their own working lives. Yet, despite extensive critique, flexibility has retained a forcefulness and power both within and without the academy.

In part, flexibility's popularity as a 'household word' (Ong 1999, 18) rests upon understandings of 'flexibility in a system and its parts...as [being] intrinsically valuable' (Martin 1994, 149). Within the workplace, seemingly 'rigid' and out-of-date labour processes, job demarcations and organisational practices could be swept away through the encouragement and promotion of adaptability, innovation and continual re-organisation and change. More broadly, skilful responsiveness to life course and personal changes began to be seen to be vital to individuals' well-being (see Giddens 1992). As Martin (1994, 149–150) writes, 'the intense desirability – even the seductiveness – of the ability to be flexible and adaptive while in constant change is registered by the simultaneous appearance of this cluster of attributes in an exceedingly wide variety of domains.'

In hindsight, the far-reaching impact of flexibility as a discourse might seem to belie its (at least partial) origins within a relatively narrow management literature, where it had been used to refer to new developments in firms and labour markets. Anglo-American economic geography in particular quickly became caught up with ideas about 'flexible specialisation' (Piore and Sabel 1984) – and, to a somewhat lesser extent, the Institute of Manpower Studies' model of 'the flexible firm' (Atkinson 1984). There was considerable preoccupation across the social sciences with 'testing' different models of flexibility at work – with determining whether or not firms and organisations really had moved towards a model of 'core' and 'peripheral' workers, or whether so-called 'multi-skilling' practices could be identified within workplaces. Analysts who focused upon specific forms of labour market change (such as increases in temporary, part-time and subcontract working) increasingly began to emphasise the diversity of 'flexible' practices in particular workplaces. Perhaps not surprisingly, employers were found to be using a wide range of strategies to deploy labour in order to match 'demand' (and, indeed, to avoid paying benefits to workers). A distinction between 'numerical' and 'functional' flexibility (see Atkinson 1984, and critiques in Walby 1989; Reimer 1994) thus was unable fully to capture the multiplicity of practices, such as zero-hours working, 'permanent' temps and part-time working with fixed but unscheduled hours.

Some critics sought to shift the terms of debate towards broader questions about the nature of contemporary economic change and restructuring. Anna Pollert (1988, 1991) and others maintained that capitalism had always sought to increase workforce exploitation and that to view flexibility as an entirely new strategy, connected to a wider sea change in economies and societies in the late twentieth century, was to ignore the prescriptive nature of the 'flexible firm' project. Similarly emphasising the starkly unequal power relations between employers and employees, John Allen and Nick Henry (1997, 183) argued that flexibility had been

> invoked to try and explain too much. In particular, the 'package' has been used to cloak new sets of uncertainties in the UK labour market experienced not by firms, but by men and women in more precarious employment positions.

Allen and Henry (1997) posited that the language of risk (as derived from Beck 1992) was more appropriate to an understanding of many employees' experiences of insecure and precarious work, particularly within contract service industries. These and subsequent evaluations of 'risky' (Reimer 1998), contingent (Peck and Theodore 2001) and 'non-standard' patterns of employment have certainly helped to shed light on the position of women and men struggling to make a living within late capitalist economies. Attempts to think beyond the confines of categories such as 'numerical' and 'functional' flexibility, and 'core' and 'peripheral' workforces, have also appeared helpful.

However, as Martin's (1994) note emphasises, the underlying assumption of many accounts – both those concerned with labour market change as well as attempts to construct broader 'transition models' of a new, post-Fordist economy and society – has been that that the notion of flexibility acts as a veil or a cloak. The 'truth' about socio-economic restructuring could be more fully understood (and, by implication, altered) if only we could make visible the underlying 'realities' of capitalism. This has been attempted in two ways. As I have indicated, some writers have sought to identify the diverse meanings associated with flexible working. In a discussion of the UK retail sector, for example, Diane Perrons (2000, 1724) highlights employers' use of part-time contracts that have fixed hours but also variable rotas throughout the year. Perrons writes:

> This provides enormous flexibility for the employer, who will not incur additional overtime costs when working hours have to be marginally extended. Thus flexibility does not necessarily imply use of temporary agencies, subcontracting or casualisation and in this sense is very different from the forms of numerical flexibility discussed by Atkinson (1985)...

Research undertaken for the Joseph Rowntree Foundation (Burchell et al. 1999; Purcell et al. 1999) also has sought to define and document different types of 'flexible' practices.

Other authors have sought to refute the notion of flexibility altogether. Although Pollert's (1991) edited collection hoped to bid *Farewell to Flexibility?*, the question mark in the title indicates the continuing power of the discourse (Reimer 1998, 125–126). For Hyman (1991, 172), flexibility is 'a one-sided, and often intentionally misleading, means of characterising what might better be described as a specific constellation of choices, advantageous to employers, among different types and patterns of rigidity'. Hyman thus concludes that social scientists should 'avoid embracing...the fetishism of flexibility' (172). Yet, in seeking entirely to reject the term, such arguments are also unable fully to conceptualise the impact of ideas about flexibility. The language of flexibility not only has worked its way deeply into discourses of work and employment but also has coloured contemporary cultural ideas about survival and 'fitness' (Martin 1994). Further, even if the outcomes of flexibility as a managerial practice are not clear – (for example, if attempts at flexible working strategies actually create organisational 'rigidities') the act of pursuing new management forms in and of itself can have compelling effects (see Thrift 2000).

One of the interesting aspects of the way in which discussions of flexibility have developed is the extent to which they parallel more recent debates surrounding the idea of commodity fetishism. Within analyses of the geographies of commodities, there has developed an awkward split between those responding to David Harvey's (1990) call to reveal the truth about power relations underpinning the production of commodities (e.g. Hartwick 2000) and those who contend 'that commodity fetishes are by no means neatly woven "veils" which simply mask the origins of consumer goods' (Cook et al. 2004, 174). Understandings of the complex webs of meanings and practice that shape the lives of commodities and consumers continue to develop, but an interesting point of departure is provided by Ian Cook et al. and Philip Crang's (1996) exhortation that analysts of consumer culture should 'get with the fetish' (after Taussig 1992). They argue that there is a need to reflect more carefully upon the ways in which commodity fetishisms are ruptured, disrupted and reworked – rather than simply seeking to 'make visible' the true meanings of commodities in late capitalist societies.

Some of the most interesting insights into the notion of flexibility have also been provided by authors who have sought to pursue and disrupt the diverse cultural meanings that make up the 'bundle of ideas' (Martin 1994, 144) associated with the term – and in ways that do not rely upon a straightforward 'unveiling'. Martin's (1994) consideration of the flexible body/flexible bodies is particularly pertinent to and fruitful for current debates about the performative aspects of workplace identity (McDowell 1997); about restructuring and injury at work (Leslie and Butz 1998); and about the gendered dimensions of flexibility (Freeman 1998). Martin (1994) develops her arguments in part through outlining the wide-ranging use of visual imagery to express the desirability of flexibility. There are gendered assumptions at work here as well. Long-established stereotypes of women's ability both to be flexible and adaptable in the workplace (see, for example, Walby's [1989] account of secretarial work as the ultimate 'flexible' job) and to be able to 'juggle' productive and reproductive responsibilities are simultaneously reflected and reinforced in academic and popular accounts. Historically, women factory workers were seen as desirable for certain jobs because of their 'nimble fingers'; in some contemporary portrayals women's whole bodies are expected to be moulded and reshaped by firms' need for flexibility. The image used to illustrate a 1995 *Guardian* feature about 'new' patterns of flexible working, for example, was a stretched figure of a woman, intertwined with a series of giant clocks (see Figure 1).

Aihwa Ong's account of the 'flexible practices, strategies and disciplines' (Ong 1999, 19) that have shaped the recent lives of overseas ethnic Chinese also offers a means of working with, rather than against, the notion of flexibility. For a particular group of 'mobile managers, technocrats and professionals' (112) seeking global economic opportunities, migration and transnational relocation have the potential to confer status and power: flexibility is preferred to stability. Ong develops the notion of 'flexible citizenship' as a means of conceptualising 'the cultural logics of capitalist accumulation, travel and displacement that induce subjects to respond fluidly and opportunistically to changing political conditions' (6). Her focus is upon the 'production and negotiation of global cultural meanings' (3) that cross-cut participation in global capitalism. Further, although Ong emphasises the strategic dimension of subjects' flexible positioning, she also draws out the institutional contexts and webs of power that shape such flexible strategies (108). Gender divisions, for example, form an important part of this story of flexibility; although female partners and families might be seen to stand outside fraternal networks of production, trade and finance, the labour of women is important in organising and maintaining what Ong terms 'familial regimes of dispersal and localisation' (128). That is, there is a flexible imperative in family life as well, with which the lives of overseas Chinese women are bound up. Benefits and disadvantage of flexibility for different groups cannot be straightforwardly aligned and measured – nor indeed may it be appropriate to attempt to do so. Ong's analysis seeks to explore different meanings and contexts of flexible citizenship, and yet also avoids a reading of flexibility as cloaking an underlying reality.

In distinctive ways, both Martin's and Ong's discussions pull debates about flexibility in different directions – certainly, away from the narrowly workplace

Figure 1: New patterns of flexible working? Source: Brewster (1995).

scale with which other analysts have been concerned. More importantly, though, they offer the possibility of highlighting the importance of power relations, but in a manner that does not simply rely – as critiques of flexibility have in the past – on a simple 'unveiling' of the power of capitalism to extract surplus value from a labour force. Exposing 'myths' at work (Bradley et al. 2000) cannot be the only end point of the discussion: future considerations of flexibility might most profitably be concerned with working on the 'surface' (à la Cook and Crang 1996; Cook et al. 2004) of the concept.

KEY REFERENCES

Martin, E. 1994. *Flexible Bodies: Tracking Immunity in American Culture.* Boston, Beacon.

Ong, A. 1999. *Flexible Citizenship: The Cultural Logics of Transnationality.* Durham, NC and London, Duke University Press.

OTHER REFERENCES

Allen, J. and Henry, N. 1997. Ulrich Beck's *Risk Society* at work: labour and employment in the contract service industries, *Transactions of the Institute of British Geographers*, 22: 180–196.

Atkinson, J. 1984. *Flexibility, Uncertainty and Manpower Management.* Report no. 89, Institute of Manpower Studies, Brighton.

Beck, U. 1992. *Risk Society: Towards a New Modernity.* London, Sage.

Brewster, C. 1995. You've got to go with the flow, *Guardian*, 22 April.

Bradley, H., Erickson, M., Stephenson, C., and Williams, S. 2000. *Myths at Work.* Cambridge, Polity.

Burchell, B., Day, D., Hudson, M., Ladipo, D., Mankelow, R., Nolan, J., Reed, H., Wichert, I. and Wilkinson, F. 1999. *Job Insecurity and Work Intensification: Flexibility and the Changing Boundaries of Work.* Joseph Rowntree Foundation, York.

Cook, I. and Crang, P. 1996. The world on a plate: culinary culture, displacement and geographical knowledges, *Journal of Material Culture*, 1: 131–153.

Cook, I., Crang P. and Thorpe, M. 2004. Tropics of consumption: getting with the fetish of 'exotic' fruit?, in A. Hughes and S. Reimer eds. *Geographies of Commodities.* London, Routledge, 173–192.

Freeman, C. 1998. Femininity and flexible labour: fashioning class through gender on the global assembly line, *Critique of Anthropology*, 18: 245–262.

Giddens, A. 1992. *The Transformation of Intimacy: Sexuality, Love and Eroticism in Modern Societies.* Cambridge, Polity.

Hartwick, E. 2000. Towards a geographical politics of consumption, *Environment and Planning A*, 32: 1177–1192.

Harvey, D. 1990. Between space and time: reflections on the geographical imagination, *Annals of the Association of American Geographers*, 80: 418–434.

Hyman, R. 1991. The fetishism of flexibility: the case of British Rail, in B. Jessop, K. Nielsen, H. Kastendiek and O. Pedersen eds. *The Politics of Flexibility: Restructuring State and Industry in Britain, Germany and Scandinavia.* Aldershot, Edward Elgar, 162–172.

Leslie, D. and Butz, D. 1998. 'GM suicide': Flexibility, space, and the injured body, *Economic Geography*, 74: 360–378.

McDowell, L. 1997. *Capital Culture: Gender at Work in the City.* Oxford, Blackwell.

Peck, J. and Theodore, N. 2001. Contingent Chicago: restructuring the spaces of temporary labour, *International Journal of Urban and Regional Research*, 25: 471–496.

Perrons, D. 2000. Flexible working and equal opportunities in the United Kingdom: a case study from retail, *Environment and Planning A*, 32: 1719–1734.

Piore, M. and Sabel, S. 1984. *The Second Industrial Divide: Possibilities for Prosperity*. New York, Basic Books.

Pollert, A. 1988. Dismantling flexibility, *Capital and Class*, 34: 42–75.

Pollert, A. ed. 1991. *Farewell to Flexibility?* Oxford, Blackwell.

Purcell, K., Hogarth, T. and Simm, C. 1999. *Whose Flexibility?: The Costs and Benefits of 'Non-standard' Working Arrangements and Contractual Relations.* York, Joseph Rowntree Foundation.

Reimer, S. 1994. Flexibility and the gender division of labour: the restructuring of public sector employment in British Columbia, *Area*, 26: 351–358.

Reimer, S. 1998. Working in a risk society, *Transactions of the Institute of British Geographers*, 23: 116–127.

Taussig, M. 1992. *The Nervous System.* London, Routledge.

Thrift, N. 2000. Performing cultures in the new economy, *Annals of the Association of American Geographers*, 90: 674–692.

Walby, S. 1989. Flexibility and the changing sexual division of labour, in S. Wood ed. *The transformation of work? Skill, flexibility and the labour process.* London, Unwin Hyman, 127–140.

— PART II —

DIFFERENCE AND BELONGING

— Introduction —

Difference and Belonging

The recognition of significant social difference is a key feature of contemporary life and underpins our sense of belonging to various kinds of collectivity. The essays in this section deal with the various ways in which identities are defined, negotiated and expressed. Rather than seeing identity as a purely individual, personal or biographical construct, the contributors all emphasise that our identities are articulated relationally across boundaries of social inclusion and exclusion. The essays also demonstrate that social identities are rarely expressed along a single 'dimension' of gender, age or ethnicity, for example. Instead, it is more useful to think about the mutual constitution of these different strands. It is virtually impossible to think of a particular social category, such as 'youth', without simultaneously thinking about how such a construct is raced, classed and gendered.

In referring to identity and difference as social constructs, there has been a tendency to overlook the more physical, embodied nature of these constructions. As Robyn Longhurst and Peter Jackson both emphasise, identities are not merely discursive constructions. While their narrative dimensions are important, they are also practical accomplishments that cannot be accessed solely through linguistic or textual means. Identities are practical achievements, expressed through material as well as symbolic means. A sense of identity or belonging is also profoundly emotional, requiring new kinds of research that go beyond the pragmatic and purely utilitarian.

This section therefore begins with the body and works 'outwards' through more subjective aspects of personal and social identity, including the range of 'dimensions' that have all too often in the past been treated as independent of each other: gender, (dis)ability, sexuality, etc. The essays by Alastair Bonnett, Robert Wilton and Mark Johnson in particular emphasise the fact that notions of identity apply as much to majorities as to minorities – hence their interest in constructions of 'whiteness', (dis)ability and (hetero)sexuality. All the essays (but particularly Tim Cresswell's and Darren O'Byrne's) emphasise the fact that notions of identity and belonging have political and moral dimensions as well as purely personal significance. And, as David Atkinson's essay on heritage highlights, contemporary identities are always rooted in the past but subject to constant reworking via the processes of (selective) remembering and forgetting.

Given its inherent complexity, it should be no surprise that identity has been so central to recent debates in critical social theory, including psychoanalysis, feminism, postcolonialism and postmodernism. Theories of performance and performativity have been particularly significant in recent work on identity (as emphasised in the essays by Robyn Longhurst, James Martin and Peter Jackson). While this work has sought to subvert traditional notions of identity as the surface reflection of some stable, inner self, its emphasis on the discursive limits of identity construction has generated waves of new research on the relationship between discourse and practice that have been highly productive and energising. This new generation of identity studies has been particularly effective in de-naturalising ideas of gender and race that have, in the past, been all too readily traced back to a sense of primordial (biological or genetic) difference. Wrested away from this fictitious sense of certainty and stability, identities emerge as plural and contested, a site of struggle in practical as well as discursive terms. Robert Wilton's essay provides a good illustration of this point, where the hegemony of medical definitions of the disabled individual are increasingly under attack, redefining (dis)ability in social terms without erasing the embodied experience of those who are defined as disabled.

While the nation state remains a key arbiter in the definition of identity (as Darren O'Byrne reminds us in his essay on citizenship), contemporary identities are becoming ever more complex in an increasingly globalised world. With increasing mobility, fewer and fewer people have a stable sense of belonging to one particular place. More and more individuals have transnational identities, either through having migrated from one place to another themselves or because they have been caught up in the various transnational forces that are generated by such experiences. The language of identity and belonging increasingly reflects this unstable world, with its emphasis on hybridity and diaspora, centres and margins, borders and boundaries. These spatial metaphors remind us that questions of identity and belonging are eminently geographical phenomena, where social constructions do not merely reflect pre-formed geographies; they are spatially as well as socially constituted. That is what makes ideas of difference and belonging such central issues in the development of a critical cultural geography.

— The Body —

Robyn Longhurst

In some ways, attempting to define the body seems ludicrous. After all, we all *have* bodies; or at least, we all *are* bodies – they are more than just possessions (Nast and Pile 1998, 1). Surely, therefore, we all know what the body is. Yet philosophers from the Ancient Greeks to the postmodernists have been preoccupied with attempting to understand and define the body. Over the centuries, and in different places, there has been little agreement about the meaning of the body, or even what the body is. For example, Anthony Synott (1993) asks: does it include the shadow, nail clippings and faeces?

Many feminists, including Moira Gatens (1991a), have made the seemingly obvious point that there is no one body; *the* body is an illusion. There are only bodies in the plural. There are complex processes through which female and male bodies are differentiated. Bodies are *sexed* and gendered. The multiplicity that surrounds and inhabits the body, or bod*ies*, makes it impossible to settle on any one straightforward definition. The body – whether it be infant, child or adult – is a surface of social and cultural inscription; it houses subjectivity; it is a site of pleasure and pain; it is public and private; it has a permeable boundary that is crossed by fluids and solids; it is material, discursive and psychical. Vicki Kirby (1992, 1) describes the body as 'a terra incognita'. Ironically, it seems that the only thing we can know about the body is that we can't know it. It cannot be treated as obvious and taken for granted. The meaning of the body is 'equivocal, often ambiguous, sometimes evasive and always contested' by those who attempt to understand more fully its meaning (Pile and Thrift 1995, 6).

While the body has long been a matter of social concern, over the last few decades it has come to occupy an even more prominent position in social theory (see Featherstone 1983; Foucault 1980; Shilling 1993; Turner 1984, 1992). Kathy Davis (1997) puts forward a range of possible reasons for this upsurge in interest in the body. First, she argues that bodies no longer simply represent how we fit into the social order, but instead, are a vehicle for self-expression. Second, '[i]nterest in the body also goes hand in hand with recent medical advances and improved sanitation.

Life expectancy is greater than in previous centuries…' (2). Third, scholars have been interested in the body as a '*theoretical* intervention', and this has been fuelled by the fact that 'both modernist and postmodernist scholars alternately propose the body as secure ground for claims of morality, knowledge or truth *and* as undeniable proof for the validity of radical constructionism' (4, emphasis in original).

In the 1970s and 1980s many feminists were hesitant about focusing on the body. Women's bodies – their desires and physical attributes – were often used as proof of Woman's essential (and inferior) difference from Man. Many feminists were fearful that reference to the physical body would serve only to naturalise what was in fact social difference. Feminists at this time preferred to talk about gender (the social construction of roles and relations) rather than about sex (the biological body). This distinction between sex and gender, employed by many feminists in the 1970s and 1980s, was derived from the work of psychologist Robert Stoller. Stoller (1968) argued that the biological sex of a person augments but does not determine the appropriate gender identity for that person. A person's gender identity is primarily the result of post-natal psychological influences. Many feminists took up this distinction between sex and gender as a way of arguing that it is possible to change gendered behaviours. In the 1990s feminists came to theorise sex and gender not as discrete and separate entities but as mutually constituted (see Gatens 1991b). In fact, during the 1990s feminists were often at the forefront of debates on the body (see Bordo 1993; Butler 1990, 1993; Grosz 1994).

Feminists deconstructed not only the dualism between sex and gender but also that between mind and body. Gatens (1988 61) argues that: 'not only have mind and body been conceptualised as distinct in western knowledges but also the divisions have been conceptually and historically sexualised'. The mind has been associated with Man, the body with Woman (Lloyd 1993).

> In western culture, while white men may have presumed that they could transcend their embodiment (or at least have their bodily needs met by others) by seeing it as little more than a container for the pure consciousness it held inside, this was not allowed for women, blacks, homosexuals, people with disabilities, the elderly, children and so on. This masculinist separation of minds from bodies, and the privileging of minds over bodies, remains a dominant conception in western culture (Longhurst 1997, 491).

Feminist geographers, such as Gillian Rose (1993), have argued that the discipline of geography has not been immune to dualistic thinking. The mind, masculinity, rationality and Sameness have been given priority over the body, femininity, irrationality and Otherness in geography (Longhurst 1997). Some geographers, therefore, have focused on the body as a way of contesting dominant discourses in the discipline. There has been 'a growing concern with the bodily' in geography (Rose 1995, 545). Felicity Callard (1998, 387) claims: '"The body" is becoming a preoccupation in the geographical literature, and is a central figure around which to base political demands, social analyses, and theoretical investigations.' There has been a 'dash towards things corporeal' (Callard 1998, 388), which is evident in a range of studies (see Ainley 1998; Bell et al. 2001; Butler and Parr 1999; Duncan 1996; Longhurst 2001; McDowell and Court 1994; Nast and Pile 1998; Teather 1999).

Social scientists, including geographers, have adopted a variety of approaches to understanding the body, including psychoanalytical, phenomenological (the 'lived body') and cultural (the body as a surface of inscription) approaches. One of the most popular approaches with geographers and others interested in issues of space and place has been, and continues to be, the cultural approach, which draws on post-structuralist theory to understand the body as a surface to be etched by cultural and social systems (Turner 1992) or discourses (Foucault 1980).

This approach affords an opportunity for understanding further bodies and spaces as mutually constituted. Elizabeth Grosz (1992) argues that there is a two-way linkage between bodies and cities, which could be defined as an *interface*, perhaps even a co-building. 'The city in its particular geographical, architectural, spatializing, municipal arrangements is one particular ingredient in the social constitution of the body' (Grosz 1992, 248). Bodies and spaces construct each other in complex and nuanced ways. It is impossible to talk about bodies without talking about space, and visa versa. Bodies are performed, resisted, disciplined and oppressed not simply in but *through* space. Heidi Nast and Steve Pile (1998, 1) remind us that 'we live our lives – through places, through the body'. They explain that there is a pressing need to examine the interconnections between bodies and places because the ways in which we live out these interconnections, these relationships, are political.

Judith Butler (1990, 136) argues that the body is 'performative' – that is, it 'has no ontological status apart from the various acts which constitute its reality'. Similarly, geographers have begun to argue that space has no ontological status, no fixed characteristics. This is not to suggest that spaces are immaterial (for example, someone in a wheelchair is likely to face very 'real' material challenges when attempting to negotiate spaces in most city centres) but, rather, that space is not simply a backdrop for social relations. Space plays an important role in constituting and reproducing social relations (see Massey 1999). Both bodies and spaces are simultaneously real, material, imaginary and symbolic.

Understanding bodies and spaces as performative has offered geographers a new way of understanding power relations. Liz Bondi and Joyce Davidson (2002) note: 'Some important studies in cultural geography have argued that people and places are imagined, embodied and experienced in ways that are...radically and inextricably intertwined with each other.' They continue: 'To *be* is to be some*where*, and our changing relations and interactions with this placing are integral to understandings of human geographies' (emphasis in original). This suggests that bodies are entwined in multiple power relations realised through space. These power relations may be differentially organised through varying relations of race, sexuality, gender and so on, but in all instances they are written on and through the bodies and spaces under discussion. Bodies cannot be snatched from the spatial relations that constitute them.

In the future it is likely that feminist and cultural geographers, and others interested in spatial relations, will increasingly interrogate bodies as multiple, fluid and situated in particular spaces. Instead of focusing on just one facet of identity and subjectivity, geographers and others are increasingly weaving together various aspects of embodiment, such as age, sexuality, class, race and/or ethnicity. At times political purpose may instigate a decision to prioritise one aspect of embodiment over another, but for the most part there seems to be emerging understandings of bodies as complex amalgamations that are multiply situated.

Coupled with this growing understanding of bodies as complex amalgamations is an understanding of bodies as 'lived'. A common criticism of post-structuralist theorising on the body over the last decade has been that the bodies under consideration appear as fleshless linguistic territories. Bodies are not portrayed as having specific capacities, a specific skin colour, weight, age, genitalia or sexual orientation. These fleshless theoretical bodies, argue feminists, are a masculinist illusion. Denying the weighty materiality and specificity of flesh enables the unmarked body (the white, able-bodied, heterosexual, masculine body) to retain its hegemonic position. Focusing on bodies that have no specified materiality will not necessarily further feminist, socialist, anti-racist or disability activists' agendas. Denying the weighty materiality of flesh and fluid is likely to help preserve hegemonic bodily practices and politics (Longhurst 2001).

Many critical geographers, for example feminist, socialist, anti-racist, postcolonial and queer geographers, are now focusing on the body as one possible route to changing social, cultural and economic relations for the better. These geographers are increasingly recognising that bodies (bodies that have a particular skin type and colour or shape, or that have particular genitalia or impairments, or that are a specific age, etc.) are always placed in particular temporal and spatial contexts. Situating the body at the centre of empirical and theoretical enquiries has been one of the most exciting moves in geography over the last decade. Questions of the body – its materiality, discursive construction, regulation and representation – are absolutely crucial to understanding spatial relations at every scale. It is likely that, in the future, the body will be on the agendas not just of critical geographers but also on the agendas of a range of others interested in teasing out relations between people and places.

KEY REFERENCES

Butler, R. and Parr, H. eds. 1999. *Mind and Body Spaces: Geographies of Illness, Impairment and Disability*. London, Routledge.

Butler, J. 1993. *Bodies That Matter: On the Discursive Limits of Sex*. New York, Routledge.

Grosz, L. 1994. *Volatile Bodies: Towards a Corporeal Feminism*. St Leonards, NSW, Allen and Unwin.

Longhurst, R. 2001. *Bodies: Exploring Fluid Boundarie*s. London, Routledge.

Nast, H. and Pile, S. 1998. Introduction: makingplacesbodies, in H. Nast and S. Pile eds. *Places Through the Body*. London, Routledge, 1–19.

Rose, G. 1993. *Feminism and Geography: The Limits of Geographical Knowledge*. Cambridge, Polity.

Teather, E. ed. 1999. *Embodied Geographies: Spaces, Bodies and Rites of Passage*. London, Routledge.

Turner, B. 1984. *The Body and Society: Explorations in Social Theory*. Oxford, Blackwell.

OTHER REFERENCES

Ainley, R. ed. 1998. *New Frontiers of Space, Bodies and Gender*. London, Routledge.

Bell, D., Binnie, J., Holliday, R. Longhurst, R. and Peace, R. 2001. *Pleasure Zones: Bodies: Cities, Spaces*. New York, Syracuse University Press.

Bondi, L. and Davidson, J. 2003. Troubling the place of gender, in K. Anderson, M. Domosh, S. Pile and N. Thrift eds. *Handbook of Cultural Geography*. London, Sage, 325–343.

Bordo, S. 1993. *Unbearable Weight: Feminism, Western Culture, and the Body*. Berkeley, University of California Press.

Butler, J. 1990. *Gender Trouble: Feminism and the Subversion of Identity*. New York, Routledge.

Callard, F.J. 1998. The body in theory, *Environment and Planning D: Society and Space*, 16: 387–400.

Davis, K. ed. 1997. *Embodied Practices: Feminist Perspectives on the Body*. London, Sage.

Duncan, N. ed. 1996. *Body Space*. London, Routledge.

Featherstone, M. 1983. The body in consumer culture, *Theory, Culture and Society*, 1, 2: 18–33.

Foucault, M. 1980. *The History of Sexuality* (vol. 1) *An Introduction* (trans. by R. Hurley). New York, Vintage/Random House.

Gatens, M. 1988. Towards a feminist philosophy of the body, in B. Caine, E. Grosz and M. de Lepervanche eds. *Crossing Boundaries: Feminisms and Critiques of Knowledges*. Sydney, Allen and Unwin, 59–70.

Gatens, M. 1991a. Corporeal representation in/and the body politic, in R. Diprose and R. Ferrell eds. *Cartographies: Poststructuralism and the Mapping of Bodies and Spaces*. Sydney, Allen and Unwin, 79–87.

Gatens, M. 1991b. A critique of the sex/gender distinction, in S. Gunew ed. *A Reader in Feminist Knowledges*. New York and London, Routledge, 139–157.

Grosz, E. 1992. Bodies–cities, in B. Colomina ed. *Sexuality and Space*. New York, Princeton Architectural Press, 241–253.

Kirby, V. 1992. *Addressing Essentialism Differently ...Some Thoughts on the Corpo-real*. Occasional Paper no. 4, Department of Women's Studies, University of Waikato, New Zealand.

Lloyd, G. 1993. *The Man of Reason: 'Male' and 'Female' in Western Philosophy*. London, Routledge.

Longhurst, R. 1997. (Dis)embodied geographies, *Progress in Human Geography*, 21, 4: 486–501.

Massey, D. 1999. Spaces of politics, in D. Massey, J. Allen and P. Sarre eds. *Human Geography Today*. Cambridge, Polity, 279–294.

McDowell, L. and Court, G. 1994. Performing work: bodily representations in merchant banks, *Environment and Planning D: Society and Space*, 12: 727–750.

Pile, S. and Thrift, N. eds. 1995. *Mapping the Subject: Geographies of Cultural Transformation*. London, Routledge.
Rose, G. 1995. Geography and gender, cartographies and corporealities, *Progress in Human Geography*, 19, 4: 544–548.
Shilling, C. 1993. *The Body and Social Theory*. London, Sage.
Stoller, R. 1968. *Sex and Gender*. London, Hogarth.
Synott, A. 1993. *The Body Social: Symbolism, Self and Society*. London, Routledge.
Turner, B. 1992. *Regulating Bodies: Essays in Medical Sociology*. London, Routledge.

— Identity —

James Martin

'Identity' implies an undifferentiated unity or sameness, one that constitutes the essential 'being' of an entity. In Western thought since Plato it has often been assumed that to 'have an identity' is to make the claim that being – what an object fundamentally is – equates to some essential quality (or qualities). For Plato, and also for later Christian theologians, for example, human identity consisted fundamentally in an immaterial, immortal 'soul', the body being merely a temporary container for this enduring essence. Similarly, though with different implications, Descartes and other rationalists of the seventeenth century conceived the essence of human identity as the faculty of reason – that is, the ability to discern truth from falsehood. Thus, reference to individual identity frequently involves the idea of an interior 'self' or subjectivity that is equal to certain core characteristics that give it integrity and coherence. These characteristics define and unify the parameters of individual meaning and experience, and provide the basis upon which personality is built. The great challenge of identity, however, lies in how to seal off this intimate, interior, subjective space from the supposedly exterior world of objects, passions and fleeting experiences, which are treated merely as its context. With the development of social thought in the nineteenth and twentieth centuries, the contextual and historical influences upon human identity have increasingly come to be emphasised.

Though human identities are typically 'held' individually, they are regarded as having distinctively social origins and expression. For instance, 'class', 'gender' or 'national' identities imply individual selves fashioned around the shared content of these social categories and the practices associated with them. Social conditions are assumed to imprint themselves upon identity but are ultimately separable from it. Features such as language, values, dress, social roles and functions, etc. are argued to be secondary, external phenomena that 'reveal' or 'express' the primary identity to a greater or lesser extent. Identity, therefore, is often understood to precede and guide human interactions, to be relatively fixed, an invariant principle distinguishable from contingent and variable characteristics. Thus, to define an identity is to communicate the essential aspect of a self or personality (individual or collective) that gives meaning and value to what it does, and, typically, to request a certain respect and understanding for issues and problems that relate to its essence.

The proliferation of cultural and political identities in recent decades has aroused immense interest among social, political and cultural theorists. Claims, for example, to distinct regional, ethnic and sexual identities have challenged an earlier preoccupation by sociologists and psychologists with individual and class identities. Theoretical concern has turned towards grasping the various ways that different identity types are constructed in specific social contexts and how experience and action are structured by 'external' conditions (see Calhoun 1994). This is the case especially in the field of social psychology, where shared languages and meanings in 'everyday life' are analysed as factors in the 'rhetorical' construction of identity (see, for example, Billig 1987). In political philosophy, Charles Taylor (1989) documents the development over time of a 'modern' identity in moral and political philosophy. He traces the formation of the self, conceived as the occupant of 'moral space', from atomistic individualism through to contemporary multiculturalism. Different historical traditions, he argues, construct our orientation towards the evaluation of 'good' and 'bad' in different ways. Anthony Giddens (1991) also examines the changing nature of identity in what he calls 'late modernity'. Increasingly, he argues, individuals are constructing a 'reflexive self-identity'; that is, traditional sources of identity (e.g. the patriarchal family, religion, nation) are being replaced by a greater degree of purposive negotiation in individual lifestyles.

Spatiality is widely recognised as a key dimension in the formation of social identities: identities are understood to be generated in relation to specific places, both territorial and social (Keith and Pile 1993; Carter et al. 1993). National or regional identity, for instance, involves subjects' perception of the importance of territorial location and history in the formation of elements that make up their common identity. 'National characteristics' may also be specified, perhaps controversially, in terms of regional cultural and social 'traditions': the customs and culture of southern Italians as 'amoral' and individualistic, for instance (see Banfield 1958). Likewise, class identities are specified by Marxists in relation to place within a structure of production and property relations. The habits, assumptions and customs of different classes are believed to derive to a great degree from an individual's occupation within the division of labour. Capitalist production relations are also distributed geographically, and this results in regional variations in the patterns of belief, behaviour and class consciousness within and across classes (see Massey 1995). Spatial location is important, not only in generating shared experiences and customs that form identities but also in providing a 'position' from which resistance can be made against power, inequality and other forms of perceived oppression. Thus the factory, the locality, the urban neighbourhood or colonial territory furnish individuals with a relatively enclosed space that intensifies experiences, both of commonality and distance. These may become the basis of new forms of collective identity and civic life (Sennett 1973; Castells 1983).

Recently, theoretical studies have explored the intrinsically problematic character of the concept of identity. Interventions from various fields, such as psychoanalysis, feminism, postcolonial theory and various postmodern theories, have challenged the idea of identity as an internally unified order the meaning of which can be more or less accurately captured and represented (see Hall 1996; Woodward 2000). Identity has come to be understood not only as temporally and spatially variable but as intrinsically plural and contradictory. This contrasts with the received notion of identity as a stable 'container' rooted 'inside' the subject and separated off from external contingencies. Instead, it is increasingly conceived not as marking out some inherent or essential features (e.g. reason, racial characteristics, class position, etc.) but as a fractured, overlapping, sometimes unstable condensation of various social influences.

The 'internal' space of the subject, for example, is increasingly regarded as porous, fluid, open to modification. Rather than having a fixed or preconstituted identity that guarantees persons authorship of their actions, or being the unmodified expression of social structures, the subject is understood more as an unfinished entity, one that is an active force in its own construction. In Lacanian theory, for instance, the subject is conceived as an empty place or 'lack'. It is the very absence of a closed identity that compels individual subjects to seek ways of 'filling the gap' by acts of *identification* (Stavrakakis 1999; Laclau 1994). The secret of identity, therefore, lies in an ongoing struggle to conceal an intrinsic absence by entry into the symbolic order or the world of fantasy. Thus claims to an essential 'belonging' to a homeland, a nation or ethnic group are efforts to invoke the mythical unity and stability of a closed identity rather than expressions of something that actually already exists. Fascists in the 1930s, for example, appealed to idealised notions of racial or national purity with terms such as *das Volk* (the people) or *Italianitá* (Italianness). Identity, therefore, is 'retroactively' constituted, presenting itself in its various formations as if it preceded the moment of its formation. For Slavoj Zizek (1989), this 'as if' is the true mechanism of ideology, for it constructs the subject as having an identity that is in fact contingent, changing and always incomplete.

The notion of identity as a 'discursive' construction – that is, one constructed in and through language (see Howarth 2000) – has shifted attention away from founding principles such as 'human nature' or social structures and, simultaneously, towards a 'politics of identity' in which *difference* is perceived as a fundamental dimension (see Woodward 1997). Closure and unity are effects produced by differentiation, by the raising of a symbolic barrier of meaning to distinguish one thing from another. Thus the 'male' identity is distinguished by its difference from 'female', or 'Englishness' is given content by its opposition to the Irish or French. Differences such as these mark out the limits of identity by referring to what it is not, and, in so doing, actively produce coherence by 'framing' certain characteristics in a hierarchical manner. Distinctions such as these are not simply conceptual but are materially produced (e.g. the association of women with domesticity and the 'private' space of the home, the ghettoisation of certain ethnic groups, etc.) and are organised such that certain differences (and spaces) are regarded as superior and others as inferior or 'abject' (see Sibley 1995). 'Having an identity', therefore, comes with a series of associated practices through which it is concretised and involves relations of power, subordination and exclusion.

These ideas inform broadly post-structuralist theories, which look to practices and operations of power that fashion identity in various ways. Judith Butler's use of Michel Foucault's notion of 'subjectification' to critique heterosexual notions of gender identity is one such example. Butler (1999, 1993) argues against the idea that gender identity is founded on a natural, sexual division between 'male' and 'female'. Rather, that distinction is 'performed' through a multiplicity of institutionalised social practices and sites of 'expert' power that invoke, materialise and naturalise sexual identity. Their effect, however, is also to marginalise gay and lesbian identities that do not fit the dominant frame, which she terms 'hetero-normativity'. Abjection, she argues, seems intrinsic to any effort to assert a dominant type of identity. But it is also productive of various forms of transgressive identity that subvert the assumed naturalness of social norms. In her famous example, cross-dressing is a parody of sexual identity that both reinforces the idea of sexual difference and reveals its contingency upon performance and hence its openness to (discursive) manipulation.

If identities are discursively constructed, multiple, contradictory and open to transgression, it is rare nevertheless, for them to be explicitly experienced as such. Identity is often invoked to signify an internal order that, however illusory according to contemporary cultural theory, implies the notion of a stable self that pre-exists specific social interactions. When filling in forms, many of us unquestioningly tick the box indicating our 'nationality' or 'sex'. When we go abroad, we often understand our sense of cultural differences in the common-sense terms of 'them' and 'us'. Thus, identities are often not perceived by those who hold them as transitory and artificial but as essential and intensely personal. Ernesto Laclau (1990) argues that it is precisely because identities lack essential coherence that they are experienced as an aspiration to fullness. All identities, he claims (following Lacan and Derrida), are 'dislocated' – that is, experienced as partially incomplete because they can be formed only through a differentiation that simultaneously limits the identity by making it dependent on the presence of an 'Other'. Dislocation does not automatically involve crisis or total instability, yet in certain contexts – of great social and economic disruption, for example – challenges to personal and collective identity can multiply dislocations to the degree that a reassertion of a full identity becomes imperative. It is at such moments, argues Laclau (1996), that individual subjects are open to the appeal of 'empty signifiers' – that is, key principles that symbolise a stable order-to-come. Empty signifiers include notions of 'justice', 'freedom', 'national independence', etc.; they are empty precisely because they do not have any specific content as such but function as the 'horizon' for *all* meaning. Signifiers such as these offer dislocated identities a powerful, if illusory, sense that their identity is merely 'blocked' by the arbitrary interference of others (e.g. 'foreigners', 'infidels', capitalists, etc.). Once this blockage is removed identity can, it is supposed, return to its natural and full expression.

According to Manuel Castells (1997), dislocation and resistance in the politics of identity has its most profound expression in the context of globalisation. For him, globalisation involves the formation of a 'network society' around high-speed information technology and capitalist restructuring. This produces a 'space of flows' and 'timeless time', which disrupt and weaken local cultural traditions, national state institutions and economic systems to the advantage of capitalist elites and at the expense of indigenous populations (see Castells 2000). These processes have multiple effects on the formation of social identities throughout the world (see also Massey 1994, Part II). Contra Giddens (see above), identity politics in the network society, argues Castells, is increasingly based on the communal resistance to disembedded and individualised global culture. In its 'reactive' or defensive form, this is witnessed in the rise of religious (e.g. Christian and Islamic) fundamentalism and ethnic and racial movements that seek 'refuge and solidarity' in communal identity. Alternatively, a more positive, 'proactive' type of resistance is found in social movements that challenge global processes in the name both of their local identities and 'humanity'. These groups – as diverse as environmentalist movements and Mexico's *Zapatistas* – campaign by linking the local to the global and seek to invoke the idea of global responsibility.

KEY REFERENCES

Calhoun, C. ed. 1994. *Social Theory and the Politics of Identity*. Oxford, Blackwell.

Castells, M. 1997. *The Power of Identity. The Information Age: Economy, Society and Culture* (vol. 3). Oxford, Blackwell.

Hall, S. 1996. Introduction: who needs identity?, in S. Hall and P. du Gay eds. *Questions of Cultural Identity*. London, Sage.

Keith, M. and Pile, S. eds. 1993. *Place and the Politics of Identity*. London, Routledge.

Laclau, E. 1996. *Emancipation*(s). London and New York, Verso.

OTHER REFERENCES

Banfield, E. C. 1958. *The Moral Basis of a Backward Society*. New York and London, Free Press.

Billig, M. 1987. *Arguing and Thinking: A Rhetorical Approach to Social Psychology*. Cambridge, Cambridge University Press.

Butler J. 1993. *Bodies that Matter: On the Discursive Limits of 'Sex'*. New York and London, Routledge.

Butler, J. 1999. *Gender Trouble* (2nd ed.). New York and London, Routledge.

Carter, E., Donald, J. and Squires, J. eds. 1993. *Space and Place: Theories of Identity and Location*. London, Lawrence and Wishart.

Castells, M. 1983. *The City and the Grassroots: A Cross-cultural Theory of Urban Social Movements*. London, Arnold.

Castells, M. 2000. *The Rise of the Network Society The Information Age: Economy, Society and Culture* (vol. 1) (2nd ed.). Oxford and Malden, MA, Blackwell.

Giddens, A. 1991. *Modernity and Self-Identity: Self and Society in the Late Modern Age*. Cambridge, Polity.

Howarth, D. 2000. *Discourse*. Buckingham, Open University Press.

Laclau, E. 1990. *New Reflections on the Revolution of Our Time*. London and New York, Verso.

Laclau, E. ed. 1994. *The Making of Political Identities*. London and New York, Verso.

Massey, D. 1994. *Space, Place and Gender*. Cambridge, Polity.

Massey, D. 1995. *Spatial Divisions of Labour: Social Structures and the Geography of Production* (2nd ed.). Basingstoke, Macmillan.

Sennett, R. 1973. *The Uses of Disorder: Personal Identity and City Life.* Harmondsworth, Penguin.

Sibley, D. 1995. *Geographies of Exclusion: Society and Difference in the West*. London and New York, Routledge.

Stavrakakis, Y. 1999. *Lacan and the Political*. London, Routledge.

Taylor, C. 1989. *Sources of the Self.* Cambridge, Cambridge University Press.

Woodward, K. ed. 1997. *Identity and Difference*. London, Sage (in association with the Open University).

Woodward, K. ed. 2000. *Questioning Identity: Gender, Class, Nation*. London, Routledge (in association with the Open University).

Zizek, S. 1989. *The Sublime Object of Ideology*. London and New York, Verso.

— Gender —

Peter Jackson

Having served as the central category in feminist research for many years, gender has come to be regarded as an increasingly problematic concept, with critics such as Susan Bordo identifying 'a new scepticism about the use of gender as an analytical category' (1990, 135). Among literary theorists, in particular, gender is regarded as an inherently unstable, continually self-deconstructing discursive formation. Among social scientists, too, gender is assuming less centrality as its complex interweaving with other social differences has been increasingly explored. As members of the Women and Geography Study Group (WGSG) conclude, while gender is not the only category for feminist research, gender remains a useful, politically and intellectually necessary category in exploring contemporary difference and diversity (WGSG 1997). This essay traces how we have got to this point, beginning with the critical distinction between sex and gender in early feminist work, moving on to discuss the current dissolution of the concept, and ending with some suggestions for its possible reformulation in future research.

SEX AND GENDER

Although the distinction between sex and gender was already apparent in the nineteenth century, the pioneering French feminist Simone de Beauvoir made a revolutionary contribution to our understanding of the political implications of this distinction. De Beauvoir famously began the second volume of her book *The Second Sex* (originally published in French in 1949) with the arresting assertion that '"*on ne nâit pas femme on le devient*" (one is not born, but rather one becomes a woman)' (1972, 295). The modern feminist agenda of redressing the inequalities between men and women was born from this recognition, focusing on the historical process of 'becoming' rather than assuming that the sexual division of labour was fixed and unmoveable. According to Raymond Williams' discussion of 'sex' in *Keywords* (1976, 285), 'gender' has its roots in the Latin word *generare*, 'to beget'.

This etymological connection between gender and biological reproduction hints at some of the complexities of the word and at its contested history. While sex and gender are often regarded as interchangeable in colloquial use, distinguishing between the terms was a fundamental manoeuvre in feminist thought, helping to prise apart biological notions of sexual reproduction and culturally constructed notions of identity. An emphasis on gender as a social and cultural construction enabled feminists to highlight the neglect of women's histories and geographies (Rowbotham 1977; WGSG 1984). It also helped to demonstrate that masculine and feminine gender roles were the product of particular social relations rather than being rooted in biological or God-given differences between men and women. Research by Linda McDowell and Doreen Massey (1984), for example, effectively demonstrated how specific constructions of class and gender have shaped distinctive labour markets in the East End of London, the agricultural fens of East Anglia, the Lancashire textile towns and the coal mining areas of North-East England. The distinction between sex and gender was vital to the success of the women's movement in urging social and political change in women's health and childcare issues, in equal opportunities legislation and employment rights, in striving for fairer political representation and greater social equality. The force of these political imperatives makes the current rethinking of gender within feminist research a highly contentious issue. Yet there are both political and theoretical grounds for urging such a rethinking.

The insistence on gender as a unifying category in the promotion of women's rights came under increasing criticism as differences between women were highlighted within the women's movement. A greater sensitivity to racialised difference, urged with particular vehemence by Black and Latina women in the United States and later by a range of postcolonial theorists, forced a recognition that there is no universal category of Woman (Anzaldúa 1987; hooks 1981; Spivak 1988). Feminist geographers have also contributed to these debates, with a recognition of the importance of racialised and generational differences among women (Radcliffe and Westwood 1993; Katz and Monk 1993). Other dissenting voices have joined the debate, challenging the bedrock of a common experience of gender among women, whether on the grounds of sexuality, age, ethnicity or disability.

More recently, the separation of sex from gender has been subjected to another line of critique, from those who are calling into question the distinction between nature and culture. While much social science has been premised on the notion that human culture and society are somehow outside or above nature, recent work by feminists and others has sought to challenge the human/non-human divide and to re-instate our place within a more-than-human world (Haraway 1991; Whatmore 2002). Judith Butler's work makes a related case, questioning the 'discursive limits of sex' and arguing that there is no pre-discursive 'sex' on which a culturally constructed notion of 'gender' then sets to work. Drawing on a range of post-structuralist theorists such as Foucault, Kristeva and Wittig, Butler argues that our sexed bodies can be the occasion for a number of different genders (1990, 112). Gender-as-identity is a performative accomplishment rather than an expressive act. In Butler's account, there are no pre-existing identities. Rather, our gendered identities are based on routinised practices. As such, gender is conceived of as 'a sustained and repeated corporeal project...an identity tenuously constituted in time, instituted in an exterior space through a *stylised* repetition of acts' (139–140, emphasis in original). Our gendered identities are cultural fictions, made intelligible within the punitive framework or 'regulatory grid' of compulsory heterosexuality. Butler herself focuses on dissonant juxtapositions of gender and sex, such as lesbian butch-femme identities or the cross-gender performances of drag queens. This 'queering' of the conventional sex–gender order is particularly visible in contexts such as gay, lesbian and bisexual identities. But it is equally applicable to any performance of gender that disrupts the regulatory fictions of compulsory heterosexuality (Bell et al. 1994). While Butler has been criticised by those who feel that her work underplays the agency of historically and geographically embedded subjects (Nelson 1999), her argument has been highly influential in the current re-theorisation of gender as a central analytical category in feminist thought.

GENDER AS A SITE OF STRUGGLE

Clearly, then, the concept of gender is a contested term with a rich and complex history. This definitional history has political implications, with more at stake than semantic niceties. If our identities as men and women are thought to be immutably connected to biological differences, the scope for political and social change is limited. If gender is regarded as a social and cultural construction that varies from time to time and from place to place, then the scope for political change is immense. A simple reading of the historical evidence could be construed as showing a progressive winning back to 'culture' of distinctions that were formerly regarded as 'natural'. So, for example, the Victorian cult of domesticity, which insisted that a woman's place was in the home, was rooted in notions of the 'weaker sex', with women's perceived need for protection and nurturance effectively restricting their independent participation in public life beyond the home. While these ideas applied principally to bourgeois women, and the notion of 'separate spheres' for men and women can clearly be challenged, a whole regime of gender relations was elaborated on this fragile basis, encompassing many sections of society. As Christine Stansell's work on nineteenth-century New York demonstrates, these ideas could have devastating material consequences, such as the enforced removal of children from their mothers, when translated into legislative form through vagrancy and truancy laws or attempts to control the spread of contagious diseases (Stansell 1986).

The current dissolution of gender as a central category within feminist thought is therefore highly contested, with some authors advocating a 'strategic' use of essentialised notions of gender in order not to undermine political struggles in support of women's rights. For others, however, the de-centring of gender is not a sign of weakness but may actually strengthen the feminist project, as argued by the WGSG (1997). From this perspective, the recognition that gender is part of a wider set of social forces replaces an untenable way of thinking about gender as a fixed or stable binary. In Beverley Skeggs' work, for example, based on a longitudinal ethnographic study of white working-class women in the North-West of England, gender is a key analytical category but one that is closely interwoven with other social formations in complex and contested constructions of respectability (Skeggs 1997).

In such empirically grounded accounts, gender clearly emerges as a vital analytical category, infused with social relations of power. Clearly, too, such constructions apply to men as well as to women, with power in one domain readily spilling over into other domains. The use of a spatial metaphor here is not accidental, as Bob Connell (1987) shows in his analysis of the gender regimes that operate through a range of institutions and social structures, including the family, the state and the street. Likewise, in his study of contemporary masculinities, Connell (1995) demonstrates that men's power in the domestic realm is closely related to their absence from home during the working day. Much ideological work, over centuries, has been required to maintain the relative value attached to paid employment as a 'masculine' sphere and to devalue the 'feminine' sphere of domestic work and childcare. Hence the complex sexual politics that follow from male unemployment, where men's conventional source of power in the labour market is undermined and where they can be made to feel socially as well as economically redundant (McDowell 1991).

GENDER AS POSITIONALITY

Finally, I wish to argue that the concept of gender raises a series of important issues concerning the politics of position. One way of thinking about these issues is to reflect briefly on the 'masculinist' power of a discipline such as geography. This power, though often barely visible, has infused the history of the discipline for generations. It is most obviously apparent in the exclusion of women from powerful positions within the discipline, with women only admitted as Fellows of the Royal Geographical Society on equal terms with men in 1913, and with male professors still vastly outnumbering their female colleagues (Rose 1993). But it is also apparent in more subtle ways, in terms of what are considered appropriate topics of study, in the choice of research methods and approaches, and in modes of disseminating research findings. While there may be no specifically 'feminist method', adopting a feminist approach has clear epistemological implications, including the adoption of a position that is on the same analytical plane as those we choose to research (Stanley and Wise 1993). Addressing questions of positionality is, however, notoriously difficult to accomplish in practice, since many issues are involved, some of which we may be consciously aware of but others of which are hidden deep within our subsconscious (Rose 1997). At the very least, however, geographers now rarely seek to shelter behind the positivist shield of scientific objectivity and political neutrality, grappling with the consequences of our human subjectivity as part of the process of research.

Taking these arguments about positionality into account represents a key challenge for future research on geographies of gender. On the basis of current trends, research in this field is increasingly likely to focus on multiple, place- and time-specific constructions of masculinity and femininity, including the intersection between different 'dimensions of difference' (Laurie et al. 2000). Theorising the interplay between constructions of gender and sexuality has been particularly productive of new ideas and approaches, with hegemonic notions of gender clearly dependent upon hetero-normative assumptions. Heterosexuality is so firmly inscribed in space that it is virtually invisible, until its boundaries are transgressed (Valentine 1993). Similar arguments apply to constructions of 'whiteness' – where men as well as women need to be constantly reminded that we all lead racialised lives (Frankenberg 1993). Research on gender has also been at the forefront of recent debates about embodied geographies (Teather 1999), challenging the conventional and highly gendered separation of mind and body.

Research on these issues has only recently begun to permeate the boundaries of geography. Much remains to be done before discursive constructions of gender can be successfully traced through specific social practices and linked to particular embodied identities and material forms. While gender may have been de-centred as an analytical category within feminist research, it must surely continue to play a key role in the production of more critical cultural geographies.

KEY REFERENCES

Glover, D. and Kaplan, C. 2000. *Genders*. London, Routledge.

Jackson, S. and Scott, S. 2001. *Gender: A Sociological Reader*. London, Routledge.

McDowell, L. and Sharp, J.P. eds. 1999. *A Feminist Dictionary of Human Geography*. London, Arnold.

WGSG 1997. *Feminist Geographies: Explorations in Diversity and Difference*. London, Longman.

OTHER REFERENCES

Anzaldúa, G. 1987. *Borderlands/La Frontera: The New Mestiza*. San Francisco, Aunt Lute Books.

Bell, D., Binnie, J., Cream, J. and Valentine, G. 1994. All hyped up and no place to go, *Gender, Place and Culture*, 1: 31–47.

Bordo, S. 1990. Feminism, postmodernism, and gender-scepticism, in L.J. Nicholson ed. *Feminism/Postmodernism*. London, Routledge, 133–156.

Butler, J. 1990. *Gender Trouble*. London, Routledge.

Connell, R.W. 1987. *Gender and Power*. Cambridge, Polity.

Connell, R.W. 1995. *Masculinities*. Cambridge, Polity.

de Beauvoir, S. 1972. *The Second Sex* (trans. by H. Parshley). Harmondsworth, Penguin.

Frankenberg, R. 1993. *White Women: Race Matters*. London, Routledge.

Haraway, D. 1991. *Simians, Cyborgs and Women: The Reinvention of Nature*. London, Free Association Books.

hooks, b. 1981. *Ain't I a Woman? Black Women and Feminism*. London, Pluto.

Katz, C. and Monk, J. eds. 1993. *Full Circles: Geographies of Women over the Life Course*. London, Routledge.

Laurie, N., Smith, F., Dwyer, C. and Holloway, S. 2000. *Geographies of New Femininities*. London, Longman.

McDowell, L. 1991. Life without father and Ford: the new gender order of post-Fordism, *Transactions of the Institute of British Geographers*, 16: 400–419.

McDowell, L. and Massey, D. 1984. A woman's place, in D. Massey and J. Allen eds. *Geography Matters!* Cambridge, Cambridge University Press, 128–147.

Nelson, L. 1999. Bodies (and spaces) do matter: the limits of performativity, *Gender, Place and Culture*, 6: 331–353.

Radcliffe, S.A. and Westwood, S. eds. 1993. *Viva: Women and Popular Protest in Latin America*. London, Routledge.

Rose, G. 1993. *Feminism and Geography: The Limits of Geographical Knowledge*. Cambridge, Polity.

Rose, G. 1997. Situating knowledges: positionality, reflexivities and other tactics, *Progress in Human Geography*, 21: 305–320.

Rowbotham, S. 1977. *Hidden from History* (3rd ed.). London, Pluto.

Skeggs, B. 1997. *Formations of Class and Gender*. London, Sage.

Spivak, G.C. 1988. Can the subaltern speak?, in C. Nelson and L. Grossberg eds. *Marxism and the Interpretation of Culture*. Urbana, University of Illinois Press, 271–313.

Stanley, L. and Wise, S. 1993. *Breaking out Again: Feminist Ontology and Epistemology*. London, Routledge.

Stansell, C. 1986. *City of Women: Sex and Class in New York, 1789–1860*. New York, Alfred A. Knopf.

Teather, E.K. ed. 1999. *Embodied Geographies*. London, Routledge.

Valentine, G. 1993. (Hetero)sexing space: lesbian perceptions and experiences of everyday spaces, *Environment and Planning D: Society and Space*, 11: 395–413.

WGSG 1984. *Geography and Gender*. London, Hutchinson.

Whatmore, S. 2002. *Hybrid Geographies*. London, Sage.

Williams, R. 1976. *Keywords*. London, Fontana.

— Whiteness —

Alastair Bonnett

The language of geography is often indistinguishable from the language of race and ethnicity. 'European', 'Asian', 'Caribbean', 'Irish': such labels, like innumerable others, are both geographical and ethnic designations. This dual identity explains, in part, why geography is – whether geographers like it or not – intimately involved in debates on the causes and consequences of racism and ethnic discrimination. Yet it also highlights the curiosity of the 'critical concept' addressed here. For, although it is usually understood as a synonym for 'European heritage', 'white' belongs to that group of racial terms (more specifically, that group of colour-based categories, which includes red, black and yellow, originally sanctioned by the science of Linneaus and Cuvier) that cling to the imagination, in part because they appear abstracted from the politics and history of territory and, hence, seem obvious and natural. I shall be arguing that it is precisely this ability to appear natural that establishes whiteness as a significant concept within cultural geography. More specifically, it is the way that white identity has (a) been used to construct normative geographies and (b) acted to naturalise modernity, in different ways in different societies around the world, that demands our attention.

The theme of whiteness is not new to geography (for example, Woodruff 1905; Trewartha 1926; Kennedy 1990 [1931]). The imperial geographies of the late nineteenth and early twentieth centuries constantly strove to map out the limits and possibilities of white settlement and colonial control. However, it would be a mistake to read these applications of racial environmental determinism as indicative of a confident and unchallenged white supremacism. Rather, they formed part of a larger debate on a perceived crisis of white authority and colonial legitimacy (Bonnett 2000a). The focus within this body of geographical research was, after all, upon the *limits* of white rule. From 1880 to 1930 a considerable literature arose on the 'perils' and problems of whiteness; its vulnerability to a myriad of challenges (see, for example, Pearson 1894; Putnam Weale 1910; Money 1925; Stoddard 1922). Common sites of crisis identified were internal racial strife (the 'fratricidal' nature of World War I emerged as the prime illustration), the rising power of the non-white world (the outcome of the 1904–1905 Russo–Japanese war quickly became the principal example), the racial treason of Bolshevism, and the rise of the 'under-man' (i.e. the white proletariat). Geographers, then, were contributing to a *literature of white crisis*. It is interesting to note that, from the late 1930s onwards, the idea of openly celebrating whiteness – of talking about it as a positive identity, as something to be proud of – was gradually dropped within British public discourse. At the same time, the idea of 'the West' and 'Western' (terms that had been developing contemporaneously with the crisis of whiteness literature; see Kidd 1902 and Spengler 1926) began to come to the fore. The same pattern can be witnessed within academic geography. White attitudes became things to be studied, and eventually 'whiteness' became a term to be problematised. But 'the West' and 'Western' emerged as categories to be believed in; understood not as constructs but as coherent and meaningful expressions.

Despite its declining status within public discourse, white identity continues to be significant, both explicitly within everyday and popular culture and in coded or euphemistic forms within government discourse. This pattern is apparent in many societies. The everyday rhetoric of the white ideal has been discussed in detail in a number of ethnographic and historical studies of Latin American societies (for example, Lancaster 1991; Nutini 1997; and Weismantel and Eisenman 1998). Similar if less conclusive work, focusing mainly on advertising and other forms of popular culture, has been undertaken in China (Johansson 1998) and Japan (Wagatsuma 1968; Creighton 1995). Such studies are integral to the cultural geography of whiteness, if by that phrase we understand the comparative and international study of the cultural impacts and forms of white identity. However, the other potentially significant aspect of a cultural geography of whiteness – the study of the role of whiteness in 'place making' – has attracted little research outside Western (or do I mean white?) countries (Dwyer and Jones 2000; Watt 1998). Part of the reason may lie with the fact that the theme that has structured this work is the way whiteness acts to 'normalise' certain places and register others as exotic. This particular focus is not necessarily unhelpful within non-Western societies (for example, it may be applied to the spatial aspects of ethnic self-exoticisation). However, it is likely that it will need to be supplemented (for example, through the consideration of the Westernised city as white space, or the white spaces produced by globalised popular culture) in order to produce forms of enquiry into the 'place-making' role of whiteness in 'non-white societies' that are appropriate and substantive.

The function of whiteness in symbolising or producing 'normal' space in the West rests upon the social fact that non-white people are far more likely to be visible, to be considered to be 'out of place', than whites. Ingrid Pollard's (see Kinsman 1995) photographic meditation on her (black British) presence in the English countryside provides a straightforward illustration. Her images work by producing an immediate but uncomfortable thought: that black Britons' place is in the city. John Urry (1995, 27) asserts that the '"racialisation" of the phenomenology of the urban works partly in England through the contrasting high valuation which is placed upon the English countryside, which is taken to be predominately white'. Yet, even within the 'cosmopolitan' and 'multicultural' (or do I mean non-white?) city, whiteness has its territories and spatial limits. Recent studies affirm that it is only when 'white places' and 'non-white places' come into contact that the former become visible, the reality of white space becoming legible against a darker background. Thus, for example, Wendy Shaw's (2000, 2001) ethnographic research on Sydney suggests that

> [a]way from the stark black/white racialised boundary near The Block [i.e., the Aboriginal identified area of Redfern], where the space of whiteness absorbs other ethnicities, whiteness appears to fade into ethnic neutrality. Away from the Aboriginal 'other', whiteness is not so visible ... whiteness strengths and consolidates against the presence of The Block. (2001, 8)

The geography of Britain, the United States and Australia is also racialised at other spatial levels, such as the street (McGuinness 2000), the shopping centre (Jackson 1998), the suburb (Watt 1998; Back and Nayak 1999; Twine 1996) and the town. The role of the town as a kind of haven of the white urban, defined against the menacing presence of the 'cosmopolitan' city, appears to be particularly important in parts of the United States (Dwyer and Jones 2000; Kobayashi and Peake 2000).

Whiteness is a slippery topic: to try and 'pin it down' can easily lead to the very things critical cultural geography seeks to escape: reification and essentialism. Our interest in the topic should not lead to a fetishisation – in which whiteness is seen everywhere and used to explain everything – nor allow us to fall back into the increasingly discredited anti-racist tradition of casting white people as the sole agents of discrimination. However, when considered alongside other processes and patterns of social differentiation, an attention to whiteness can be invaluable to understanding modern places and spaces.

The significance of whiteness is even more apparent when we turn our attention to the international dimensions of white identity. It is one of the ironies of both contemporary ethnic and racial studies and cultural geography in the West that the two traditions have tended to restrict the focus of their enquires to Western countries. It is an irony because, if any areas of scholarship might be hoped to provide a resolutely anti-parochial frame of reference, it is surely these two. The shift in the latter half of the twentieth century, away from the racist assumptions of colonial era geography and anthropology, may help to explain this reticence to 'explain other societies' (Asad 1973). Yet this flight from 'Otherness' has become another form of 'Othering', a process that might be claimed to produce its own form of Eurocentrism and certainly leads to an unacceptable level of ignorance about ethnic divisions and racialisations around the world.

Despite the almost universal abandonment of explicit doctrines of white supremacy, and the adoption of anti-racist rhetoric as the lexicon of legitimacy by institutions the world over, whiteness continues to the reified as a racial and cultural norm. The patterns and paths of resistance to this process are diverse, yet if any one attribute of the white racial norm stands out from the last century it is its capacity for adaptation and survival. The durability of whiteness is a function of its close relationship with modernity. More specifically, the white ideal has been used, in various and changing ways, to naturalise modernity, to 'fix' it within the cultures and the bodies of certain European identified groups. Although this is a complex and global process, two major forms of white modernity may be identified (Bonnett 2000b). First, a biologically identified view of 'the white race' as the physical carrier of modernity, through both colonialism and post-colonial emigrations. This currently is most starkly apparent within the successive campaigns of governments throughout South America to modernise both their economies and their social structure by 'pouring in white blood' through assisted immigration schemes for Europeans (see, for example, Skidmore 1974 and Wright 1990). In the latter half of the twentieth century this phase declined in significance and a new point of emphasis within the relationship between whiteness and modernity was forged. In contemporary non-Western societies the white ideal is 'enforced', not necessarily through the physical presence or even the agency of white people, but rather through a close association between the aspirational lifestyle of consumer capitalism and the actual lifestyle and culture of the white West. A literature on this association is emerging within many area specialisms. Two important examples are Perry Johansson's (1998, 1999) studies on consumer identities as white identities in China and Millie Creighton's (1995, 1997) analyses of the role of 'the white' in Japanese advertising. However, to date, Latin Americanists have provided the most thoroughly researched explications of this process (Simpson 1993; Laurie and Bonnett 2002). The Peruvian activist Patricia Oliart (1997) has identified an association of the internationalisation of economic and media interests with the re-invention of the white European as the symbol of modernity, as the corporeal marker of social progress and physical attractiveness.

> What is happening now is that racism is coming back stronger...Money counts again now and the way you look, we have lots of gyms, that we never had before, all classes doing aerobics and dying their hair, like a blond hair...it doesn't matter if you're not white, you can look white, you can become white, you can wear nice shoes, you can dye your hair, you can get a great body, and if you don't do that, you have a ponytail, wear ethnic skirts or whatever, then that's your problem.

As Oliart's observations indicate, whiteness is being connoted as a lifestyle, symbolically tied to the pleasures of a consumption-led identity (pleasures such as 'freedom' and 'choice'). A further implication of this process is that, far from being an archaic ideology from a discredited past, the white ideal is being re-imagined. Moreover, in its new guise, this racial and cultural archetype is less identifiable as the foreign belief system of a discrete group of nasty white supremacists. It is now part and parcel of a widely disseminated aspirational agenda – a process that entails its availability to local re-interpretation, mutation and transgression as well as emulation.

KEY REFERENCES

Bonnett, A. 1997. Geography, race and whiteness: invisible traditions and current challenges, *Area*, 29, 3: 193–199.

Bonnett, A. 2000b. *White Identities: Historical and International Perspectives.* Harlow, Pearson Education.

Dwyer, O. and Jones III, J. 2000. White socio-spatial epistemology, *Social and Cultural Geography*, 1, 2: 209–222.

Jackson, P. 1998. Constructions of 'whiteness' in the geographical imagination, *Area*, 30, 2: 99–106.

Johansson, P. 1998. White skin, large breasts: Chinese beauty advertising as cultural discourse, *China Information*, 12, 2/3: 59–84.

Watt, P. 1998. Going out of town: youth, 'race', and place in the South East of England, *Environment and Planning D: Society and Space*, 16: 687–703.

OTHER REFERENCES

Asad, T. ed. 1973. *Anthropology and the Colonial Encounter.* London, Ithaca Press.

Back, L. and Nayak, A. 1999. Signs of the times? Violence, graffiti and racism in the English suburbs, in T. Allen and J. Eade eds. *Divided Europeans: Understanding Ethnicities in Conflict*. The Hague, Kluwer Law International, 243–283.

Bonnett, A. 2000a. The first crisis of whiteness, *History Today*, 50, 12: 38–40.

Creighton, M. 1995. Imaging the other in Japanese advertising campaigns, in J. Carrier ed. *Occidentalism: Images of the West*. Oxford, Oxford University Press, 135–160.

Creighton, M. 1997. Soto Others and uchi Others: imaging racial diversity, imagining homogenous Japan, in M. Weiner ed. *Japan's Minorities: The Illusion of Homogeneity.* London, Routledge, 211–238.

Johansson, P. 1999. Consuming the other: the fetish of the western woman in Chinese advertising and popular culture, *Postcolonial Studies*, 2, 3: 377–388.

Kennedy, D. 1990 (1931). The perils of the midday sun: climatic anxieties in the colonial tropics, in J.M. MacKenzie ed. *Imperialism and the Natural World*. Manchester, Manchester University Press.

Kidd, B. 1902. *Principles of Western Civilisation: Being the First Volume of a System of Evolutionary Philosophy.* London, Macmillan.

Kinsman, P. 1995. Landscape, race and national identity: the photography of Ingrid Pollard, *Area*, 27, 4: 300–310.

Kobayashi, A. and Peake, L. 2000. Racism out of place: thoughts on whiteness and an antiracist geography in the new millennium, *Annals of the Association of American Geographers*, 9, 2: 392–403.

Lancaster, R. 1991. Skin colour, race, and racism in Nicaragua, *Ethnology*, 30, 4: 339–353.

Laurie, N. and Bonnett, A. 2002. Adjusting to equity: anti-racism and the contradictions of neo-liberalism in Peru, *Antipode*, 34, 1: 28–53.

McGuinness, M. 2000. Geography matters? Whiteness and contemporary geography, *Area*, 32, 2: 225–230.

Money, L. 1925. *The Peril of the White.* London, W. Collins.

Nutini, H. 1997. Class and ethnicity in Mexico: somatic and racial considerations, *Ethnology*, 36, 3: 227–238.
Oliart, P. 1997. Interview with Alastair Bonnett, 3 April, Catholic University of Peru, Lima. Unpublished.
Pearson, C. 1894. *National Life and Character: A Forecast*. London, Macmillan.
Putnam Weale, B. 1910. *The Conflict of Colour.* London, Macmillan.
Shaw, W. 2000. Ways of whiteness: Harlemising Sydney's Aboriginal Redfern, *Australian Geographical Studies*, 38, 3: 291–305.
Shaw, W. 2001. *Way of Whiteness: Negotiating Settlement Agendas in (Post)colonial Inner-Sydney.* Unpublished Ph.D., University of Melbourne.
Simpson, A. 1993. *Xuxa: The Mega-marketing of Gender, Race, and Modernity.* Philadelphia, Temple University Press.
Skidmore, T. 1974. *Black into White: Race and Nationality in Brazilian Thought*. New York, Oxford University Press.
Spengler, O. 1926. *The Decline of the West:* (vol. 1) *Form and Actuality.* New York, Alfred A. Knopf.
Stoddard, L. 1922. *The Revolt Against Civilization: The Menace of the Under-man.* London, Chapman and Hall.
Trewartha, G. 1926. Recent thought on the problem of White acclimatization in the wet tropics, *Geographical Review*, 16: 467–478.
Twine, F.W. 1996. Brown skinned white girls: class, culture and the construction of white identity in suburban communities, *Gender, Place and Culture*, 3: 205–224.
Urry, J. 1995. *Consuming Places*. London, Routledge.
Wagatsuma, H. 1968. The social perceptions of skin color in Japan, in J. Franklin ed. *Colour and Race.* Boston, Houghton Mifflin, 129–165.
Weismantel, M. and Eisenman, S. 1998. Race in the Andes: global movements and popular ontologies, *Bulletin of Latin American Research*, 17, 2: 121–142.
Woodruff, C. 1905. *The Effects of Tropical Light on White Men*. New York, Rebman, Co.
Wright, W. 1990. *Café con leche: Race, Class and National Image in Venezuela*. Austin, University of Texas Press.

— (Dis)ability —

Robert Wilton

How people assign meaning to disability and bodily difference plays a key role in shaping the spatial arrangement of social life, and vice versa. We can illustrate this relationship using examples of conflicts over the location of homes and services for people with disabilities drawn from my research. Often the prospect of housing or services for disabled people being developed nearby generates some concern among community members. In one sense, fears are prompted by concerns over property values and neighbourhood character, but these conflicts also offer insight into cultural constructions of disability that provoke efforts to exclude. Community opposition can be interpreted as an effort to reaffirm the distinction between self and Other – an inherently spatial strategy in which exclusion helps to define the identity of community and residents alike. In one conflict, neighbours organised against a residence for people with mental illness. How were the people with mental illness constructed in the conflict? One neighbour complained:

> The problem with [the facility] is that they have an open-door policy so they let their people come and go as they please. Well, when you go into the post office down [there], there's large groups of people from this particular facility hanging out by the door, panhandling, urinating, doing whatever out in public, and that's out of control.

This person implies that residents had suffered a complete loss of control over their bodies. Spending time at the facility, however, I rarely saw more than one or two people outside the nearby post office, and these were homeless people asking for spare change. Residents of the facility often congregated outside their home, sitting on benches, smoking or strolling along the street. The notion that facility residents were 'urinating in the street' and doing 'whatever' dehumanises residents and distinguishes their behaviour from that of normal people. The attribution of a loss of control colours public perceptions and perpetuates stereotypes about people with mental illness as unpredictable, unsafe and potentially violent.

In another community, residents opposed the construction of an AIDS hospice. People cited concerns about local property values as the basis for opposition, but closer analysis of neighbours' discourse and actions points to other anxieties about the control of local space and the exclusion of difference. The hospice director recalled that, shortly after the hospice opened, one neighbour called repeatedly to complain about the facility and her fears about breathing the 'AIDS air'. Other neighbours also expressed concerns about the hospice. As the director recalled:

> We started getting some calls about the patio… we have an open patio out there [by the hospice]. We started getting complaints from people walking by, they didn't want to see, they didn't want to see these people with AIDS, these sick people.

The proximity of AIDS disturbed taken-for-granted understandings of neighbourhood space and, at the same time, made vulnerable people's own sense of identity.

How do we make sense of these and other cultural constructions of 'disabled' difference? And what is their relation to the organisation of social space? It's important to begin by considering competing definitions of disability. Disabled people include individuals with physical (including chronic illness), mental and/or intellectual impairments. While this is a diverse population, there are some similarities in the way members are defined. In contemporary society, definitions tend to focus on the 'disabled' individual. In no small part, this is due to the overwhelming influence of medical institutions and professionals who emphasise the physiological nature of disability and the need to 'fix' individuals who are disabled. These definitions (re)produce what is often termed the *medical model of disability*. Disabled people's inability to participate in social life is understood as a product of individual failing.

Recently, activists and scholars have challenged the hegemony of the medical model. They advance an alternative in which *impairment* is characterised as a functional limitation caused by physical, mental or sensory impairment while *disability* is characterised as the loss or limitation of opportunities to take part in the life of the community due to physical and social barriers. By separating the conditions experienced by individuals from the difficulties they encounter in particular social contexts, the *social model of disability* positions disablement as a form of social oppression rather than personal tragedy.

The social model is politically and theoretically powerful. However, in early formulations, it tended to focus heavily on material social conditions. Vic Finkelstein, for example, placed particular emphasis on industrialisation and the exclusion of impaired people from wage labour as a key moment in the 'production' of disability in Western society. While attributing greater significance to an ideology of individualism that grew up with industrial capitalism, Michael Oliver also sees material change as a driving force behind the disablement of physically impaired people. More recently, there has been greater attention to the way in which cultural representations sustain the material production of disability. Scholars have critically examined representations of disabled bodies and interrogated the 'able-body' as a cultural norm that influences society's treatment of (in both senses of the term) disabled people.

To understand constructions of disabled and able bodies, scholars draw insight from feminist theory, specifically the unpacking of dominant representations of the female body and norms of physical beauty. Iris Marion Young uses the term 'cultural imperialism' to describe the way in which certain norms are positioned as universal and taken for granted. For Young, groups subject to cultural imperialism are 'rendered invisible as subjects, as persons with their own perspective and group-specific experience and interests. At the same time, they are marked out, frozen into a being marked as Other, deviant in relation to the dominant norm.' This is a key point: while disabled people are erased as subjects capable of representing themselves, they are simultaneously culturally positioned as Other.

Cultural representations of disability as Other typically do not portray disability as *just* disability. Rather, disabilities are given a broader significance, and in this sense serve as metaphors. Thus, scholars argue that, within popular culture, disability often comes to signify evil, social disorder, moral degeneracy and fear of dependency, among other things. In the early 1990s, Jennie Morris argued that disability was either absent from, or distorted in, all mainstream forms of cultural representation. Seeking an explanation, she suggested that 'it is fear and denial of the frailty, vulnerability, mortality and arbitrariness of human experience that deters us from confronting such realities. Fear and denial prompt the isolation of those who are disabled, ill or old as "other," as "not like us".'

Ultimately, dominant cultural representations of disability communicate less about disability per se, and are more concerned with the validation of its opposite – what is 'good' and 'normal' in social, physical, mental, moral and sexual terms. Tom Shakespeare suggests that cultural representations of disability can be conceived as 'dustbins for disavowal'. This excerpt from an advertisement for a Nike shoe offers one example of the way in which fear of vulnerability and mortality is *disavowed* through the cultural construction of disability as Other.

> Right about now you're probably asking yourself, 'How can a trail running shoe with an outer sole designed like a goat's hoof help me avoid compressing my spinal column into a Slinky® on the side of some unsuspecting conifer, thereby rendering me a drooling, misshapen, non-extreme-trail-running husk of my former self, forced to roam the earth in a motorized wheelchair…?'

As the earlier examples demonstrate, representations of people with mental illness as out of control and potentially violent, or of people with HIV/AIDS as potentially contagious and morally compromised, severely constrain people in their efforts to occupy social space. More generally, cultural norms about (dis)ability reproduce, and are reproduced by, the exclusion of disabled people from everyday places. In public space, poorly designed environments mark out (in Young's terms) disabled people, while cultural norms emphasise the difference of disabled bodies, reaffirming the 'normality' of the environment. Likewise, constructions of disabled people as unreliable and unproductive emerge from and legitimate the exclusion of people from sites of mainstream education and work.

The marginalisation of disabled people is not universal or unchanging. Cultural norms emerge in particular historical and geographical contexts. As a consequence, the way disability is understood varies significantly over time and space. In most

Western cultures the medical model remains a dominant interpretive frame, but its dominance is a relatively recent achievement. In other settings disability has been understood as punishment for sin, a sign of moral weakness or grounds for legal punishment, and to some extent these conceptions of (dis)abled bodies continue to exist today.

As we saw above, scholars such as Michael Oliver argue that fundamental changes in the lives of people with physical impairments occurred with the structural transformation wrought by industrialisation. Similarly, the work of Michel Foucault illustrates the transformation of madness into 'mental illness' occurring alongside shifts in European societies from medieval society into a pre-industrial era. Foucault argues that, from the seventeenth century on, the mad were removed from society, first as members of a broader population of 'unruly peoples', and then as a more specialised category to be treated by newly founded professions such as psychiatry. The spatial transformation wrought by the insane asylum profoundly altered society's understanding of madness.

If we look more closely at specific historical and geographical contexts, we can identify both differences *and* similarities in the meanings of disability. Martha Edwards in her research on physical impairment in classical Greece suggests that there may not have been an automatic correlation between being impaired and being classified as '*adunatos*', or unable, as is often the case today. At the same time, Robert Garland argues that disabled difference was used in Graeco-Roman times as a scapegoating device in times of social uncertainty, something that has parallels in contemporary society. Writing about medieval society, Brendan Gleeson argues that people with physical impairments who belonged to family economies in this period experienced greater social and spatial inclusion than they would with the rise of industrial capitalism. However, the following excerpt from Sebastian Brant's *Ship of Fools,* written in 1494, bears an uncanny resemblance to the demonisation of disabled 'beggars' on today's city streets.

> He limps, he's hunched and very sick
> He ties his leg to crutch or stick
> Or hides a bone 'neath garment thick
> Should anyone inspect his wound
> He'd find it very shrewdly bound
> As beggars many men live high,
> Who have more coin than you or I.

Cultural constructions of (dis)ability hold implications not only for people with disabilities but for a majority of people who struggle to approximate contemporary cultural norms of physical attractiveness, youth and bodily performance. Harlan Hahn argues that anxieties about disability and death 'are reflected in both the propensity to shun those with unattractive bodily attributes and the extraordinary stress that modern society devotes to its quest for supernormal standards of bodily perfection'. The cultural construction of the able-body and its antithesis, the disabled body, erase the heterogeneity of bodily form and function in the population as a whole. While disabled women and older women are most clearly marked out by impossible standards of youth and beauty, the pervasiveness of these norms has very real implications for many girls and women. In some cases pressure to achieve an acceptable appearance can cause illness and impairment; eating disorders such as anorexia serve as an obvious example. It is also true that the achievement of a certain kind of hegemonic masculinity – to be a real man – rests on an ability to demonstrate masculine qualities of strength and fitness. Moreover, these issues have implications for constructions of (dis)abled sexuality, with the able-body and mind positioned as the sine qua non of desirable sexuality and 'normal' sexual relations for both women and men.

There also remains a strong moral dimension to the cultural construction of the able-body. In contemporary society there is a widespread assumption that health, youth and beauty can be achieved with appropriate effort. Michael Featherstone, for example, argues that in late capitalist society 'the penalties of bodily neglect are a lowering of one's acceptability as a person, as well as an indication of laziness, low self-esteem and even moral failure'. Advances in 'body work' techniques such as plastic surgery create a tendency to regard the body as increasingly malleable. Advertisements from gyms and fitness centres to 'be yourself only better' or 'look and feel great', while partly concerned with health, provide one example of the moral imperative to approximate the ideal of the able-body.

Constructions of disabled people as unproductive, dependent, dangerous or pitiful remain pervasive, but disabled people create alternative ways of understanding mental and physical difference. An important part of the disability rights movement in Western countries has been the emergence of what some activists term 'crip' culture. 'Crip' culture, like queer culture, appropriates, and re-assigns meaning to, dominant discourse. It seeks alternatives to dominant representations of disabled bodies and minds. Crip culture involves what Cheryl Wade calls 'reclaiming history' – working against the erasure of disabled people in times past. Challenging dominant representations of disability also involves efforts to reclaim geographies. An interesting example of this can be found in the controversy over the memorial to Franklin Delano Roosevelt in Washington, DC. In its original design, the memorial featured a number of sections or spaces representing different periods in FDR's presidency. Each section contained statues and inscriptions containing his words. Although Roosevelt experienced polio as a child and used a wheelchair during his presidency, the closest the memorial came to recognising his disability is shown in Figure 1, where a cape almost entirely conceals the fact that the president is seated in a wheelchair. After disability activists organised to protest the memorial, a new statue was added at the entrance to the memorial (Figure 2). Although concerns continue to be raised about the inscription behind the statue (a quotation from his wife, Eleanor, about his 'illness'), the new statue both reclaims history and challenges the exclusion of disability from this public space.

Many geographers are also reclaiming the 'place' of disability. Ruth Butler, for example, has begun to explore the spaces of disabled sexuality, while Vera Chouinard offers important insight into the spaces disabled women create for themselves through political activism. Work by Hester Parr draws attention to 'mad' identities to distinguish individuals' sense of self from externally imposed biomedical constructions of mental illness. She uses ethnography to examine how people navigate public, institutional and semi-institutional spaces in the contemporary city. Taking a historical focus, Chris Philo challenges the assumption that the mentally ill have been universally excluded, identifying historical moments at which 'mad people' have found themselves both within and beyond the 'normal' spaces of social life.

Figure 1

Figure 2

In sum, able-ist cultural representations reproduce and normalise the marginalised socio-economic status of disabled people and their lack of full citizenship. Moreover, these cultural norms sustain, and are sustained by, the spatial exclusion of disabled people from everyday life. Yet the exclusion of disabled people is not in any sense inevitable. In recent decades activists have challenged the assumption that people with physical and mental impairments cannot participate fully in society. Recognising that there are other ways to make sense of, and value, physical and mental difference is a key part of ongoing struggles for inclusion.

KEY REFERENCES

Butler, R. and Parr, H. 1999. eds. *Mind and Body Spaces: Geographies of Illness, Impairment and Disability.* New York, Routledge.

Gleeson, B. 1999. *Geographies of Disability.* New York, Routledge.

Imrie, R. 1996. *Disability and the City: International Perspectives.* London, Chapman.

Park, D., Radford, J. and Vickers, M. 1998. Disability studies in human geography, *Progress in Human Geography*, 22: 208–223.

Shakespeare, T. 1994. Cultural representations of disabled people: dustbins for disavowal, *Disability and Society*, 9: 249–266

OTHER REFERENCES

Butler, R. 1999. Double the trouble or twice the fun? Disabled bodies in the gay community, in R. Butler and H. Parr eds. *Mind and Body Spaces: Geographies of Illness, Impairment and Disability.* New York, Routledge, 203–220.

Chouinard, V. 1999. Body politics: disabled women's activism in Canada and beyond, in R. Butler and H. Parr eds. *Mind and Body Spaces: Geographies of Illness, Impairment and Disability*. New York, Routledge, 269–294.

Edwards, M. 1997. Constructions of physical disability in the Ancient Greek world, in D. Mitchell and S. Snyder eds. *The Body and Physical Disability.* Ann Arbor, University of Michigan Press, 35–50.

Featherstone, M. 1991. The body in consumer culture, in M. Featherstone, M. Hepworth and B. Turner eds. *The Body: Social Process and Cultural Theory.* London, Sage, 170–196.

Finkelstein, V. 1980. *Attitudes and Disabled People.* New York, World Rehabilitation Fund.

Garland, R. 1995. *The Eye of the Beholder: deformity and disability in the Graeco-Roman world*. Ithaca, New York, Cornell University Press.

Hahn, H. 1988. The politics of physical difference: disability and discrimination, *Journal of Social Issues*, 44: 39–47.

Morris, J. 1990. *Pride Against Prejudice: Transforming Attitudes to Disability.* London, Women's Press.

Oliver, M. 1990. *The Politics of Disablement*. New York, St. Martin's Press.

Parr, H. 2000. Interpreting the 'hidden social geographies' of mental health: ethnographies of inclusion and exclusion in semi-institutional places, *Health and Place*, 6: 225–237.

Philo, C. 1997. Across the water: reviewing geographical studies of asylums and other mental health facilities, *Health and Place*, 3: 73–89.

Wade, C. 1995. Disability culture rap, in B. Shaw ed. *The Ragged Edge: The Disability Experience from the Pages of the First Fifteen Years of the Disability Rag.* Louisville, KY, Avocado Press.

Wilton, R. 1998. The constitution of difference: space and psyche in landscapes of exclusion, *Geoforum*, 29: 173–185.

Young, I. M. 1990. *Justice and the Politics of Difference.* Princeton, Princeton University Press.

— Sexuality —

Mark Johnson

As Kath Weston (1998) has elsewhere noted, sexuality often appears to be a hot topic of academic enquiry: hot both in the sense of being a topic that has recently been a growth industry, and in the sense that it is still regarded with a certain degree of distance and ambivalence. As she demonstrates, the first step towards developing a critical understanding of sexuality is to understand both the reasons for and the consequences of sexuality being construed as a hot topic. The seeming emergence of sexuality as a hot topic of academic enquiry is conventionally seen to be an effect of an increasingly open, sexually tolerant and liberated society, spearheaded, among others, by lesbian and gay political movements in the West. What are the consequences or effects of this reading of events? Firstly, this 'just so' story too often obscures the way in which the study of sexuality continues to be marginalised or ghettoised as an interest of and for sexual others. That is to say, it not only ignores the discrimination that individuals studying sexuality in geography and other social sciences have often encountered (Valentine 1998) but also, just as importantly, construes the study of sexuality as variously being either about the identity politics of sexual minorities and subcultures in the West or the exotic sexual practices of 'far-flung natives'. Certainly, the emerging focus on heterosexuality can be seen as a positive development in the field, in the sense that the hegemonic status of the norm is being subjected to similar processes of analysis and deconstruction to that which has been perceived as 'Other'. Parallels can be drawn here with the way in which academics are beginning to directly interrogate whiteness as the hegemonic 'race' in ethnic and racial studies, which had previously focused primarily on the study of non-white ethnicities. However, just as it is important to remember that the study of 'race'/ethnicity in Western academia has always to a certain extent been premised on – even as it has variously challenged – the hegemony of whiteness as the 'unmarked' category, studies of sexuality have always been about policing, enforcing and variously re-inscribing the hegemonic status of heterosexuality. So, the study of (hetero)sexuality is certainly not new, and has been at the very centre of social science investigation and theory since the late nineteenth century.

LOCATING SEXUALITY IN HISTORY

So what exactly is sexuality? To answer this question there is perhaps no better starting point than Michel Foucault's (1980) *The History of Sexuality*, vol. 1. Foucault argues that the starting point for understanding sexuality is not to treat it as a set of 'natural' desires and instincts that society and culture variously organises, makes sense of and suppresses in different ways. Rather, sexuality is to be understood and treated as a discursively constructed set of social facts/fictions that not only creates and sustains desire and bodily pleasure but also, and more fundamentally, creates particular kinds of desiring subjects. In fact, for Foucault, sexuality is a particularly Western discourse that emerged in the nineteenth century as a central part of a new historical epoch in which power is defined and exercised in relation to the creation, ordering and regulation of individual reproductive bodies. Of course, there had previously been discourses about different kinds of sexual behaviours. What changed was that the sexual not only came to be seen as both a biological and a social imperative but also as the underlying truth about the individual.

Foucault, for example, famously demonstrates how the categories 'homosexual' and 'heterosexual' were nineteenth-century inventions, and argues that this was not simply a relabelling and categorisation of sexual practices but, more fundamentally, marked a shift from religious and moralising discourses on sexual behaviour to legal, bureaucratic and medicalised discourses of sexual identity that could be and were located in particular bodies. Countering the conventional view of the Victorian era as somehow repressed and silent on sexuality, Foucault shows in precisely the opposite manner how there was, as he puts it, an 'incitement to discourse' about sexuality. If the continual rediscovery of sexuality as a 'hot' topic is anything to go by, it is an incitement that has not failed to diminish over the past century and a half.

RELOCATING SEXUALITY IN THE GEOGRAPHICAL IMAGINATION

Foucault's insights continue to inform and underpin contemporary writing and research on sexuality, and in particular the articulations and disarticulations of sexuality in terms of both identity and identity politics and erotic practice. However, there have been important developments and criticisms of his work, most notably from feminist scholars. In particular, while feminists have largely taken on board Foucault's fundamental point about sexualities history, they have repeatedly shown the way in which Foucault glosses over the differential effects or consequences of compulsory (hetero)sexuality for women and men, and on formations of masculinity and femininity. Just as importantly, he fails to consider the extent to which the discourse of sexuality itself emerges in the first place as an effect of hetero*gendered* power and patriarchy (e.g. Balbus 1986; Bartky 1990, 63–82; Butler 1990, 93–110; Diamond and Quinby 1988; Hartsock 1990, 157–175).

Indeed, a recent review of 'sexuality in geography' (Elder et al. 2003) suggests that, while there is a growing body of increasingly sophisticated theoretical and empirical work on sexuality in relationship to space and place,

> most geographers sidestep the procreational norms through which the world is sexually structured and known. By procreational, we mean the many practical and symbolic ways in which notions of modern motherhood, fatherhood, and (nuclear, heterosexed) family life insinuate their ways into cultural bodies, places and imaginings: from constructions of normative nuclear familial life and goals, to heteropatriarchal framings of the nation-states, to the sexualized language through which many of us write or explain the world.

However, what I wish to point to is yet another equally problematic and paradoxical lacuna in Foucault's work and writing, and one that has equally profound implications for the study of sexualities. Foucault (1980, 57–58) is very careful to suggest in *The History of Sexuality* that his project is concerned with the development of a particularly Western discourse of sexuality and the emergence of, as he puts it, the *scientia sexualis* – the sexual sciences. Foucault contrasts the sexual sciences of the West with what he calls the *ars erotica*, the erotic arts, associated with such places as China and the Orient more generally. At first glance one might accept this as Foucault's way of simply delimiting his project to a specific social and historical location, and of insisting that what is meant and intended by sexuality in one particular place cannot be universally assumed to apply in another social or cultural situation (Jackson 2000). Hence, human geographers and anthropologists alike have been arguing that what we understand by sexuality or even assume to be different kinds of sexual identities are understood in the same way, or even understood to belong to a separate domain of the sexual (Elder 1995, 1998).

This apparently straightforward explanation of Foucault's distinction between the *scientia sexualis* and *ars erotica* too easily falls into a kind of essentialist and essentialising occidentalist/orientalist, East/West divide, which is not only politically suspect but also empirically dubious and theoretically unproductive. Firstly, the so-called history of Western sexuality is located as much in the periphery of colonial empires as it is in the urban centres of Europe. As Weston (1998, 15) suggests, the development of Western heterosexual norms were premised on and supported not just by the creation of homosexual 'Others'. Rather, 'Western' (hetero)sexuality was created and sustained by contrasts drawn with the practices of 'Others' imagined to fall outside the norm's cultural and geographical parameters.

Moreover, it was not simply, as in Freud's case, of drawing on extant ethnographic descriptions of native practices in different times and places to produce a catalogue of *The Sexual Aberrations* (1975 [1938]). As Ann Stoler (1995; see also Nast 1999, 2000) demonstrates, the development of Western bourgeois sexuality was inextricably linked with colonial entanglements and racial ideologies. Stoler suggests, (1995, 47) 'One could argue that the history of Western sexuality must be located in the production of historical Others, in the broader force field of empire where technologies of sex, self, and power were defined as European and Western as they were refracted and remade.' She argues, for example, that the repressive hypothesis was neither, in a simple Freudian analysis, the driving motor behind the violent misogynistic practices of White colonisers nor, *à la* Foucault, simply an incitement to discourse about sexuality but, rather, an effect of the attempt to delimit and police the bodily boundaries of nation, race and class among both coloniser and colonised. The irony of this is that what emerges as a discursive effect of colonialism later becomes the explanation as to why those very same individuals acted in the way they did towards colonised women and men: namely, the attribution, by mainly white bourgeois men to various colonised others (both within and outside Western Europe), of a socially debilitating sexual excess and primitive promiscuity that, in certain accounts, rendered these others not only lower in the human evolutionary scale but also in need of the civilising influence of those who had mastered – or, at least, sublimated or repressed – their own sexualities (Stoler 1997).

Secondly, another major problem with Foucault's opposition between the *ars erotica* and the *scientia sexualis* is that the effects and consequences of the development of the sexual sciences continues to extend far beyond the formation of bourgeois sexuality in the West. For example, among others, Neil Garcia (1996) and Antonia Chao (2000) have argued in the case of the Philippines and Taiwan, respectively, that various erotic practices and gender identifications are increasingly being sexualised in terms of Western identity categories of 'homosexual' and 'heterosexual'.

Some scholars have seen this proliferation of Western identity categories, including the terms 'lesbian' and 'gay', as indicative of the globalisation of lifestyle and identity politics (Altman 1996). However, simply because there has been an increasing proliferation of Western discourses of sexuality (part of the movement and flows of goods and ideas and people across the globe), it does not mean to say that everybody is becoming a subject of or subjected to modernist discourses of sexuality and identity in any simple way. To suggest otherwise is redolent of a kind of evolutionary and naïve diffusionist narrative that re-inscribes the hierarchies of coloniser/colonised, cultured/uncultured, etc. (Blaut 1992, cited in Elder et al. 2003; Johnson et al. 2000).

In summary, then, what Foucault has taught us is that sexuality is not an originary thing but, rather, that it has come to occupy this position as containing an exciting and seductive truth about both our self and Others. In order to extend Foucault's insights, however, it is important to expand its unfolding history, to treat 'sexuality' not as a discrete set of discourses and practices that arise *sui generis* in one particular historical locale, but rather – as I have argued elsewhere (Johnson 1998) – as unfurling across even as it is discursively employed to re-inscribe various cultural, ethnic and national boundaries (see also Paur, Rushbrook and Schein 2003; Binnie 2004).

KEY REFERENCES

Bell, D. and Valentine, G. eds. 1995. *Mapping Desire: Geographies of Sexualities*. London, Routledge.

Foucault, M. 1980. *The History of Sexuality.* vol. 1: *An Introduction* (trans. by R. Hurley). New York, Vintage Books.

Stoler, A. 1995. *Race and the Education of Desire: Foucault's History of Sexuality and Colonial Order of Things*. Durham, NC, Duke University Press.

Weston, K. 1998. *Long Slow Burn: Sexuality and Social Science*. London, Routledge.

OTHER REFERENCES

Altman, D. 1996. Rupture or continuity? The internationalization of gay identities, *Social Text*, 48: 77–94.

Balbus, I. 1986. Disciplining women: Michel Foucault and the power of feminist discourse, in S. Benhabib and D. Cornell eds. *Feminism as Critique*. Cambridge, Polity, 110–127.

Bartky, S. L. 1990. *Femininity and Domination: Studies in the Phenomenology of Oppression*. New York, Routledge.

Binnie, J. 2004. *The Globalization of Sexuality*. London, Sage.

Blaut, J. 1992. *The Colonizer's Model of the World: Geographical Diffusionism and Eurocentric History*. New York, Guilford.

Butler, J. 1990. *Gender Trouble*. New York, Routledge.

Chao, A. 2000. Global metaphors and local strategies in the construction of Taiwan's lesbian identities, *Culture, Health and Sexuality*, 2, 4: 377–390.

Diamond, I. and Quinby, L. 1988. *Feminism and Foucault: Reflections on Resistance*. Boston, Northeastern University Press.

Elder, G. 1995. Of moffies, Kaffirs, and perverts: male homosexuality and the discourse of moral order in the apartheid state, in D. Bell and G. Valentine eds. *Mapping Desire*. London, Routledge, 56–65.

Elder, G. 1998. The South African body politic: space, race and heterosexuality, in H. Nast and S. Pile eds. *Places through the Body*. New York, Routledge, 153–164.

Elder, G., Knopp, L. and Nast, H., 2003. Sexuality and Space, in Gary L. Gaile and C. J. Willmott eds. *Geography in America at the Dawn of the 21st Century*. Oxford University Press.

Freud, S. 1975 (1938). *The Sexual Aberrations*. Book III in *The Basic Writings of Sigmund Freud*. New York, Random House.

Garcia, N. 1996. *Philippine Gay Culture: The Last Thirty Years*. Quezon City, University of the Philippines Press.

Hartsock, N. 1990. Foucault on power: a theory for women?, in L. J. Nicholson ed. *Feminism/Postmodernism*. New York, Routledge, 154–172.

Jackson, P.A. 2000. An explosion of Thai identities: global queering and re-imagining queer theory, *Culture, Health and Sexuality*, 2, 4: 405–424.

Johnson, M. 1998. Global desirings and translocal loves: transgendering and same-sex sexualities in the southern Philippines, *American Ethnologist*, 25, 4: 695–711.

Johnson, M., Jackson, P. and Herdt, G. 2000. Critical regionalities and the study of gender and sexual diversity in South East and East Asia, *Culture, Health and Sexuality*, 2, 4: 361–375.

Manderson, L. and Jolly, M. 1997. Introduction, in L. Manderson and M. Jolly eds. *Sites of Desire, Economies of Pleasure: Sexualities in Asia and the Pacific*. London, University of Chicago Press, 1–26.

Nast, H. J. 1999. 'Sex', 'race' and multiculturalism: critical consumption and the politics of course evaluations, *Journal of Geography in Higher Education*, 23, 1: 102–115.

Nast, H. J. 2000. Mapping the 'unconscious': racism and the Oedipal family, *Annals of the Association of American Geographers*, 90, 2: 215–255.

Paur, J., Rushbrook, D. and Schein, L. eds. 2003. Sexuality and space: queering geographies of globalization, *Environment and Planning D: Society and Space*, 21: 383–387 (special issue).

Stoler, A. 1997. Educating desire in colonial Southeast Asia: Foucault, Freud, and imperial sexualities, in L. Manderson and M. Jolly eds. *Sites of Desire, Economies of Pleasure: Sexualities in Asia and the Pacific*. London, University of Chicago Press, 27–47.

Valentine, G. 1998. Sticks and stones may break my bones: a personal geography of harassment, *Antipode,* 30, 305–332.

— Moral Geographies —

Tim Cresswell

A moral geography, simply put, is the idea that certain people, things and practices belong in certain spaces, places and landscapes and not in others. This deceptively simple definition underlines the centrality of an understanding and theorisation of the interdependence of the geographical objects of space, place, landscape, territory, boundary and movement with the sociological/cultural objects of class, race, gender, sexuality, age, (dis)ability, etc. The word 'moral', therefore, indicates a fairly contingent set of rules and expectations dressed up as though it was common sense. Central to all these discussions is the role of power in constituting the relationship between geography on the ground and the practices of social groups and individuals. Central also is the role of the non-compliant in disturbing these taken-for-granted relationships and opening them up to question. The constitution of what counts as moral is infused with a geographical imagination and shot through with ideology. Moral geographies, as conventionally defined, are ideological geographies.

Although Felix Driver (1988) was the first to use the term 'moral geographies', its lineage can be traced through the work of Chris Philo (1987), David Sibley (1981, 1995) and Cresswell (1996, 1997). These works focus on the role of the geographical imagination to the production of 'outsiders' – people (and, more recently, animals [Philo 1995]) who are said to be 'out of place'. They are out of place because they do not fit into an already established (even if only temporarily) set of expectations about the link between geographical ordering and behaviour. Thus, mad people (Philo 1987; Parr and Philo 1995), gypsy travellers (Sibley 1981), children (Philo 1992; Valentine 1997), political protestors (Cresswell 1996), non-white people (Anderson 1991; Craddock 2000), gays, lesbians and bisexuals (Bell and Valentine 1995; Brown 2000), the homeless (Veness 1992; Cresswell 2001), prostitutes (Hubbard 1998), the disabled (Kitchin 1998) and a plethora of 'Others' are constituted as 'deviant' and outside 'normal' society. Theorists outside geography variously inform this work. The most significant of these are Erving Goffman's work on stigma (Goffman 1968; Philo 1987), Michel Foucault's theorisations of ordering and discipline (1979, 1980), the psychoanalytic theorisations of 'object relations theory' associated with Melanie Klein (Klein 1990; Sibley 1995), the ideas of Pierre Bourdieu surrounding 'doxa' and 'habitus' (Bourdieu 1990; Cresswell 1996) and the older formulations of the Chicago School of Sociology and their descendants (Park and Burgess 1925) concerning 'moral order' and 'deviance' (Becker 1966; Suttles 1968; Ley 1974; Cohen 1980; Jackson 1984). David Matless' *Landscape and Englishness* (1998) takes a more general look at moral geographies. Rather than focusing on the role of geography in the production of social difference along lines of race, class or gender, he links the idea of landscape to morality through a detailed account of how visions of the English landscape promoted various forms of order at the expense of the 'immoral geographies' of such things as untidiness and bungalows. Crucial to Matless' argument is the way that visions of landscape are connected with ideas of appropriate behaviour that constitute 'citizenship'. A moral geography begets moral citizens.

Any discussion of moral geographies has to touch on heretical or immoral geographies. Following Georges Canguilhem's observation that we only become aware of the 'normal' when we experience the 'pathological' (Canguilhem 1989), it is clear that the study of forms of transgression in geography points towards the often unspoken existence of normative mappings of human groups and behaviours into those that are 'in place' and those that are 'out of place'. The metaphor of disease mobilised by Foucault is often used to denote an immoral geography. Foucault uses plague as a metaphor for disorder – the imagined disorder in the mind of all planners.

> The plague as a form, at once real and imaginary, of disorder had as its medical and political correlative discipline. Behind the disciplinary mechanisms can be read the haunting memory of 'contagions', of the plague, of rebellions, crimes, vagabondage, desertions, people who appear and disappear, live and die in disorder. (1979, 178–179)

Disease often appears as a metaphor for perceived transgressions of moral geographies (Cresswell 1997; Craddock 2000). It underlines the anxiety and disgust felt by those who identify with the particular moral geography that has been transgressed. Sibley explains this disgust with reference to Klein's 'object-relations theory', which takes the fear of mixing unlike categories to be rooted in the childhood experience of separation from the mother and the dangers associated with impurity and dirt (Sibley 1995). In the background here is the work of Richard Sennett on the production of maintenance of order in the city (Sennett 1971). Sennett also took a psychoanalytical approach to the processes of ordering in social life, stating that the insecurity of modern (sub)urban dwellers is a result of a kind of halted development that refuses to embrace encounters with difference that a full (disordered) urban experience might provide.

Some recent work has attempted to deal with the issue of moral geographies in a less ambivalent manner. Robert Sack and Yi-Fu Tuan have concerned themselves with how geography is central to the construction of a genuinely moral society (Tuan 1989; Sack 1997). To them, a theory of morality can be satisfactorily constructed only through the awareness of the centrality of space and place to our existence. Rather than looking to instances of transgression to see how geography has constituted normality under the guise of the taken for granted, these writers have sought to show how there are geographies to what is, in fact, moral. David Smith and David Harvey have sought to engage with moral philosophy to ask questions about social and spatial justice (Harvey 1996; D. M. Smith 1997, 1998, 2000). Smith notes the use of the term 'moral geographies' to describe normative assumptions about people and place but suggests that geographers have been slow to engage with what morality actually is. Moral geographies, more often than not, are ideological geographies (Smith calls them 'descriptive ethics'). The word 'moral' is used in an entirely contextual way and effectively becomes the object of critique – a particular set of suppositions about people and place that serves some form of vested interest. Indeed, the implicitly radical approach taken to most cases of moral geography serves to suggest that there is nothing moral about them at all in any absolute sense. In other words, the very idea of a genuinely moral geography is constantly subverted. This is in contrast to the ideas of moral philosophers, who seek to define general senses of good and bad, just and unjust. Examples include Jurgen Habermas' notion of ideal speech acts, John Rawls' theorisations of justice and Michael Walzer's conception of 'thick' or contextual morality (Habermas 1990; Walzer 1994; Rawls 1999). Walzer in particular introduces a way of thinking that contrasts a 'thin', evenly spread, notion of universal justice with a contextually embedded 'thick' morality. This is taken up by Harvey (1996) in his discussion of the politics of difference, and what he sees as the need for a foundational conception of justice that takes difference and diversity into account without succumbing to what he perceives as postmodernism's ethical relativism (Young 1990). Smith suggests that the exploration of moral geography might be about the negotiation between this universality and thick contextuality around the local mobilisation of ideas of the 'good' and the 'just' through geographical themes such as distance and proximity, location, access, public and private space and nature/environment.

In many cases general geographical categories have become laden with moral narratives. Take the binary of place and mobility. While place has been painted as a location of rooted morality (alongside identity and authenticity), a centre of meaning and field of care (Tuan 1977; Sack 1997), mobility has often been seen as disruptive and furtive – morally suspicious. The development of this sedentarist metaphysics (Malkki 1992) in modernity can be seen in the portrayal and treatment of all manner of mobile people in modern society. The homeless, refugees, gypsies, travelling salespeople and nomads have all been either symbolically and politically marginalised or forced to fit into clearly bounded and rationalised sedentarist geographies (Sibley 1981; Atkinson 1999). Moral geographies of mobility are also clearly evident in multiple representations of the figure of the tramp in the United States at the end of the nineteenth century (Cresswell 2001). Following a series of economic downturns in the American economy in the 1870s and 1880s, the number of homeless, mobile people looking for work increased dramatically. A number of new forms of knowledge (tramp laws, sociology, eugenics, vaudeville comedy, etc.) attempted to make sense of them, firstly by producing a set of labels (tramp, hobo, etc.) and then by portraying their mobility as an immoral geography that threatened the rosy glow of sedentary existence (home, work, leisure). So, while legal knowledge made the geography of the tramp not only immoral but illegal (being without a home, from another state and without a means of support became a specific crime) sociologists in Chicago saw the tramp as a 'social problem' that needed their expertise to solve. Eugenicists, meanwhile, were busy describing the mobility of the tramp as a deeply ingrained genetic malfunction labelled 'nomadism'. The moral meanings given to mobility also featured in the more sympathetic portrayals of Charlie Chaplin as the Little Tramp, performing a mobile critique of Taylorism in *Modern Times,* and the photographer Dorathea Lange, who sought to use images of the fruit tramp and the dust bowl migrant to attract sympathy to their plight. In each of these cases a long-standing set of ideas about the good and the just (and their inverse) inform specific knowledges about geographical practice (in this case, mobility). In other words, general questions of normative ethics that transcend the particular issue of the tramp in the United States infuse the process of making up the tramp through the geographical imagination that underlies the specific forms of knowledge that brought the tramp into being.

A similar process is at work when long-standing and widespread ideas about nature combine with 'race' to produce particular, located, moral geographies. Just as women have been said to be close to 'nature' so non-white people have been constantly constructed as culture's Other. Indigenous Americans are one group of people who have been constructed as part of nature. In Frederick J. Turner's frontier thesis (Turner 1947) America's indigenous community is invisible only because it is subsumed within a general notion of the savage wilderness, which European Americans inevitably transform. This particular geography was utilised by documentarians such as Edward Curtis and Robert Flaherty, who sought to portray the indigenous community as rooted in nature – unchanging and sepia-toned, with the tell-tale signs of modernity airbrushed out (Jackson 1992; L. Smith 2001). The connection that links nature to indigenous communities and particular moral geographies was more recently mobilised in arguments over treaty rights in northern Wisconsin, where white protestors objecting to the rights of the indigenous community to fish off-reservation mobilised a set of expectations about aboriginality to suggest that the American Indians had become modern (by using electric torches and motorised boats) and had therefore abrogated their rights (Silvern 1995). Once again, the very specific located story of human/environment interaction is underlain by more general narratives of environmental ethics.

A similar logic is central to the construction of gender. Where men and, more particularly, women are said to belong is key to our understanding of how men have constituted women and themselves through time. The most prominent 'thin' moral geography of all is, arguably, the distinction of public and private space and the association between the public and masculinity. The expectation, for most of the nineteenth century, that women 'belong' at home led to women who were visibly public being labelled prostitutes (among other things) and being compelled to dress up as men in order to enact their transgression. Studies of prostitutes, poor women on the road, the *flâneuse* and the explorer/traveller all make this point

(Ryan 1989; Wolff 1990; Blunt 1994; Cresswell 1999). Others developed more subtle ways of inhabiting the public sphere and getting away with it (Domosh 1998). Far from being a relic of the nineteenth century, the equation that links women with the private and men with the public still structures much of what passes for public discourse about women's involvement in the public sphere. Reactions to the peace protestors of Greenham Common are a case in point (Cresswell 1996).

The ideas covered by the term 'moral geographies' (and 'heretical geographies') help us to analyse the taken-for-granted relationship between the geographical ordering of the world and ideas about what is good, right and true. They reveal how central geographical objects (space, place, landscape, etc.) are to the ordering of seemingly natural expectations about who and what belong where and when. The transgression of these expectations often succeeds in bringing the power relations behind such geographies into sharp relief. At another level, the idea of moral geographies points towards the possibility of a more general understanding of the role of geographical elements of human experience, such as place or mobility, in a higher-level construction of the moral.

KEY REFERENCES

Cresswell, T. 1996. *In Place/Out of Place: Geography, Ideology and Transgression*. Minneapolis, University of Minnesota Press.

Cresswell, T. 2001. *TheTramp in America*. London, Reaktion.

Harvey, D. 1996. *Justice, Nature and the Geography of Difference*. Cambridge, MA, Blackwell.

Sibley, D. 1995. *Geographies of Exclusion: Society and Difference in the West*. London, Routledge.

Smith, D. M. 2000. *Moral Geographies: Ethics in a World of Difference*. Edinburgh, Edinburgh University Press.

OTHER REFERENCES

Anderson, K. 1991. *Vancouver's Chinatown: Racial Discourse in Canada, 1875–1980*. Montreal, McGill-Queen's University Press.

Atkinson, D. 1999. Nomadic Strategies and Colonial Governance: domination and resistance in Cyrenaica, 1923-1932, in J. Sharp, P. Routledge, C. Philo and R. Paddison eds. *The Entanglements of Power: Geographies of Domination/Resistance*, London, Routledge, 93-121.

Becker, H. S. 1966. *Outsiders: Studies in the Sociology of Deviance*. New York and London, Free Press and Collier Macmillan.

Bell, D. and Valentine, G. eds. 1995. *Mapping Desire: Geographies of Sexualities*. London, Routledge.

Blunt, A. 1994. *Travel, Gender and Imperialism: Mary Kingsley and West Africa*. New York, Guilford.

Bourdieu, P. 1990. *The Logic of Practice*. Stanford, Stanford University Press.

Brown, M. P. 2000. *Closet Space: Geographies of Metaphor from the Body to the Globe*. London and New York, Routledge.

Canguilhem, G. 1989. *The Normal and the Pathological*. Cambridge, MA, Zone Books.

Cohen, S. 1980. *Folk Devils and Moral Panics: The Creation of the Mods and the Rockers*. Oxford, Blackwell.

Craddock, S. 2000. *City of Plagues: Disease, Poverty, and Deviance in San Francisco*. Minneapolis, University of Minnesota Press.

Cresswell, T. 1997. Weeds, plagues and bodily secretions: a geographical interpretation of metaphors of displacement, *Annals of the Association of American Geographers*, 87, 2: 330–345.

Cresswell, T. 1999. Embodiment, power and the politics of mobility: the case of female tramps and hobos, *Transactions of the Institute of British Geographers*, 24: 175–192.

Domosh, M. 1998. Those 'gorgeous incongruities': polite politics and public space on the streets of nineteenth-century New York City, *Annals of the Association of American Geographers*, 88, 2: 209–226.

Driver, F. 1988. Moral geographies: social science and the urban environment in mid-nineteenth-century England, *Transactions of the Institute of British Geographers*, 13: 275–287.

Foucault, M. 1979. *Discipline and Punish: The Birth of the Prison*. New York, Vintage Books.

Foucault, M. 1980. *Power/Knowledge*. New York, Pantheon.

Goffman, E. 1968. *Stigma: Notes on the Management of Spoiled Identity*. Harmondsworth, Penguin.

Habermas, J. 1990. *Moral Consciousness and Communicative Action*. Cambridge, MA, MIT Press.

Hubbard, P. 1998. Community action and the displacement of street prostitution: evidence from British cities, *Geoforum*, 29, 3: 269–286.

Jackson, P. 1984. Social disorganization and moral order in the city, *Transactions of the Institute of British Geographers*, 9: 168–180.

Jackson, P. 1992. Constructions of culture, representations of race: Edward Curtis's 'way of seeing', in K. Anderson and F. Gale eds. *Inventing Places: Studies in Cultural Geography*. Melbourne, Longman, 89–106.

Kitchin, R. 1998. 'Out of place', 'knowing one's place': space, power and the exclusion of disabled people, *Disability and Society*, 13, 3: 343–356.

Klein, R. S. 1990. *Object Relations and the Family Process*. New York, Praeger.

Ley, D. 1974. *The Black Inner City as Frontier Outpost: Images and Behavior of a Philadelphia Neighborhood*. Washington, D.C., Association of American Geographers.

Malkki, L. 1992. National Geographic: the rooting of peoples and the territorialization of national identity among scholars and refugees, *Cultural Anthropology*, 7, 1: 24–44.

Matless, D. 1998. *Landscape and Englishness*. London, Reaktion.

Park, R. and Burgess, E. 1925. *The City: Suggestions for Investigation of Human Behaviour in the Urban Environment*. Chicago, University of Chicago Press.

Parr, H. and Philo, C. 1995. Mapping mad identities, in S. Pile and N. Thrift eds. *Mapping the Subject*. London, Routledge, 199–225.

Philo, C. 1987. 'The Same and the Other': On Geographies, Madness and Outsiders. Occasional Paper no. 11, Loughborough University of Technology Department of Geography.

Philo, C. 1992. The child in the city, *Journal of Rural Studies*, 8, 2: 193–207.

Philo, C. 1995. Animals, geography, and the city: notes on inclusions and exclusions, *Environment and Planning D: Society and Space*, 13, 6: 655–681.

Rawls, J. 1999. *A Theory of Justice*. Cambridge, MA, Belknap Press of Harvard University Press.

Ryan, M. P. 1989. *Women in Public: From Banners to Ballots, 1825–1880*. Baltimore, Johns Hopkins University Press.

Sack, R. 1997. *Homo Geographicus*. Baltimore, Johns Hopkins University Press.

Sennett, R. 1971. *The Uses of Disorder: Personal Identity and City Life*. New York, Vintage Books.

Sibley, D. 1981. *Outsiders in Urban Societies*. New York, St. Martin's.

Silvern, S. 1995. Nature, territory and identity in the Wisconsin Treaty rights controversy, *Ecumene*, 2, 3: 267–292.

Smith, D. M. 1997. Geography and ethics: a moral turn, *Progress in Human Geography*, 21, 4: 583–590.

Smith, D. M. 1998. Geography and moral philosophy: some common ground, *Ethics, Place and Environment*, 1, 1: 7–33.

Smith, L. 2001. Chips off the old ice block: Nanook of the North and the relocation of cultural identity, in T. Cresswell and D. Dixon eds. *Engaging Film: Geographies of Identity and Mobility*. Lanham, MD, Rowman and Littlefield, 94–122.

Suttles, G. D. 1968. *The Social Order of the Slum: Ethnicity and Territory in the Inner City*. Chicago, University of Chicago Press.

Tuan, Y.-F. 1977. *Space and Place: The Perspective of Experience*. Minneapolis, University of Minnesota Press.

Tuan, Y.-F. 1989. *Morality and Imagination: Paradoxes of Progress*. Madison, University of Wisconsin Press.

Turner, F. J. 1947. *The Frontier in American History*. New York, Holt, Rinehart and Winston.

Valentine, G. 1997. Angels and devils: moral landscapes of childhood, *Environment and Planning D: Society and Space*, 14, 5: 581–599.

Veness, A. 1992. Home and homelessness in the United States: changing ideals and realities, *Environment and Planning D: Society and Space*, 10, 4: 445–468.

Walzer, M. 1994. *Thick and Thin: Moral Argument at Home and Abroad*. Paris, University of Notre Dame Press.

Wolff, J. 1990. The invisible flaneuse: women and the literature of modernity, in J. Wolff ed. *Feminine Sentances: Essays on Women and Culture*. Oxford, Polity, 34–50.

Young, I. M. 1990. *Justice and the Politics of Difference*. Princeton, Princeton University Press.

— Citizenship —

Darren O'Byrne

The debates and controversies surrounding the nature, meanings and possible futures of citizenship have been among the most exciting to have taken place within the social sciences during the last twenty years. Various collected volumes containing contributions from some of the most influential social and cultural commentators on the concept and problems of citizenship today are frequently cited (Turner 1993a; van Steenbergen 1994). This revitalisation of the citizenship debate within academic discourse is particularly refreshing given that for much of the twentieth century it had been rather static, dominated by liberals inspired by the work of T.H. Marshall, and Marxists who took their inspiration primarily from Antonio Gramsci's writings on civil society. The renewed interest in citizenship has in part been a reflection of wider trends within the cultural and social sciences, which have allowed for the dislodging of the nation state as the central unit of analysis. Interest among academics in such trends and concepts as globalisation, postmodernity, the politics of identity, and emerging nationalisms has breathed new life into the citizenship debate, and forced academics to reconsider some of the assumptions that previous generations may have taken for granted.

We should be careful, though, not to deduce from this that Marshall's contributions are no longer relevant; merely that they were situated within a specific framework and that criticisms have exposed their limitations. Marshall took for granted the role of the nation state in establishing citizenship rights, and in particular the establishment of the welfare state during the twentieth century (Marshall 1950). He suggested that the process of developing citizenship in capitalist democracies could be read as a three-stage evolution, resulting in the recognition of three distinct sets of citizenship rights: civil rights, political rights and social rights. Civil rights, he argued, include those individual freedoms – to speak one's mind, to form opinions and beliefs, to own property – that are provided for by the modern legal system. Political rights, formed around the freedom to participate in the process of government, are made possible by the modern democratic political system. Social rights, such as the rights to welfare, education and 'well-being', are catered for by the emergence of the modern welfare state. As Maurice Roche has rightly suggested, Marshall's understanding of the shaping of modern citizenship is closely connected to the ongoing efforts at forging an integrated nation state system – what Roche refers to as 'national functionalism' (Roche 1992, 22).

While Marshall's thesis has continued to this day to inspire subsequent academics (Bulmer and Rees 1996), the criticisms that have been directed at it have come from all corners. Marxists have criticised the absence of economic rights from his scheme, while otherwise sympathetic liberals, such as Talcott Parsons, have suggested the addition of cultural rights (Parsons and Platt 1973). The inherent evolutionism of his model has been particularly susceptible to criticism (Giddens 1982), as has his commitment to the integrative capacity of citizenship (Hindess 1987). Feminists have pointed out that, whatever other shortcomings Marshall's three-stage framework might have, it is, at best, applicable solely to men. Sylvia Walby, for instance, reminds us that, by the time citizenship had, according to Marshall, been extended to include social rights, women had still not achieved basic civil or political rights. Furthermore, in some cases, women achieved political rights before civil rights; indeed, these political rights formed the power base necessary for the subsequent establishment of civil rights (Walby 1994). Ursula Vogel provides a sharper critique, suggesting that women's exclusion from citizenship was a direct consequence of the emergence of such entitlements for men (Vogel 1994).

To best situate Marshall within current debates on citizenship, we should bear in mind two biases in his work. First, Marshall operated within a distinctly *liberal* tradition that understands citizenship solely within the context of rights and duties. Theoretical developments within the social sciences have drawn attention to other components, such as participation, membership and identity, that need to be taken into consideration. Second, the conditions that Marshall took for granted, in particular the centrality of the modern nation state, appear to have been eroded by processes of 'globalisation'. The emerging recognition of ethnic and cultural identities not reducible to the nation state, and of transnational practices and networks that challenge nation state sovereignty, has prompted academics to engage in debates on the possibility (or reality) of *global* citizenship. The remainder of this essay will focus on these two developments.

A recognition common to both of these contemporary discourses is that we need to move beyond the limited conceptualisation of citizenship associated with Western modernity. Liberalism and nation-statism are among the dominant ideologies of the 'modern age', but citizenship itself is not a product of modernity. It is common practice to accept that the origins of the citizenship ideal can be traced back to Ancient Greece (Clarke 1994). For sure, neither the Greek nor the subsequent Roman traditions were to any extent universal or wholly democratic, but they did establish the conditions that allowed 'active citizens' to participate in the process of political administration.

In the Greek tradition, particularly as it was articulated by Aristotle, citizenship was viewed as a process of self-fulfilment, achieved through *membership* and *participation*. It took on a *legal* status, with associated *rights* and *duties*, primarily under the Roman system. It is not difficult for us to see, then, not only that the ideal of citizenship predates the emergence of the modern nation state but that its 'key components' extend beyond the simple reciprocity of rights and duties prioritised by Marshall and the liberal tradition to incorporate more complex issues of membership, participation, identity and identification (Hall and Held 1989; Delanty 2000; O'Byrne 2003). These additional components have best been articulated within a communitarian tradition that locates citizenship not within the market or the state but within an autonomous political and ethical community (Delanty 2000, 23; van Gunsteren 1994, 41).

Nevertheless, despite these classical origins, it is fair to say that the dominant model of citizenship emerged alongside the onset of modernity and its associated projects of capitalism, democratisation and the bureaucratisation of political power in the centralised nation state (Roche 1992, 16; Turner 1993b, 12). Insofar as modernisation has often also been equated with individualisation, the dominance of the liberal tradition, with its emphasis on the citizen as the 'calculating bearer of rights and preferences' (van Gunsteren 1994, 38), can be read as part of the process that made possible 'the success of the individualistic concept of society over the traditional perception of it as an organic whole' (Bobbio 1996, ix). However, this process of individualisation also has to be understood within the context of the formalisation of nation states as autonomous territories. Thus, the communitarian emphasis on 'belonging' was transformed into a *republican* tradition that emphasised membership of a single community, the 'republic', from which both individuality and community strength emerge (van Gunsteren 1994, 42). In other words, the liberal tradition exemplified by Marshall's work was always intertwined with a republican tradition that was susceptible to nationalistic and patriarchal tendencies.

The second, by no means unconnected, problematic involves the extent to which that very nation state has lost its role as the defining source of political identification. While we might conceivably wish to accept this to be a true reflection of the 'post-modern condition' and accordingly consign the redundant narrative of citizenship to the conceptual scrap heap, perhaps our energies would be better employed in seeking to understand what kinds of citizenship might exist *beyond* the nation state. In the spirit of such endeavour, we could identify 'strong' and 'weak' attempts to define what me might controversially call *global citizenship*.

A *weak* version would identify the various *forms* of action or lifestyle that might constitute the practice of global citizenship. Thus, Richard Falk has usefully suggested five distinct *types* of global citizen (Falk 1994), each of whom takes advantage in different ways of the increasingly borderless world. Falk has in his list the 'global reformer', who actively campaigns for a strongly politicised concept of 'one world'; the 'global capitalist', whose various networks transcend the limitations of specific nation states; the 'global manager', who is functionally involved in the administration of planetary environmental or economic concerns; the 'global regionalist', whose transnational identity is located primarily within the emergence of such political communities as 'Europe' but who is at the same time necessarily conscious of that community's relationship to the wider world; and, finally, the 'global activist', whose advocacy of a global civil society is performed in a politicised way through involvement in such social movements as Greenpeace and Amnesty International.

Alternatively, a *strong* version would require a very clear definition of the term in contrast not only to nation state citizenship but also to the ancient idea of *world* citizenship. In other words, it would locate the theory and practice of citizenship within contemporary conditions of globalisation, thus highlighting its distinct characteristics within the context of social change (O'Byrne 2003). In contrast to the rigid legalism of the liberal perspective, the communitarianism of the Ancient Greeks allowed for a more flexible, abstract notion of citizenship relating to humanity and the known world. Thus, the history of *world* citizenship is in many respects older than that of the more territorial counterpart. Indeed, it is a fascinating history, which can be traced from Aristotlean communitarianism, through Stoicism to the religious universalism of St Augustine, and then, with the advent of modernity and the Enlightenment, to the more politicised moral universalism of Kant and the emergent human rights movement (Heater 1996). However, throughout this history, world citizenship has remained a somewhat abstract, ideal commitment to membership of a common humanity, strong in *moral* force as an appeal to a common good but lacking in *legal* force by virtue of its detachment from positive law. When the 1948 Universal Declaration of Human Rights was signed by the member states of the United Nations, a set of ethical guidelines was introduced that, while grounded in no small way in the traditions of moral universalism and natural law, also served as a coercive, if not legally binding, framework for state behaviour; a blueprint for a cosmopolitan constitution. This is one of the defining moments in post-war political globalisation, and it – together with subsequent developments in international law – makes possible a new kind of citizenship in both the liberal and the communitarian senses; a citizenship in which rights are *human* rights, protected not necessarily by nation-state constitutions but by intergovernmental agreements and international positive law, and in which duties are not necessarily towards the 'national interest' but towards the survival of the planet and its inhabitants. In the same breath, we can rethink the concept of participation beyond liberal democracy towards a globalised, *radical* democracy made possible by information technology, while adapting our sense of membership away from the limitations of the political nation state towards a more flexible, multicultural concept of society. All this is possible because the external conditions within which political action – the performance of our citizenships – takes place are globalised. Thus, *global citizenship* is world citizenship under the impact of globality, and it is both pragmatic and real (Albrow and O'Byrne 2000, 74).

But is it citizenship? If we accept that citizenship is far more than a simple legal contract that binds an individual to a political-administrative state via the reciprocity of rights and duties, then it almost certainly is. Indeed, in the historical discourse on citizenship, for every Marshall working within the liberal, nation-state tradition there are a dozen or so Aristotleans, Kantians or feminists seeking to expose the limitations of this narrow definition. There is nothing inherent in the nature of citizenship that suggests it must involve some kind of social contract between an individual and a political authority, never mind that that authority has to be the relatively new invention we call the nation state. Some might argue that if we limit citizenship to this narrow definition we necessarily purge it of any emancipatory or empowering potential. Others might point out the extent to which nation state citizenship has always been a project of *exclusion*. After all, citizenship has long been used as a tool for *nation building* – that is, for attempting to mould a common identity among residents of a given political territory, never mind their differences. Insofar as this *assimilationist frame* has sought to create a sense of homogeneity, it has done so at the expense not only of the *external* 'Other' but of the multitude of *internal* 'Others' – those who do not conform to the monocultural aspirations of the nation state – as well.

On the other hand, there is some validity in the charge that, by extending the meaning of citizenship too far beyond the liberal contractarian perspective, we run the risk of rendering it meaningless. Citizenship in legal terms is at least empowering insofar as it identifies a formal 'contract' between the citizen and the state, thus protecting rights in positive law. Too much emphasis on 'identity' or 'belonging' might serve only to detach citizenship from the formal politics of everyday life. Indeed, it is noticeable that much of the work carried out within contemporary communitarianism – with its laudable project of rebuilding the idea of the 'good society' – tends to operate within the framework of *civil society* rather than citizenship (Walzer 1995).

Citizenship is at a crossroads. The term is used repeatedly in debates over European integration, the rights of refugees, participation in competitive sport, and countless other areas of contestation. At the same time, while Western academics urge us to dispense with, globalise or rethink citizenship as a framework for political identity, newly emerging nationalisms in many parts of the world continue to turn to such concepts as citizenship and civil society in order to mould a sense of national identity and overcome the problem of social order. What is at least clear is that any discussion of citizenship now has to take into consideration the possibility of multiple citizenships and allegiances in a world in which the nation state is only one of many possible sources of identification, and that, for a model of citizenship to be applicable, it has to extend beyond the legalism and exclusivity of the liberal model.

KEY REFERENCES

Bulmer, M. and Rees, A.M. eds. 1996. *Citizenship Today: The Contemporary Relevance of T.H. Marshall.* London, UCL Press.

Delanty, G. 2000. *Citizenship in a Global Age: Society, Culture, Politics.* Buckingham, Open University Press.

Marshall, T.H. 1950. *Citizenship and Social Class.* Cambridge, Cambridge University Press.

Roche, M. 1992. *Rethinking Citizenship: Welfare, Ideology and Change in Modern Society*. Cambridge, Polity.

Turner, B. S. ed. 1993a. *Citizenship and Social Theory*. London, Sage.

van Steenbergen, B. ed. 1994. *The Condition of Citizenship*. London, Sage.

OTHER REFERENCES

Albrow, M. and O'Byrne, D. 2000. Rethinking state and citizenship under globalized conditions, in H. Goverde ed. *Global and European Polity? Organizations, Policies, Contexts*. Aldershot, Ashgate, 65–82.

Bobbio, N. 1996. *The Age of Rights*. Cambridge, Polity.

Clarke, P.B. 1994. *Deep Citizenship*. London, Pluto Press.

Falk, R. 1994. The making of global citizenship, in B. van Steenbergen ed. *The Condition of Citizenship*. London, Sage, 127–140.

Giddens, A. 1982. Class division, class conflict, and citizenship rights, in A. Giddens ed. *Profiles and Critiques in Social Theory*. London, Macmillan, 164–180.

Hall, S. and Held, D. 1989. Citizens and citizenship, in S. Hall and M. Jacques eds. *New Times: The Changing Face of Politics in the 1990s*. London, Lawrence and Wishart, 173–188.

Heater, D. 1996. *World Citizenship and Government: Cosmopolitan Ideas in the History of Western Political Thought*. London, Macmillan.

Hindess, B. 1987. *Freedom, Equality and the Market*. London, Tavistock.

O'Byrne, D. 2003. *The Dimensions of Global Citizenship: Political Identity Beyond the Nation-State?* London, Frank Cass.

Parsons, T. and Platt, G.M. 1973. *The American University*. Cambridge, MA, Harvard University Press.

Turner, B.S. 1993b. Contemporary problems in the theory of citizenship, in B.S. Turner ed. *Citizenship and Social Theory*. London, Sage, 1–18.

van Gunsteren, H. 1994. Four conceptions of citizenship, in B. van Steenbergen ed. *The Condition of Citizenship*. London, Sage, 36–48.

Vogel, U. 1994. Marriage and the boundaries of citizenship, in B. van Steenbergen ed. *The Condition of Citizenship*. London, Sage, 77–89.

Walby, S. 1994. Is citizenship gendered?, *Sociology*, 28, 2: 379–395.

Walzer, M. 1995. The concept of civil society, in M. Walzer ed. *Toward a Global Civil Society*. Oxford, Berghahn, 7–28.

— Heritage —

David Atkinson

Raphael Samuel has called heritage a 'nomadic term'; one that 'travels easily', it is increasingly prevalent throughout our contemporary world and crops up in some of the most unexpected places (Samuel 1994, 205). David Lowenthal agrees, identifying a 'cult' of heritage, evidenced by a plethora of sites scattered across the globe, 'busy lauding – or lamenting – some past, be it fact or fiction' (Lowenthal 1998, xiii). By emphasising its heterogeneity, both authors undermine the casual but persistent assumption that societies may identify a singular, coherent 'heritage' that articulates their collective social memory, and that is manifest in unique places or preserved landscapes. Instead, they conceptualise 'heritage' as socially constructed. And it follows that there is no single 'heritage' but, rather, plural *versions* of the past constructed in contemporary contexts. Moreover, as Brian Graham (2002, 1004) states: '[I]f heritage is the contemporary use of the past, and if its meanings are defined in the present, then we create the heritage that we require.' Thus, critical cultural geographers can help identify the partial versions of heritage that particular social groups require and produce; they can also explore how these heritages are materialised in space and place.

In addition, critical approaches also expose how heritage and heritage sites are mobilised increasingly as important cultural, political and economic resources in our contemporary world (Graham 2002). At times the process appears unstoppable, as localities scramble to market a distinctive identity that might earn a share of the global tourist trade (MacCannell 1992). In many cases 'heritage' becomes part of the deal, and a local past is mobilised to sell a place in the present. Therefore, what some call 'the heritage industry' is often embedded in the consumption of 'historic' places. Yet these articulations of heritage can be surprisingly fixed in their readings of time and space, selling partial representations of history in discrete, bounded sites.

Accordingly, we have two problems with heritage. First, powerful groups often promote 'sectarian claims upon the past' for their own ends (Landzelius 2003, 208). As I mentioned, many heritage initiatives are designed by local authorities to suit place-promotion strategies and attract tourism and investment. Perhaps inevitably, they often sanitise local histories, seldom focusing on their controversial, uncomfortable or mundane aspects but celebrating their notable, distinctive elements instead. And, although intended to promote a collective heritage identity, these tales are limiting in other ways too. They can exclude difference by masking plural, complex and diverse histories beneath one-dimensional narratives; they can elide the broader spatial connections of places via these fixed heritage representations, rooted in bounded sites. Naturally, excluded groups sometimes contest these 'official' stories with alternative readings of heritage (although these too can be factional). But, once an essentialised heritage identity is formally sanctioned and promoted by powerful actors, there is always the risk that it may reproduce categories of belonging and sameness, and parallel exclusionary projections of difference and otherness.

The second problem is that these partial narratives also find material form, helping to constitute heritage sites and spaces in our contemporary world (and making this process of direct concern to geographers). Again, the selective tales of the powerful have the advantage: the capital invested in supporting their heritage strategies has lasting impacts on the landscape as monuments, buildings or districts deemed emblematic of an era to be celebrated are preserved (Urry 1990). Conversely, the historic fabric redolent of other periods deemed mundane or unexceptional is neglected or even demolished. Of course, local communities sometimes occupy the spaces between or beyond these 'official' sites with events, carnivals or their own monuments and murals (Graham 2002). Even museums – those traditional bastions of formal memory – are becoming more reflexive about the stories they tell and the histories they celebrate (Duncan 2003). In sum, though, all of this demonstrates that mosaics of spaces – representing certain, selected versions of heritage and eliding others – pattern our world increasingly.

This process first attracted academic complaint in Britain in the 1980s. Critics such as Patrick Wright (1985), recently returned from overseas, were struck by the increasing commodification of history and the growth of popular nostalgia. In particular, he railed against the increased marketing of an aristocratic past – accusing newly opened stately homes and gardens of pedalling a 'reactionary chic' that erased the stories and struggle of other classes. Soon afterwards, Robert Hewison (1987) also critiqued romanticised depictions of the past that served conservative visions of the present. He was scathing about the transformation of redundant industrial areas – another aspect of Britain's nascent 'heritage industry'. To his mind, the restored docks, mills and warehouses – now used for leisure, retail and 'executive' housing – masked the decay of traditional industries. More controversially, he also alleged that heritage provided 'inauthentic', 'bogus history', in contrast to the formal scholarship of academic historians. While this problematic distinction sailed close to academic elitism and disregarded the popularity of heritage sites, it also failed to acknowledge that debates surrounding heritage questions have a longer and more complicated lineage than his arguments allowed (Samuel 1994; Urry 1990). Nevertheless, these early critics did emphasise that, when one rendering of the past is prioritised over others, all too often these other groups, processes and historical periods are excluded.

WHICH 'MARITIME HERITAGE'?

I shall illustrate these themes by outlining some of the versions of maritime heritage that have materialised in the port city of Hull, England, over the past few years. The first instance I discuss dates from 1999, when redevelopment plans for the redundant fishing dock proposed a leisure and retail complex with a 'maritime heritage' theme. For many locals still smarting from the decimation of the city's once-dominant fishing industry since the 1970s, the project's commercial developers showed scant regard for the memories of the industry, its cultures and the approximately 8,000 fishermen who never returned from the Arctic fishing grounds (Lazenby and Starkey 2000). But, when the former fishing community complained, they found that the city council's tourism and place promotion strategies had little interest in remembering fishing either. Deemed a smelly, dirty, unskilled industry by the city's image consultants, this type of maritime heritage was quietly elided in favour of attempts to promote a vibrant, modern image for Hull. Here, then, was a history sanitised for an imagined international audience by capital and local authorities alike. Meanwhile, a local community and their sense of a maritime past were marginalised (Atkinson et al. 2002).

By contrast, two years later Hull was visited by Sea Trek 2001, a 'heritage spectacle' comprising six 'historic', square-rigged 'tall ships' (most of which were modern replicas). *This* version of maritime heritage earned unqualified support from the local authority and enthusiastic marketing from its tourism agencies. It was also hugely popular with the public. When the ships sailed into port late one night 40,000 spectators turned out, and 20,000 people bought tickets and queued at length to tour the ships' decks the next day. Another 80,000 looked on from the quayside. For the people of Yorkshire, these 'tall ships' from an imagined 'romantic age of sail' were something worth seeing. And this, the official tourism and promotional materials told them, was a celebration of Hull's 'proud maritime heritage'.

Yet, for those on board, this heritage spectacle was about something else entirely. Sea Trek was organised by an American venture capitalist as an elaborate celebration of the early nineteenth-century journeys that led Mormon converts from Europe across the Atlantic to North America, and then further west to their eventual, sacred, 'gathering' and settlement in Utah. Through the summer of 2001 the ships and their passengers revisited a series of key sites along this route. And, because early Mormon converts from Scandinavia and the Baltic sailed to America via Hull, Sea Trek docked here too. Consequently, for those on board this was a spiritual pilgrimage, and their website diaries recorded their pleasure at the Hull crowds who participated in their performance. However, those on shore were told nothing of this religious agenda; for them, the event was simply about Hull's 'maritime heritage'.

Moreover, when the ships, their pilgrim cargo and the tourists were gone, the event left a tangible mark on the dockside that likewise communicated a particular understanding of emigrant heritages. The Sea Trek organisers donated a bronze statue of an emigrant family to the city, one of a series of identical monuments that mark the Mormon migrations from Gothenburg, Hamburg and Copenhagen, through Hull and Liverpool, to New York, St. Louis and, finally, Utah (Figure 1). The local authorities positioned it at a prominent site by the entrance to the historic city docks. In one respect, this was an overdue recognition of Hull's role as a major transmigrant port. Between 1836 and 1914, for example, 2.2 million people passed through the city (Evans 2001). They totalled some 8% of all European migrants to North America in the period, but, until recently, there was no public commemoration of this in Hull. Here was another largely forgotten maritime heritage.

Figure 1: The 'Sea Trek' statue of an emigrant family being installed at the entrance to Hull's former docks.

The statue raises further questions, though. Monuments and sites of commemoration have attracted academic attention of late due to the ways they materialise social memory in public space. But, as with heritage sites, these too often convey selective understandings of the past, and who, or what, is worth remembering (Johnson 1995). This statue, for example, embodies a particularly conservative and patriarchal vision of an emigrant family and their gender roles. The strong, square-jawed father, staring westwards into the distance and their future, is the focal point of this idealised nuclear family. The mother sits dutifully by his side on the trunk containing their few possessions. She is plainly deferential and, fulfilling her childcaring role, minds her small daughter. Her young son, by contrast, is more independent – waving a stick at an unfeasibly large crab that rears up behind the group. The monument thus enshrines a romanticised, heroic vision of the European diaspora en route for the Americas – and, while it signals their courage and optimism, it says little of the poverty or persecution that often compelled such lengthy dislocation. Neither does it countenance the racial or religious distinctions, physical differences or diseased bodies that also impacted upon migrants' prospects. Arguably, it masks the full range of Hull's European transmigrants, with their differing travelling groups, ethnicities, motives and destinations. Equally, it implies a one-way passage and says nothing of return migration or the fluid, multicultural communities that shaped hybrid cultures as they sailed back and forth between the ports of this modern, transatlantic world (Gilroy 1993; Linebaugh and Rediker 1990; Rediker 1987). But, although this depiction of a migrant family is only one aspect of Hull's story, it is now cast in bronze and is therefore rendered more tangible, permanent and privileged than others.

Similar tales have been recounted all over the 'West' in recent years as the construction of heritage sites has continued relentlessly. These examples from Hull illustrate some of the issues raised by their partisan nature. Moreover, because constructions of heritage are usually embedded in places and landscapes, they also entail subtle yet significant geographical categories of belonging and difference. It is here especially that cultural geographers can contribute to their critique.

THINKING THROUGH THE SPACES OF HERITAGE

As the heritage business grew, its commentators and critics began to recognise the significance of the sites, places and landscapes where heritages are articulated as partially constitutive of this phenomenon. Some wrote of heritage as 'intrinsically place-based' (Ashworth 1994, 1) and inherently 'a spatial phenomenon', always located somewhere or distributed across space, and operating at a series of scales (Graham et al. 2000, 4). In a similar vein the historian Pierre Nora (1989, 1984–1992) argues that the modern period has witnessed the replacement of traditional forms of memory by 'sites of memory': specific places where both formal and popular memories are produced, negotiated and take root. He argues that when 'memory attaches itself to sites', these demand analysis (1989, 22). A growing tranche of cultural geographers agree.

Yet, given the sectarian and sanitised interpretations of the past pedalled by some heritage tales, cultural geographers have extended this agenda by exposing, undermining and complicating rudimentary readings of places and their pasts. Increasing numbers of studies have addressed heritage sites as nodes where the competing histories – or 'dissonant heritages' (Tunbridge and Ashworth 1996) – of different social groups collide. Accommodating 'dissonance' means recognising the complicated histories of our communities and their places, while simultaneously accepting parallel and competing accounts of this past. For some, this promises a more inclusive, plural heritage for our multicultural societies (Graham et al. 2000). Certainly, this approach allows us to move beyond selective, conservative accounts to consider the manifold, entangled elements that constitute our social worlds. Our heritage studies now encompass hitherto disregarded topics such as class relations, conditions of work and labour, and questions of gender and ethnicity (Edensor and Kothari 1994; Johnson 1996, 1999; Samuel 1994). Most notably, this approach has helped enable compelling accounts of the fraught contestations surrounding commemorations of the Holocaust/Shoah (Azaryahu 2003; Charlesworth 1994; Young 1993; Till 1999). At a time when even this kind of 'dark heritage' is increasingly drawn within the webs of capital and place commodification (Foley and Lennon 2000), the critical engagement with such weighty matters is an encouraging example of the ways that academics can respond usefully to pressing issues of social memory.

Cultural geographers can further critique simplistic heritage sites by recounting the complex spatial history of places. Sometimes, these sites appear to be discrete places, isolated from the broader patterns and processes of history (Massey 1995; Urry 1995). By revealing the connections and flows that constituted historic worlds, critics can destabilise the process of privileging a singular version of heritage and eliding other stories. Studies of the spatial histories of empires and their traffic of capital, power, commodities and cultures, for example, demonstrate the plural and entwined processes that connect places from local to global scales (Lester 2001; Nash 2000). Inevitably, the places presented as today's heritage sites were also subject to these influences. The country houses and estates that so irked Wright (1985), for instance, are revealed as originally enmeshed in webs of colonial power and trade, and circuits of culture and 'taste' (Seymour et al. 1998). They also expose the domestic and social relations of the period (Johnson 1996). Indeed, Nora (1989) identifies a responsibility to explore the links between apparently unconnected 'sites of memory'. Similarly Dolores Hayden (1995), examining how urban landscapes in Los Angeles manage to host the competing memories and affiliations of different ethnic and gender groups simultaneously, also argues that place memories need to engage with wider, transnational spatial processes, such as diaspora and migration. To this end, Michael Landzelius (2003) advocates a 'rhizome' history that undermines one-dimensional, static historical lineages and bounded identities, and foregrounds spatial relations and connections instead. Whichever strategy is preferred, a more sophisticated spatial reading of the past allows *intellectual* space for different and co-existing narratives. The challenge then, of course, is to realise this inclusive intellectual space in the material realm of the contemporary world.

POPULAR HERITAGE

The problem is that fixed, essentialist representations of heritage at delimited heritage sites look set to endure. Graham et al. (2000) blame its centrality to the commodification and consumption of place, and the enduring boundedness of Western society. The emergent political economies of heritage are equally unlikely to disappear in parts of the developing world (Hancock 2002). Indeed, the lure of tourism has inspired increasing numbers of pastiche 'heritage quarters', restored in the style of a selected era. Even entirely new sites have been created, built to look *like* historic places and to attract leisure spending (Graham 2002). Adopting Baudrillard, Robert Shannan Peckham suggests that these hyperreal tourist simulacra leave actual heritage places redundant – sidelined because their overlapping, dissonant stories and landscapes might dilute the 'authentic' heritage experience (Shannan Peckham 2003, 5).

In contrast to this spectre, in other, more promising ways our academic critiques are augmented by the wider, popular interests in histories and heritage that are evident increasingly throughout society. Despite Hewison's worries about 'bogus history', Samuel (1994) sees little wrong with 'popular' celebrations of local histories and identities. For him, 'memory work' is a dynamic, 'organic form of knowledge' – a democratic interest open to all kinds of people and drawing on a multiplicity of sources (Samuel 1994). For instance, Mike Crang (1994, 1996) explores the ways that individuals and groups explore and articulate their senses of heritage through performance and practices, and through everyday artefacts and ephemera such as photographs and postcards. Although sometimes mundane and small-scale, these popular expressions of social memory may nevertheless offer alternative readings to the fixed explanations of formal heritage. Besides, the visitors to, and residents of, heritage places are not necessarily passive recipients of these 'official' narratives either. Rather, they often consume these selectively, subverting some aspects while creating their own understandings of places and their histories (Urry 1990). As a result, *popular* expressions of heritage might also offer amorphous but sustained critiques of those pasts selected by heritage and marketing strategies.

One last dockside example demonstrates this point. The 1996 Festival of the Sea in Bristol, England, centred on the launch of a replica of the ship that Giovanni Cabotto sailed from there to Newfoundland in 1497 (Laurier 1998). It also showcased over 800 vessels and a huge range of maritime-related cultures to some 35,000 paying spectators over four days (Nash 2000). Yet, amidst all this evidence of a 'proud', 'seafaring' past, the festival's characterisation of history was abstracted from the wider complications of Bristol's historic links to other places. In particular, it virtually ignored the city's pivotal role in the seventeenth- and eighteenth-century triangular slave trade (Dresser 2001). Despite benefiting from considerable local authority support, this quasi- 'official' expression of Bristolian identity failed to address this uncomfortable history and the wealth the city had derived from imperialism. The event celebrated a largely white Bristolian history, excluding the local black community and other groups who jarred with the event's genteel, middle-class ethos (Atkinson and Laurier 1998; Nash 2000).

However, this partial heritage was contested by some of those who were excluded. Postcards and sachets of sugar explaining Bristol's roles in the triangular trade were scattered throughout the site by a local artist. Fly posters also drew attention to the slaving past, and the Bristol Black Writer's Group – granted a short slot on a festival stage – also addressed this hidden history of transatlantic exchange (Nash 2000). Thereafter, the critique rumbled on in the local media persistently. And although haphazard, such was its momentum that the city council eventually developed heritage trails and exhibitions that acknowledged and explored this 'obscured' slaving history (Chivallon 2001; Dresser 2001). Therefore, despite the elisions of the Festival of the Sea, these parallel, dissonant versions of Bristolian history did contest the dominant narrative and eventually found more permanent expression in the city.

Although the commodification of heritage for tourist markets and as a mechanism for place promotion remain powerful, this final example suggests that, alongside academic critiques, the increasing numbers involved in commemorating *their* local pasts means that one-dimensional, partial heritages will remain contested, and that scepticism towards 'official' heritage stories will flourish. This broader constituency also suggests that the conversations and debates that develop as a consequence will help facilitate more democratic, more inclusive and less problematic ways of thinking through multiple heritages and their spaces.

KEY REFERENCES

Graham, B. 2002. Heritage as knowledge: capital or culture?, *Urban Studies*, 39: 1003–1017.

Graham, B., Ashworth, G. and Tunbridge, J. 2000. *A Geography of Heritage: Power, Culture and Economy*. London, Arnold.

Lowenthal, D. 1998. *The Heritage Crusade and the Spoils of History*. Cambridge, Cambridge University Press.

Samuel, R. 1994. *Theatres of Memory: Past and Present in Contemporary Culture*. London, Verso.

Shannan Peckham, R. 2003. *Rethinking Heritage: Cultures and Politics in Europe*. London, I.B. Tauris.

Urry, J. 1990. *The Tourist Gaze: Leisure and Travel in Contemporary Societies*. London, Sage.

OTHER REFERENCES

Ashworth, G. 1994. Introduction: on heritage and the new Europe, in G. Ashworth and P. Larkham eds. *Building a New Heritage*. London, Routledge, 1–14.

Atkinson, D. and Laurier, E. 1998. A sanitised city? Social exclusion at Bristol's 1996 International Festival of the Sea, *Geoforum*, 29, 99–206.

Atkinson, D., Cooke, S. and Spooner, D. 2002. Tales from the Riverbank: place marketing and maritime heritage, *International Journal of Heritage Studies*, 8: 25–40.

Azaryahu, M. 2003. RePlacing memory: the reorientation of Buchenwald, *Cultural Geographies*, 10: 1–20.

Charlesworth, A. 1994. Contesting places of memory: the case of Auschwitz, *Environment and Planning D: Society and Space*, 12: 579–593.

Chivallon, C. 2001. Bristol and the eruption of memory: making the slave-trading past visible, *Social and Cultural Geography*, 2: 347–363.

Crang, M. 1994. On the heritage trail: maps of and journeys to Olde Englande, *Environment and Planning D: Society and Space*, 12: 341–355.

Crang, M. 1996. Envisioning urban histories: Bristol as palimpsest, postcards, and snapshots, *Environment and Planning A*, 28: 429–452.

Dresser, M. 2001. *Slavery Obscured: The Social History of the Slave Trade in an English Provincial Port*. London, Continuum.

Duncan, J. 2003. Representing empire at the National Maritime Museum, in R. Shannan Peckham ed. *Rethinking Heritage: Cultures and Politics in Europe*. London, I.B. Tauris, 17–28.

Edensor, T. and Kothari, U. 1994. The masculinisation of Sterling's heritage, in V. Kinnaird and D. Hall eds. *Tourism: A Gender Analysis*. London, Wiley, 115–134.

Evans, N. 2001. Indirect passage from Europe: transmigration via the UK, 1836–1914, *Journal for Maritime Research*, June.

Foley, M. and Lennon, J. 2000. *Dark Tourism*. London, Continuum.

Gilroy, P. 1993. *The Black Atlantic: Modernity and Double Consciousness*. London, Verso.

Hancock, M. 2002. Subjects of heritage in urban southern India, *Environment and Planning D: Society and Space*, 20: 693–717.

Hayden, D. 1995. *The Power of Place: Urban Landscapes as Public History*. London, MIT Press.

Hewison, R. 1987. *The Heritage Industry: Britain in a Climate of Decline*. London, Methuen.

Johnson, N. 1995. Cast in stone: monuments, geography and nationalism, *Environment and Planning D: Society and Space*, 13: 51–65.

Johnson, N. 1996. Where geography and history meet: heritage tourism and the Big House in Ireland, *Annals of the Association of American Geographers*, 86: 551–566.

Johnson, N. 1999. Framing the past: time, space and the politics of heritage tourism in Ireland, *Political Geography*, 18: 187–207.

Landzelius, M. 2003. Commemorative dis(re)membering: erasing heritage, spatializing disinheritance, *Environment and Planning D: Society and Space*, 21: 195–221.

Laurier, E. 1998. Replication and restoration: ways of making maritime heritage, *Journal of Material Culture*, 3: 21–50.

Lazenby, C. and Starkey, D. 2000. Altered images: representing the trawling in the late twentieth century, in D. Starkey, C. Reid and N. Ashcroft eds. *England's Sea Fisheries: The Commercial Sea Fisheries of England and Wales since 1300*. London, Chatham, 166–172.

Lester, A. 2001. *Imperial Networks: Creating Identities in Nineteenth-Century South Africa and Britain*. London, Routledge.

Linebaugh, P. and Rediker, M. 1990. The many-headed hydra: sailors, slaves and the Atlantic working class in the eighteenth century, *Journal of Historical Sociology*, 3: 225–252.

MacCannell, D. 1992. *Empty Meeting Grounds: The Tourist Papers*. London, Routledge.

Massey, D. 1995. Places and their pasts, *History Workshop Journal*, 39: 182–192.

Nash, C. 2000. Historical geographies of modernity, in B. Graham and C. Nash eds. *Modern Historical Geographies*. London, Pearson, 13–40.

Nora, P. 1984–1992. *Les lieux de mémoire* (3 vols.). Paris, Gallimard.

Nora, P. 1989. Between memory and history: *Les lieux de mémoire*, *Representations*, 26: 7–24.

Rediker, M. 1987. *Between the Devil and the Deep Blue Sea: Merchant Seamen, Pirates and the Anglo-American Maritime World, 1700–1750*. Cambridge, Cambridge University Press.

Seymour, S., Daniels, S. and Watkins, C. 1998. Estate and empire: Sir George Cornewall's management of Moccas, Herefordshire and La Taste, Grenada, 1771–1819, *Journal of Historical Geography*, 24: 313–352.

Till, K. 1999. Staging the past: landscape designs, cultural identity, and Erinnerungspolitik at Berlin's Neue Wache, *Ecumene*, 6: 251–283.

Tunbridge, J. and Ashworth, G. 1996. *Dissonant Heritage: The Management of the Past as a Resource in Conflict*. Chichester, Wiley.

Urry, J. 1995. *Comsuming Places*. London, Routledge.

Wright, P. 1985. *On Living in an Old Country: The National Past in Contemporary Britain*. London, Verso.

Young, J. 1993. *The Texture of Memory: Holocaust Memorials and Meaning*. Yale, Yale University Press.

— PART III —

BORDERS AND BOUNDARIES

— Introduction —

Borders and Boundaries

When, in the mid-twentieth century, geographers characterised their discipline as a chorographic science the purpose of which was areal differentiation, boundaries were generally considered to be an unproblematic aspect of taxonomy; objects were assigned to classes, including regions, according to their membership of a group – A or not-A. The inadequacy of such binary classification had already been recognised elsewhere in the social sciences, particularly in social anthropology, where transitional and ambiguous states were seen as one key to understanding other cultures. Questions of liminality, spaces of uncertainty that resist binary classification, have now become an important focus of cultural geography, although their significance for geography had been anticipated by Gunnar Olsson in his writing in the 1970s and early 1980s on the 'excluded middle'. Taken-for-granted boundaries are problematic, but boundaries can also be seen to generate theoretical questions that offer possibilities for developing a more critical cultural geography.

The essays in this section are concerned both with changing realities, with material changes in the organisation of societies in interpenetrating spaces from the local to the global, and with the reshaping of geography's theoretical terrain, partly in response to perceived changes in the material world. The first essay, by David Sibley, deals with one of the earliest boundary questions to be addressed by critical geographers, namely the distinction between public and private space. Current anxieties about public space and the valorisation of private space, particularly in the more developed western world, can be interpreted as a reaction to difference, to hybridity, and to certain kinds of movement and mobility – although it is important to recognise the culturally variable meanings assigned to the public and the private. Neil Washbourne touches on similar issues in his reflections on globalisation. Although globalisation is, on one level, concerned with the dissolution of boundaries, it is also characterised by resistance, manifest in inclusions and exclusions at national and local levels, and by the reworking of global cultures at the local level. The processes of homogenisation, domination and resistance, associated with accelerated capital flows and cultural change, present new theoretical challenges. It becomes necessary to view the world through different intellectual lenses.

Most obviously, the acknowledgement of global cultural complexity and the many voices engaged in the production of knowledge requires us to challenge the meta-narratives and fixities of modernity. This is argued by Steven Flusty in his essay on postmodernity, but the same ontological claim could be made for postcolonialism. Thus, Alison Blunt maintains that a postcolonial critique not only allows a re-evaluation of colonial projects, challenging both temporal and spatial distinctions, but, like the postmodern project, demands the decolonisation and destabilising of geographical knowledges. Seemingly stable temporal and spatial boundaries are collapsed and refigured. In a postmodern, postcolonial context, we can talk about new geographies that stimulate new kinds of intellectual inquiry that, in turn, allow a critical re-evaluation of the past. Anne-Marie Fortier's essay on diaspora demonstrates that the boundary crossings produced by forced movements of people can prompt new questions about belonging and identity. In this sense, as she argues, 'diaspora constitutes a rich heuristic device'. One of the consequences of diasporic movements, as with other movements and forms of cultural contact, has been the creation of hybrids. Hybridity is not new but its significance has been masked or denied by binary classificatory systems. However, echoing similar arguments to other essays in this section, Katharyne Mitchell sees hybridity as providing another route into post-structural understanding. In effect, all these essays are arguing for a more sensitive and humane appreciation of difference.

The challenge to conventional binary distinctions continues in the second set of essays in this section. Steve Hinchliffe demonstrates that geographers have had an important role in unsettling the divide between culture and nature. There is a long history in the West of assigning some human groups to nature – slaves and nomads, for example – in order to justify the denial of their civil rights, but modern scientific practice shows that the concepts of culture and nature interpenetrate in increasingly complex ways. This argument is reinforced by Nick Bingham in his discussion of the 'socio-technical'. Life is neither entirely social nor entirely technical. It is useful to dissolve the boundary between the two and focus on the agency and social production of things as elements in socio-technical networks. Finally, Judith Tsouvalis examines cyborgs as instances of hybridity in both science and fiction, arguing that the transgressive qualities of the cyborg oblige us to rethink conceptual boundaries.

These essays refer back to the themes of the other sections of this book, to questions of knowledge, power and difference. Thus, while the thematic structure of the book reflects some distinctive clustering of ideas, we would also argue that the essays might be usefully read in any order.

— Private/Public —

David Sibley

> Panic rooms have been installed in nearly every new home [in Los Angeles] inside the 'privileged triangle' of Bel-Air, Beverly Park and Holmby Hills (where the Playboy mansion sits) according to Bill Rigdon, one of the owners of Building Consensus, a local architectural design, engineering and security firm. Rigdon says some panic rooms are minimalist annexes and some are luxurious hideaways but every one was conceived as an impenetrable barrier between a homeowner and an armed intruder.
>
> D. Calvo, *Opening the Door to Panic Rooms*

This most recent attempt on the part of the seriously rich to defend themselves and their wealth illustrates a key element in the production of social space, namely, the concern of individuals and collectivities to establish a safe haven, secure from the uncertainties and threats associated with the public sphere. This perception of threat, coupled with the capacity to transform the built environment so that it provides defences against those who may disturb suburban tranquility, has much wider consequences for socio-spatial relations. It contributes to a psychogeography where public space is viewed negatively as a source of disorder and contamination. Those threatened others who are disordered and polluting are generally poor, often racialised, diseased or homeless. The anxieties surrounding the boundary between the public and the private are not solely a product of affluence but, as John Kenneth Galbraith recognised in 1958, the two are connected (Galbraith 1958). A historical perspective on the question suggests that it is an enduring aspect of socio-spatial relations, and one that is associated with a range of geographic locales and cultures.

One definition of *heimlich* (homely) included in Daniel Sanders' *Wörterbuch der Deutschen Sprache* of 1860 is 'intimate, friendly, comfortable; the enjoyment of quiet content, etc., arousing a sense of agreeable restfulness and security as in one within four walls of his house'. Sanders continues with a number of illustrations of both *heimlich* and *unheimlich* situations, such as: 'Is it still heimlich to you in your country where strangers are felling your woods?' (cited by Freud 1985 [1919],

342). His examples suggest the qualities of private space that might be disturbed by someone or something beyond the home and Sanders implies in this definition that the unsettling, the *unheimlich*, was a problem for rural communities in nineteenth-century Germany, the boundaries of the *gemeinschaft* threatened by the stranger – in an environment far removed from metropolitan Los Angeles at the beginning of the twenty-first century.

In human geography, this tension between private and public is a fairly recent concern, with an initial focus on the gendering of space in cities (McDowell 1983). More recent research has been concerned primarily with the disturbing effects of 'imperfect people' on domestic havens (Wilton 1998). In other social sciences, however, the construction of public space as threatening and of private space as secure has been a long-established theme of critical writing. Thus, Richard Sennett, in his *Uses of Disorder* (1970), suggests that the ordering and simplification of social relations were manifest in suburban space in the United States, with the creation of what he termed 'purified communities', which reinforced the dangerous simplifications of reality identified by psychoanalytical theorists such as Erik Erikson. In such communities, there was a heightened sense of threat from others – a threat, that is, to social homogeneity and spatial order. This was, in effect, a coding of racialised difference in the spaces of suburb and central city in the United States. The private status of the home is conferred also on the space of the suburb, a scale shift that is increasingly made concrete through the development of gated communities.

Sennett has enlarged on his thesis by examining historical changes in social relations in public space. In his narrative of bodies and cities, *Flesh and Stone*, he takes two engravings of London street scenes by Hogarth – *Beer Street* and *Gin Lane* – as indicative of eighteenth-century attitudes to social order and public space. The former shows bodies touching each other in gestures of respectable sociability, suggesting 'social connection and orderliness', whereas the inebriates in *Gin Lane* are detached and unconcerned with each other's welfare (Sennett 1994, 20–21). The values attached to public space in eighteenth-century England have clearly been inverted in late twentieth- and twenty-first-century England, bodily contact in public space now being seen as unwanted and threatening, a sign of disorder. The security of private space provides insulation from such disorder.

The theme of 'the decline of touch' has been explored further by Kevin Robins (1996). He draws on the psychoanalytical arguments of Wilfred Bion and the political philosophy of Cornelius Castoriadis in an attempt to understand why in modern societies there is a fear of touch and a valorisation of vision. Touch, he argues, signals engagement in society, involvement with others, whereas the emphasis on vision has serious negative implications, particularly distanciation, the stereo-typing of others, surveillance and the realisation of the controlled, panopticon society anticipated by Michel Foucault. These tendencies deepen the division between the public and the private, with the former spaces being both a source of anxiety and a terrain of control. Comfort and security are sought increasingly in the home and in privatised commercial spaces, such as shopping malls and children's play facilities. This trend in the production of space in the most developed societies thus returns us to the first use of 'private' in English as 'withdrawal from public life', from the Latin *privatus* (Williams 1981).

The social and psychological damage resulting from this fear of public space had been anticipated by Freud in his essay on the uncanny. Essentially, his argument was that the common urge to embrace the familiar and domestic concealed repressed desire, desire for the unfamiliar, for the 'Other', which through its repression only increases anxiety. In modern 'capsular societies' (Boomkens 1998; de Cauter 2000), we could argue that the problem of repression has worsened. Moreover, the conjunction of technologies of surveillance, high levels of dependence on the car for local transport and the capacity of the affluent to make their homes more *heimisch* (familiar or comfortable) has serious practical consequences. These include the emptying of the streets and, particularly, the removal of children from public space because of fear of the Other, notably the predatory paedophile. This withdrawal of children from the public sphere reduces their ability to cope outside the home, and it may affect their physical health and development through lack of exercise, a lack of stimuli provided by the built environment, and reduced opportunities to cope with the unexpected, to become 'streetwise' (Hillman et al. 1990; Valentine and McKendrick 1997). This is one of a number of social and political problems that have their origins in the changing relationship between the public and the private. One more specific issue, which was given brief prominence in Britain as a result of the murder of a young Traveller-Gypsy by a rural homeowner during an attempted burglary by the former and his companion, concerns the acceptable level of force in the defence of home space. This case had all the right ingredients: a supposedly mobile, demonised Other (the Gypsy), an unhomely house (Vidler 1996) in a remote rural area, and a house owner obsessed with security (Biressi and Nunn 2002).

The dystopian vision of some of the above authors – de Cauter, Robins, Hillman et al. – is supported to some extent by historical and cross-cultural analyses, although contradicted in some of Sennett's writing. By the early nineteenth century, Engels was arguing that people displaced their need for full emotional relations to a single sphere, the home, because of the sterility of human relations in the productive system of capitalism (Sennett 1977). Today it is not just in the richest countries but also in the South, for example in the cities of Latin America, that suburbanisation involves a retreat from communal life or, at least, movement to a more exclusive form of community. However, looking elsewhere, mostly but not exclusively beyond the highly developed West, we can find other possibilities, which stem from cultural differences in attitudes to both public and private space. Writing in 1925, Walter Benjamin and Asja Lacis noted the difference between the ordered landscape of Berlin, where the orthogonal geometries of architects and planners were transforming the city (Riley and Bergdoll 2001) and the porous boundary between the home and the street in Naples, where 'the house is far less the refuge into which people retreat than an inexhaustible reservoir from which they flood out' (Benjamin and Lacis 1997 [1925], 174). Similarly, the communal life of European Romanies today encompasses both the home and the street, with much weaker boundaries between the inside and the outside than those maintained by most *gaje* (non-Gypsies).

For some, there is no private space to defend. Many drug users, alcoholics and mentally ill people are also homeless and, in Western cities, subject to harassment or exclusion through 'community policing' (Fischer and Poland 1998, 191). As Fischer and Poland put it, '"community policing" has come to entail governance of local space by targeting "problem hosts" or "carriers of disorder"'. Behaviour that may be acceptable in home space, such as smoking or drinking alcohol, become deviant in increasingly regulated public space. This has long been a problem for indigenous people, such as the Inuit and Australian Aborigines, subject to the gaze of censorious whites and labelled as alcoholic for doing what the white people would do in the privacy of their own homes. However, the increasing regulation of practices such as smoking in public spaces extends the terrain of stigmatisation, squeezing out marginalised people who populate public space, amplifying their deviance. In effect, rules that might be applied in the well-ordered private space of the home are extended to public space, so that all space becomes *heimlich* for the powerful. The idea of public space as a space of difference, of encounters with strangers as well as with familiars, is erased. But anxieties about threatening others can never be erased – they are only displaced.

One of the problems with social science perspectives on public and private has been the common failure to capture the world-views of those 'Others' against whose transgressions private space is defended. Ethnographies that convey the experience and anxieties of those who live their lives primarily in public space thus provide an important complement to research that focuses on the paranoia of well-heeled suburban residents. An understanding of how the mentally ill in a Western city cope on the street (Parr 1997), for example, is useful in developing a more nuanced view of the socio-spatial relations produced by illness. This kind of ethnography serves to delineate the complex geographies of public space. Similarly, Lawrence Taylor and Maeve Hickey (2001) are able to convey the humanity of street children on the Mexico–US border, demonstrating how storm drains and other spaces along the border constitute resources for survival and how their use by marginalised and desperately poor children underlines their resourcefulness. The fears and anxieties of racialised 'Others' are also conveyed effectively in Helen Lucey and Diane Reay's work with inner-city children in London. This research uses Melanie Klein's ideas on object relations to understand what is 'Other' for Others (Lucey and Reay 2000). This emphasis on the world-views of the marginalised in geographical and anthropological research is very important if we are to produce alternative, humane visions.

Panic rooms are just the most recent manifestation of the failure of people to cope with social and cultural difference and the failure of states to eliminate economic inequality. 'Private' suggests certainty and familiarity and a retreat from the less predictable encounters of the public sphere, a reluctance to engage with others. This binary geography, in many respects imaginary, becomes real through the production of purified and strongly bounded spaces, to the detriment of a communal life that is inclusionary rather than exclusionary. However, the devaluation of public space and the uncritical appreciation of the private are difficult to resist, despite the social costs of this distinction in terms of heightened fear and expanded surveillance.

KEY REFERENCES

Freud, S. 1985 (1919). *The Penguin Freud Library* (vol. 14) *The Uncanny*. Harmondsworth, Penguin.

Lucey, H. and Reay, D. 2000. Social class and the psyche, *Soundings*, 15: 139–154.

Parr, H. 1997. Mental health, public space and the city: questions of individual and collective access, *Environment and Planning D: Society and Space*, 15: 435–454.

Robins, K. 1996. *Into the Image: Culture and Politics in the Field of Vision*. London, Routledge.

Sennett, R. 1994. *Flesh and Stone: The Body and the City in Western Civilization*. London, Faber and Faber.

Taylor, L. and Hickey, M. 2001. *Tunnel Kids*. Phoenix, University of Arizona Press.

OTHER REFERENCES

Benjamin, W. and Lacis, A. 1997 (1925). Naples, in W. Benjamin ed. *One Way Street*. London, Verso, 168–176.

Boomkens, R. 1998. *Een drempelwereld: moderne ervaring en stedelijke openbaarheid*. Rotterdam, Nai Uitgevers.

Biressi, A. and Nunn, H. 2002. 'An Englishman's home': reflections on the Tony Martin case, *Soundings*, 20: 37–45.

Calvo, D. 2002. *Opening the Door to Panic Rooms*, events.calendarlive.com/top/1,1419,LATimes-Movies-X!ArticleDetail-54602,00.html (accessed 7/02).

de Cauter, L. 2000. *The Capsule and the Network: Notes for a General Theory*. Unpublished paper, Department of Anthropology, University of Amsterdam.

Fischer, B. and Poland, B. 1998. Exclusion, risk and social control: reflections on community policing and public health, *Geoforum*, 29, 2: 187–198.

Galbraith, J.K. 1958. *The Affluent Society*. London, Hamish Hamilton.

Hillman, M., Adams, J. and Whitelegg, J. 1990. *One False Move: A Study of Children's Independent Mobility*. London, Policy Studies Institute.

McDowell, L. 1983. Towards an understanding of the gender division of urban space, *Environment and Planning D: Society and Space*, 1: 59–72.

Riley, T. and Bergdoll, B. 2001. *Mies in Berlin*. New York, Museum of Modern Art.

Sennett, R. 1970. *The Uses of Disorder*. Harmondsworth, Penguin.

Sennett, R. 1977. Destructive gemeinschaft, in N. Birnbaum ed. *Beyond the Crisis*. Oxford, Oxford University Press, 171–200.

Valentine, G. and McKendrick, J. 1997. Children's outdoor play: exploring parental concerns about children's safety and the changing nature of childhood, *Geoforum*, 28, 2: 219–235.

Vidler, A 1996. *The Architectural Uncanny: Essays in the Modern Unhomely*. Cambridge, MA, MIT Press.

Williams, R. 1981. *Keywords: A Vocabulary of Culture and Society*. London, Fontana.

Wilton, R. 1998. The constitution of difference: space and the psyche in landscapes of exclusion, *Geoforum*, 29, 2: 173–186.

— Globalisation/Globality —

Neil Washbourne

Globalisation is the interconnection of cultural, social, political and economic processes across the world. These interconnections vary by how extended they are, by how intense they may be and by how aware of them the global public is (Amin 1997; Held et al. 1999, 14–16). It is of vital importance to note that they do not add up to one overall process, nor to a single way of understanding it; nor does the invocation of interconnection of itself offer explanation of the origins, intensity or direction of such interconnection. The combination of processes producing incremental change does, however, constitute a historical transformation to globality, understood here to refer to the 'total set of inscriptions or references to the global' (Albrow 1996, 82; Beck 2000).

Globalisation is not, then, either a single process or predominantly economic. Intrinsically, interconnection favours the 'exchange' of symbolic goods for *any purposes*, including, but not exclusively, economic ones (Walters 2001). Although these 'exchanges' are often carried out by global corporations they are also involved in forms of 'globalisation from below' (Brecher et al. 1993). Here they are stretched across localities in the construction of diasporas (Cohen 1997) and transnational villages (Levitt 2001) and they are engaged in by individuals negotiating and structuring their lives (Durrschmidt 2000). We need therefore to reject any singular and any merely neo-liberal account of globalisation, itself more a product of globalising politics than economic globalisation per se (Gray 1999), and instead articulate globalisation as the bearer of global cultural-political challenges and opportunities. In spite of the analysis of economic globalisation as the ever-present and increasing domination of capital (or US capital, or Westernisation), our reality has contained many other experiences too.

Cultural geography has been at the forefront of disciplines relating these experiences and their consequences for thinking society and the global circumstance. Cultural geography, articulating post-structuralist and postmodern critiques, has encouraged the telling of rich and multiple stories of difference (sexualities, genders, 'racings', ethnicities, ages) that would otherwise be excluded, by omission or commission, by dominant narrations of modernity. This we may call the postmodernisation of geography (Sibley 1993; Shurmer-Smith and Hannam 1994; Crang 1998).

Modernity is the historical constitution of the institutions and identities that have structured Western and non-Western societies in the period since the sixteenth century. These institutions are the nation state, the urban world, capital and empire, and they all required for their success the threat and use of violence. They were key in structuring the world through discipline, conceptual narrowing, the management of emotion, gender, sexuality and ethnicity. The standpoint of modernity can be seen as being expressed through meta-narratives such as the onward march of progress (Lyotard 1984).

Postmodernisation is the multi-stranded practical and conceptual challenge to modernity. Modernity presented itself to the world as a hierarchy and unity, and declared that the tools for understanding and thereby controlling it were rational and arose from a single centre. Postmodernisation is the effect of successive critiques of claims to the rational grounding and centring of knowledge, in concert with real-world changes in the position of the formerly colonised. One important aspect of postmodernisation is the active generation of distaste for the meta-narratives of modernity.

Cultural geography has extended postmodernising approaches into the analysis of globalisation at both the empirical and theoretical levels. The main outlines of this analysis of globalisation may be presented under the following synoptic headings.

Questioning the culture and knowledge of the globally powerful

This occurs through anthropologising the West: treating the West and the powerful as objects of scrutiny and critique, revealing exclusionary tactics at the centre of Western cultures even in the West (Sibley 1993, ix) and emphasising the binary oppositions through which Otherness is exoticised (Crang 1998, 137). The impact of these forms of critique has, for example, led to the transformation of institutions, such as colonialist histories and museum spaces, and the attempt to transform them to invoke dialogism, hybridity and reflexive representation rather than the closed hierachies and narrations of modernity (Pieterse 1997; Bernstein 1994).

Investigating global geographies of culture

Pamela Shurmer-Smith and Kevin Hannam (1994, 76, 77–78, 79, 88) raise questions about the interpretive understanding of 'the global'. They question monocausal theories of society, denying that the globalisation of capital inevitably leads to the globalisation of culture. They address the processual globalising of culture, rather than assuming the existence of a global culture, and suggest that the contemporary construction of culture takes place at multiple levels and is characterisable by the multidirectionality of cultural flow rather than old models of centre–periphery relationships (76, 77–78, 79). Mike Crang (1998), in questioning economic globalisation, emphasises the cultural mediation of global capitalist firms and makes the case that culture is always embedded in real-life situations in temporally and spatially specific ways (97–98, 153, 155).

Developing concepts of culture adequate to global realities

The investigation of new cultural geographies, in relation to globalisation, opens up the question of what culture is and how it should be investigated. Though some cultural geographers have sought to downplay the independent role of culture (Mitchell 2001), in general cultural geographers have made the cultural mediation of all action at least a central proposition of their work (Crang 1998, 153). They have theorised culture's action independent of the economy (Shurmer-Smith and Hannam 1994, 9) and its existence as an environment for working with meaning (9, 82, 88). These new concepts of culture have had to be adequate to new relations between individuals, groups and geographical scales (cf. Albrow et al. 1997), the flow and movement of peoples and identities (Pile and Thrift 1995), the cultural praxis of social movements (Eyerman 1999) and the entanglement and intermixing of intra- and extracultural relations (Welsch 1999).

Analysing virtual geographies

New spaces of virtuality have been investigated for their creation of virtual geographies as well as their intersection with other geographies (Crang 1998, 97–98, 164). This has been a crucial area for the deployment of imaginative geographies, trying out new geographical perspectives (Crang et al. 1999). Virtual geographies, such as cyberspace, may require analysis using complexity theory and actor network analysis (Thrift 1999), thereby extending the range of geographical theory in its postmodernising moment. Wakeford (1999) discusses 'translation landscapes of computing' as part of the explanation for constructions of gender in and via an internet café through people's access to and reflection on both global and local frames of reference.

Thinking space

Doreen Massey (1999) has made great contributions to thinking on the relationship between globalisation and spatiality. Part of her theoretical conclusions, arising from the empirical investigation of youth cultures, consists in critiquing scalar analyses – in which geographical scales such as local, national and global are nested neatly inside one another – as inadequate to the multiplicity and relationality of global–local cultures. She focuses instead on social relations organised as 'constellations of temporary coherence', within which some locations are more powerful than others (124–125, 126). Crang and Nigel Thrift (2000a) analyse globalisation and its association with new spatialities as open to 'counter-memories and minoritarian themes' (18), which encourages the production of a host of spatial metaphors: contact zones, hybridities, borderlands, points of encounter (18–19). The rest of the edited collection (Crang and Thrift 2000b) multiplies the modes of spatial analysis without, however, attempting the specific constructive work of putting them to use in any shared project.

The limits of globalocentric narratives

As we have seen, then, although globalisation is often associated – or even partially identified – with capitalist (or economic) globalisation (Sibley 1993, x, 36; Shurmer-Smith and Hannam 1994, 87; Crang 1998, 134–137, 146–155), in the literature of cultural geography there is clearly a profound questioning of this association. However, there are limitations inhering in the way it has taken up the globalisation theme.

First, however rich and well-informed the analyses have been they have not attended to the narratives by which accounts gain their intelligibility. Jennifer Light (1999) claims that there is a problem of leaving the analysis open to the narrative of decline, of what she calls 'postmodern pessimism'. Suzanne Bergeron (2001) analyses a related, but globalocentric, narrative. Globalocentric narratives are those 'assuming the existence of a power structure in which global capital dominates its others' (984), which is shared alike by approvers and disapprovers of this domination (cf. Gibson-Graham 1996). While cultural geography has been good at complexifying the viewpoint of this narrative it has been much less good in unhooking from globalocentric narratives *tout court*. The point, for Bergeron, is to articulate other narrative possibilities that posit and develop the notion of agency outside the logic of global capitalist expansion. A single example of the problems of not addressing that narrative within cultural geography will have to suffice.

In his textbook on cultural geography (1998, 113, 158–159), Crang associates McDonald's with standardisation, a common trope (cf. Bell and Valentine 1997, 18; Ritzer 1993, 1998), and with the production of scripted encounters that routinise customers through a transnational consumer space that 'processes new social identities'. The notion that identities are 'processed' neglects the human action that is required for the cultural and economic production even of McDonald's, synonymous as it is, in some accounts, with the global standardisation of food culture. Anthropological studies of South-East Asian societies demonstrate people self-customising McDonald's through their own cultural production strategies, such as chatting and treating fast food places as locations to while away the hours. In Japan and Hong Kong this leads to the conception of a McDonald's meal as 'local cuisine'. In Taiwan consumption of McDonald's represents attitudes towards the relationship with mainland China. In addition, the restaurants are used as sanctuaries for women escaping male-dominated environments (Watson 1997, 2, 6, 7, 9). Furthermore, Crang's approach does not even allow for the cultural-economics of McDonald's: that ownership in a franchised company is likely to be 50 per cent 'local' with the franchise being involved in the day-to-day management, making decisions about where the profits go and having some control over advertising, location and (limited) menu innovation.

Globalisation and general narratives

What Kate Nash (2000, 71–87) calls globalisation as postmodernisation is closer to our perspectival experiences of the relativisation of modernity combined with its expression in, rather than withdrawal from, narratives. What I understand by this is in critical tension to Jean-François Lyotard's (1984) rejection of the closed meta-narratives of modernity. Lyotard produces an analysis asking us to choose between meta-narratives or little stories, a bipolarity that squeezes out of the grounds of possibility general or public narratives through which connection could be made across difference without the imposition of a single, dominant, closed (meta) narrative.

Globalisation as postmodernisation has put pressure on power holders of modernity, nation states and corporations, and thereby challenges the institutional inequalities of power characteristic of modern societies. Furthermore, access to travel and communications by non-elites allows for political coalitions across the planet (see also Walters 2001, 231; Washbourne 1999). What is afforded by this critique and the enablement of action is opportunities for the development and elaboration of concrete critiques of inequality, via the discourse of human rights, of environmental values and feminist challenges to patriarchalism. Linda McDowell (1995) specifically argues within cultural geography for a focus on these broader forms of inclusion of others as a necessary concomitant of the deep concern cultural geography demonstrates with exclusion.

Planetary Universalism as a response to globality

Martin Albrow (1996) and Paul Gilroy (2000) may be seen as advocates of this approach. They argue for a planetary (strategic, pragmatic) universalism as a broader form of inclusion, building on critiques of abstract universalisms. For both, the possibility for planetary universalism arises out of a combination of the polyvalence brought by contemporary conditions (globality) and the recognition of limits. These limits are the globe as material habitation of life, for Albrow, and the identity of the human body cell, rather than its differential racial inscription, as the measure of the common frailty of humans, for Gilroy.

For Albrow, the relativisation of the modern opens up the intellectual and cultural heritage of humankind as resources for the common endeavour of pragmatic humanism – living on this small planet. Gilroy likewise associates planetary humanism with 'rooted cosmopolitanism' (276), to which 'the narratives and poetics of cultural intermixture already alive inside Europe's postcolonial popular cultures' (253) can make their contribution in relation to an interculturalism critiquing, and bypassing '[t]he modernist obsession with origins' and purity (251, also 275). Thus, the cellular identity of humans denies the discourse of modern raciology as much as transculturality does of the notion of fixed cultures. Neither Albrow (1996, 1997) nor Gilroy (2000) reduces everything to the global or planetary, but, rather, they encourage the development of intermediate concepts. In this way they are able to grasp, respectively, contiguity without social involvement in a global city (socioscapes) and reaching beyond the merely local through everyday action (translocal; cf. Washbourne 2001 for another use of translocal and translocalism).

Albrow and Gilroy both argue that humans, beyond the faults and defaults of modernity, should come together and narrate their multiple stories in relation to the global condition. We need public general narratives of survival and common goods.

Conclusion

Thus, cultural geography falls short in analysing globalisation in two ways. First, in its acceptance of the postmodern critique of narratives, conceived as a denial of general or public narratives, cultural geography removes from its purview important analytical and agentic possibilities. We are committed to employing something more than small narratives anyway, by the public and general nature of the concepts we necessarily use. Further, one of the dominant modern narrative frames, the ever-dynamic expansiveness of capital as human history, is still inscribed in the language of some cultural geographers, yet it provides few resources for discussing trans-cultural dialogue and can be replaced only by an alternate, more inclusively based narrative.

Second, cultural geography has led more to the deployment and less to the sensitising development of new concepts through which such a public narrative could analyse the world of people's cultural-political production. One such conception, the translocal, has been mentioned with regard to Gilroy's (2000) work. But the constructive cultural work of humans all around the world will require a richer vocabulary for its comprehension as cultural production. Thus, we can picture the demands that this account lays at the door of cultural geography as a series of tasks.

1. To develop open general narratives (Bernstein 1994) of the global present.

2. To bring to the fore non-modern or non-Western, and formerly excluded modern conceptions, not just as objections or as the museumisation of culture (cf. Pieterse 1997) but as contributions to understanding of ourselves and our world.

3. Research the development of planetary (strategic, pragmatic) universalism in the variety of spheres in which it operates, in human rights, anti-patriarchalism, environmental justice and global labour regulation.

4. Develop new theoretical categories to grasp global interconnectedness via concrete empirical analyses in relation to general narratives of the present.

KEY REFERENCES

Albrow, M. 1996. *The Global Age*. Cambridge, Polity.

Amin, A. 1997. Placing globalization, *Theory, Culture and Society*, 14, 2: 123–137.

Gilroy, P. 2000. *Between Camps*. London, Penguin Books.

Massey, D. 1999. Imagining globalization: power geometries of time-space, in A. Brah, M. Hickman and M. Mac an Ghaill eds. *Global Futures: Migration, Environment and Globalization*. Basingstoke, Macmillan, 27–44.

Watson, J. L. 1997. Introduction: transnationalism, localization, and fast foods in East Asia, in J. L. Watson, ed. *Golden Arches East: McDonald's in East Asia*. Stanford, Stanford University Press, 1–38.

OTHER REFERENCES

Albrow, M. 1997. Travelling beyond local cultures: Socioscapes in a global city, in J. Eade ed. *Living the Global City: Globalization as Local Process*. London and New York, Routledge.

Albrow, M., Eade, J., Durrschmidt, J. and Washbourne, N. 1997. The impact of globalization on sociological concepts: community, culture and milieu, in J. Eade ed. *Living the Global City: Globalization as Local Process*. London and New York, Routledge, 20–36.

Beck, U. 2000. *What is Globalization*? Cambridge, Polity.

Bell, D. and Valentine, G. 1997. *Consuming Geographies: We Are What We Eat*. London, Routledge.

Bergeron, S. 2001. Political economy discourses of globalization and feminist politics, *Signs: Journal of Women in Culture and Society*, special issue on 'Globalization and Gender', 26, 4: 983–1006.

Bernstein, M.A. 1994. *Foregone Conclusions: Against Apocalyptic History*. Berkeley, University of California Press.

Brecher, J., Childs, J. B. and Cutler, J. eds. 1993. *Global Visions: Beyond the New World Order*. Boston, South End Press.

Cohen, R. 1997. *Global Diasporas: An Introduction*, London, UCL Press.

Crang, M. 1998. *Cultural Geography*. London and New York, Routledge.

Crang, M., Crang, P. and May, J. eds. 1999. *Virtual Geographies: Bodies, Space and Relations*. London and New York, Routledge.

Crang, M. and Thrift, N. 2000a. Introduction, in M. Crang and N. Thrift eds. *Thinking Space*. London and New York, Routledge, 1–30.

Crang, M. and Thrift, N. eds. 2000b. *Thinking Space*. London and New York, Routledge.

Durrschmidt, J. 2000. *Everyday Lives in the Global City: The Delinking of Locale and Milieu*. London and New York, Routledge.

Eyerman, R. 1999. Moving culture, in M. Featherstone and S. Lash eds. *Spaces of Culture: City, Nation, World*. London, Sage, 116–137.

Gibson-Graham, J.K. 1996. *The End of Capitalism (as We Knew it): A Feminist Critique of Political Economy*. Oxford, Blackwell.

Gilroy, P. 2000. *Between Camps: Nations, Cultures and the Allure of Race*. London, Penguin.

Gray, J. 1999. *False Dawn: The Delusions of Global Capitalism*. London, Granta.

Held, D., McGrew, A., Goldblatt, D. and Perraton, J. 1999. *Global Transformations: Politics, Economics and Culture*. Cambridge, Polity.

Levitt, P. 2001. *The Transnational Villagers*. Berkeley, Los Angeles and London, University of California Press.

Light, J. 1999. From city space to cyberspace, in M. Crang, P. Crang and J. May eds. *Virtual Geographies: Bodies, Space and Relations*. London, Routledge, 109–130.

Lyotard, J.-F. 1984. *The Postmodern Condition: A Report on Knowledge*. Manchester, Manchester University Press.

McDowell, L. 1995. Understanding diversity: the problem of/for 'Theory', in R.J. Johnston, P. J. Taylor and M. J. Watts eds. *Geographies of Global Change: Remapping the World in the Late Twentieth Century*. Oxford, Blackwell, 280–294.

Mitchell, D. 2001. *Cultural Geography: A Critical Introduction*. Oxford, Blackwell.

Nash, K. 2000. *Contemporary Political Sociology: Globalization, Politics, and Power*. Oxford, Blackwell.

Pieterse, J. N. 1997. Multiculturalism and museums: discourse about Others in the age of globalization, *Theory, Culture and Society*, 14, 4: 123–146.

Pile, S. and Thrift, N. 1995. Mapping the subject, in S. Pile and N. Thrift eds. *Mapping the Subject: Geographies of Cultural Transformation*. London and New York, Routledge, 13–51.

Ray, C. and Talbot, H. 1999. Rural telematics: the information society and rural development, in M. Crang, P. Crang and J. May eds. *Virtual Geographies: bodies, space and relations*. London and New York, Routledge, 149–163.

Ritzer, G. 1993. *The McDonaldization of Society: An Investigation into the Changing Character of Contemporary Social Life*. Thousand Oaks, CA and London, Pine Forge Press.

Ritzer, G. 1998. *The McDonaldization Thesis: Explorations and Extensions*. London, Sage.

Shurmer-Smith, P. and Hannam, K. 1994. *Worlds of Desire, Realms of Power: A Cultural Geography*. London, Edward Arnold.

Sibley, D. 1995. *Geographies of Exclusion: Society and Difference in the West*. London and New York, Routledge.

Thrift, N. 1999. The place of complexity, *Theory, Culture and Society*, 16, 3: 31–69.

Wakeford, N. 1999. Gender and the landscapes of computing in an internet café, in M. Crang, P. Crang and J. May eds. *Virtual Geographies: Bodies, Space and Relations*. London and New York, Routledge, 178–202.

Walters, M. 2001. *Globalization* (2nd ed.) London and New York, Routledge.

Washbourne, N. 1999. *Beyond Iron Laws: Information Technology and Social Transformation in the Global Environmental Movement*. Ph.D. thesis, University of Surrey.

Washbourne, N. 2001. Information technology and new forms of organising? Translocalism and networks in Friends of the Earth, in F. Webster ed. *Culture and Politics in the Information Age: A New Politics?* London and New York, Routledge, 129–141.

Welsch, W. 1999. Transculturality: the puzzling form of cultures today, in M. Featherstone and S. Lash eds. *Spaces of Culture: City, Nation, World*. London, Sage, 194–213.

— Postmodernism —

Steven Flusty

Postmodernism is an ontology that undermines many of geography's foundational assumptions, and necessitates a radical reconceptualisation of the field that is, as yet, ongoing. From its inception, geography has been deeply rooted in Enlightenment-cum-modernist notions of truth as objective and transparently representable. Thus, geographers from the 'Age of Discovery' onwards have undertaken the task of recording and accounting for the distribution of natural and human variation across the surface of the Earth, surveying the Earth for visible facts and mapping their relational significance so as to derive utilisable knowledge. Consonant with this mission has been geography's long and intimate engagement with the colonial project. The colonial goal of mastering all one surveys entails a prerequisite to survey (see Graham Burnett 2000), an imperative to refine one's surveillance, and a compulsion to extend one's surveillance as broadly and deeply as possible. Thus, the socio-political context of geography's disciplinary evolution has imbued the field with a distinct *raison d'être*: to lay the groundwork for, and continuously perfect, scopic regimes for the operationalisation of power. This impetus persisted, in forms both benign and less so, well into the middle of the twentieth century, whether in the instrumental urban-locational algorithms of spatial science or in the descriptive Sauerian definition and cataloguing of culture areas and their attributes.

This intersection of geography, the production of knowledge and the enactment of power, however, did not go uncontested. As early as 1885 the geographer, animal ethologist and anarco-communalist Piotr Kropotkin argued that the role of geography should not be intelligence gathering for the furtherance of empire and the subjugative exploitation of the different, but a quest to identify human commonalities and understand differences as a means of facilitating mutual co-operation among diverse people and peoples. By the beginning of the twentieth century's second half such trickles of dissent, and the persistent failure to satisfy them, became a torrent. Geographers speaking for the poor, workers, women, colonised minorities and other populations long subjected to (and treated as objects of) geographical knowledge asserted that their voices had long been silenced by geography's presumptive facts and truths. Against this injustice, alternative geographical approaches were advanced that entailed shifts in the field's standpoints, foci, methods and even epistemologies, giving rise to Marxist critical geography, feminist geography, postcolonial geography and others. In the process, the status quo consensus (however intermittently fractious) over what geography was underwent delegitimisation, and geography was pluralised: it had become geographies. These new geographies challenged what the discipline should regard as fact, what truths these facts revealed, and to what end such truths should be applied. None directly challenged underlying assumptions about the nature of factuality and the possibility of truth itself but, in the near-simultaneous proliferation of divergent geographical truths and facts, the challenge was implicit (if unintentional). In short, the new geographies explicitly questioned what geography ought to be *for*, and in their incommensurable co-presence tacitly questioned what geography ought to, and could, be. Into this opening stepped postmodernism.

Broadly stated, postmodernism is a number of related critiques of the modernist project. At its most general, this project consisted of social action informed by belief in universally discernable truth and the possibility of mobilising such truth for progressive improvement through linear time, ultimately leading to the attainment of some higher and better end state. This upward march was reliant upon a division between a unitary, distinct and separate subject capable of innocent objectivity, and a world that may be approached as a detached object of analysis. This division supposedly functioned to enable the derivation of an ever more complete, accurate and useful representation of reality ultimately in congruence with reality itself.

Postmodernism claims that this endeavour is not only mistaken, but dangerous in both theory and proven practice. Of course, 'postmodernism' as an object of description doesn't actually say anything. It is comprised of numerous voices (for an excellent summation, see Natoli 1997), many of which do not themselves identify as postmodernists, and each adopts distinct positions and areas of concentration. Taken together, however, their work converges to form postmodernism's axiomatic foci.

1. The re-assessment of truths as big legitimising stories, or 'meta-narratives'.

2. The identification of meaning as not inherent in things, but attached to things by socially and culturally situated actors.

3. The redefinition of things' immutable essences as contingent differences, always constituted in relation to what other things we choose (consciously or otherwise) to juxtapose a thing against.

4. The reconceptualisation of unproblematic perception as interpretive representation, always through the lens of a more or less conscious agenda.

5. The redefinition of knowledge as constitutive of, and constituted by, power enacted through the daily practices of bodies in space.

The implications of these precepts for undermining past certainties, revealing long-hidden agendas and their oppressive corollaries, and facilitating free-for-alls in a newly emphasised realm of discursive representation constitutes what Michael Dear (2000) terms the 'postmodernism of method'. Such a postmodernism has the effect of dissolving naturalised and, hence, unchallengeable truth, speaking paradox to power's truths, and thus assisting subordinated alternative ways of seeing the world to claim discursive space.

Complementary to this newly enlarged discursive space is a re-emphasis upon physical space. In repositioning historical truth as fragmentary narratives produced and imposed in the present, postmodernism subverts Hegelian notions of space as a residual product of idealised historical time, replacing it with a landscape of differential histories arrayed in space (Jameson 1991). Thus, physical space becomes the constitutive context for social relations in which bodies composing (in both senses) privileged and marginalised truths are produced and reproduced, and engage in strategies of domination and tactics of accommodation, appropriation and/or resistance (de Certeau 1984). In the process, the significance of emplaced specificity and views from the perspective of lived experience re-emerge from beneath abstract universals. This re-emergence of local particularity, however, is not a return to some naïve concrete. It is tempered by a focus on how such concretes are constituted through their imagining, and the acting out of those imaginings.

The postmodern foregrounding of space entails a re-centring of the discipline of geography. But, simultaneously, the corollary of new self-consciousness about how discourse produces space also entails shifts in the focus of geographical investigation. For instance, cartographical recognisance gives way to interrogations of maps, their production and their agendas (Harley 1989), and investigations into the nature of culture area and region become studies of how authoritative representations of culture and region come to constitute culture areas and regions (Häkli 1998).

Not surprisingly, the fertile chaos created by postmodernism has engendered tremendous dissent among those who remain convinced that the modernist project is requisite to generating progressive improvement in the human condition. The most substantive critiques argue that postmodernism dismembers knowing and being, twisting them into multiple layers of abstracted representations and surface reflections that can only be played with endlessly. In this proliferation of free-floating forms and arbitrarily attached meanings, coherence born of social consensus becomes impossible, thus crippling collective organisation and precluding the attainment of larger social goals. As a result, postmodernism is said to collapse society into a babbling Babel of mutually incomprehensible voices. By way of example, from the perspective of Marxist critical geography postmodernism undermines mobilisation around the shared categories of class and the shared experiences of class oppression, (e.g. see Figure 1) thus permitting the capitalist status quo to roll on undisturbed. For some feminist geographers, postmodernism renders female identity and female collectivity a logical impossibility at precisely the moment that such collective identities have begun to achieve some success in contesting their long subjugation by the largely unproblematised norm of masculinity. And, from the perspective of those allied with the sciences in general and spatial science in particular, postmodernism is something infinitely more frivolous and simultaneously more dangerous: a collection of ludicrous, unverifiable suppositions that, should they take root, have the potential to undermine the very consensus for rationality upon which modern scientific and technological progress has served to improve the material conditions of life. Thus, postmodernism becomes Eris' golden apple, which, thrown into the middle of geography's disciplinary table, undermines both resistance to the status quo *and* the status quo itself.

Whether or not postmodernism carries the potential to liberate or immobilise geography, it has indeed taken root. Postmodern theory, methods and themes now circulate widely throughout the discipline and its published output. Beyond this, a plethora of individual and collective voices in the field now demand and expect to be heard, respected and reckoned with, on their own terms and by their own standards. Further, the ramifications of postmodernism more than a decade after its infiltration among a wide subset of geographers have proven to be rather less than apocalyptic. We are still working and conversing, and frequently doing so with a heightened sensitivity to one another's positionality.

This empirical reality suggests that postmodernism does not necessarily entail immobilising fragmentation, rendering collective action impossible. The collapse of absolute truth and enforced unity has not prevented the assemblage of contingent social collectives, predicated upon common experiences in shared space, as a means of collaborating, organising, and sharing diverse knowledges. Further, to so undertake collective engagement based upon a dialogical consensus to do so finds precedent in precisely the geographical project prescribed by Kropotkin more than a century ago.

Figure 1: (by Jeff 'Ooleef' Munson).

As to the larger problem of disabling knowing by dissolving materiality into a flotilla of signs, it is indeed true that postmodern practice displays an often relentless preoccupation with the nature of representation, frequently positioning material reality as just another text to be hermeneutically deconstructed. Such entextualisation is particularly problematic from a geographical perspective, reducing place and space to systems of emptied abstract signifiers. Recent work in (arguably) postmodern human geography, however, has countered this unbearable lightness of free-floating signage by positing various types of 'discursive materialism' (Yapa 1996) or 'materialist post-structuralism' (Peet 1996). Such discursive materialisms emerge not simply as a synthesis of resolutely material and irremediably semiotic perspectives but as powerful analytical tools investigating space as the medium in which the image and the concrete reciprocally produce one another in successive iterations.

Thus, postmodernism has become deeply interwoven to the point of immanence in human geography's disciplinary practice. In the process, rejections of metanarratives and radical undecideabilities notwithstanding, postmodernism has proven to be anything but nihilistic. An ontological position doubting that any one perspective can be complete and correct with certainty, or applicable beyond a limited context, entails a conclusion that no perspective can legitimately silence another. Postmodernism thus points (or, perhaps, defers) to an egalitarian deontology and teleology, one in which each person's partial perspective gives rise to situated knowledges that can be appreciated by means of our capacity to reposition ourselves inventively in numerous divergent 'subject-positions' (Haraway 1991). Both the spatiality of these metaphors, and their applicability to geographical investigation, are apparent. Re-interpretations of spaces as multiply differentiated in relation to one another, of space as experienced and constructed differently by different occupants, and of a given space as possessed of numerous overlapping and incommensurable attributes (e.g. Soja 1996), put a progressive postmodernism into geographical practice. Such work engages others and itself dialogically, documenting mutual affect and continual renegotiation across differential positions. These negotiations in turn serve to unmask ways of seeing that, often subtly and even invisibly, inform practices whereby power operates immanently to silence and remove from sight some to the benefit of others. In that such subjugative power relations are produced, reproduced, modified and resisted by bodies that are always in relation to one another and acted upon in space, such a project is implicitly a geographical project. Thus, postmodern human geographies hold open the possibility of effectively opposing the most deeply embedded of oppressive power relations, and consciously enacting alternatives.

KEY REFERENCES

Burnett, G. D. 2000. *Masters of All They Surveyed: Exploration, Geography, and a British El Dorado*. Chicago, University of Chicago Press.

Jameson, F. 1991. *Postmodernism, or the Cultural Logic of Late Capitalism*. Durham, NC, Duke University Press.

Natoli, J. 1997. *A Primer to Postmodernity*. Oxford, Blackwell.

OTHER REFERENCES

Dear, M. J. 2000. *The Postmodern Urban Condition*. Oxford, Blackwell.

de Certeau, M. 1984. *The Practice of Everyday Life*. Berkeley, University of California Press.

Häkli, J. 1998. Discourse in the production of political space: decolonizing the symbolism of provinces in Finland, *Political Geography*, 17, 3: 331–363.

Haraway, D. 1991. *Simians, Cyborgs and Women: The Reinvention of Nature*. New York, Routledge.

Harley, J. B. 1989. Deconstructing the map, *Cartographica*, 26, 2: 1–20.

Peet, R. 1996. A sign taken for history: Daniel Shay's Memorial in Petersham, Massachusetts, *Annals of the Association of American Geographers*, 86, 1: 21–43.

Soja, E. W. 1996. *Thirdspace*. Oxford, Blackwell.

Yapa, L. 1996. What causes poverty? A postmodern view, *Annals of the Association of American Geographers*, 86, 4: 707–727.

— Colonialism/Postcolonialism —

Alison Blunt

In his recent anthology *Postcolonial Discourses*, Gregory Castle explains that he has adopted a 'regional approach' to disrupt what he calls 'the tendency toward a collectivist postcolonialism' (Castle 2001, xi). Five of the six parts of the book reflect this regional approach: 'Indian nations: conundrums of difference', 'African identities: resistance and race'; 'Caribbean encounters: revolution, hybridity, diaspora'; 'Rump Commonwealth: settler colonies and the "Second World"', and 'The case of Ireland: inventing nations' (see also Young 2001, which includes chapters entitled 'Latin America' I–II, 'Africa' I–IV and 'India' I–III). Alongside such a broad regional geography, Castle explains that Homi Bhabha's term 'vernacular cosmopolitanism' is a helpful way to recover the spatial diversity that is often subsumed by claims to a temporal universality (Bhabha 2001). As Castle explains, the idea of vernacular cosmopolitanism 'reinforces the fundamental importance of *location*, the felt experience of the local, which is not collectivized or sublated in a universal historical narrative, but coexists, with all of its local, even marginal character, within putatively universal narratives, challenging that universality by their very coexistence' (Castle 2001, xii). Location and spatial differentiation, from local to transnational scales, are important themes in *Postcolonial Discourses*, reflecting the broader importance of geography in the constitution and critique of both colonialism and postcolonialism. While postcolonialism has inspired new ideas and new theoretical inflections for a wide range of geographical research about colonialism and its effects, geographical ideas about space, place, landscape and location have helped to articulate different experiences of colonialism, both in the past and the present and both 'here' and 'there' (Blunt and McEwan 2002; Clayton 2003; Sidaway 2002). But, although spatial images such as location, mobility, marginality, and exile abound in postcolonial studies, more material geographies often remain less visible than their imaginative counterparts. In this essay I address all these themes and attempt to answer one key question: what are the differences (if any) between geographies of colonialism and postcolonial geographies?

Postcolonial studies, inspired initially by the work of Frantz Fanon and Edward Said (Young 2001), have become increasingly influential in stimulating both theoretical and substantive debate across the humanities and social sciences over the last two decades. At its broadest, postcolonialism 'deals with the effects of colonisation on cultures and societies' (Ashcroft et al. 1998, 186), and investigates such effects not only in the past and present but also within both metropolis and colony and for both coloniser and colonised. Crucially, postcolonial studies also analyse the critical connections *between* past and present, metropolis and colony, coloniser and colonised, and chart the fractures, instabilities and contradictions of colonial rule. As Robert Young explains (2001, 4),

> The postcolonial does not privilege the colonial. It is concerned with colonial history only to the extent that that history has determined the configurations and power structures of the present, to the extent that much of the world still lives in the violent disruptions of its wake, and to the extent that the anti-colonial liberation movements remain the source and inspiration of its politics.

Postcolonialism is a political discourse that addresses the workings of colonial and neo-colonial power, resists colonial and neo-colonial oppression and exploitation, and has emerged in the context of liberation movements and other anti-colonial struggles (see, for example, Fanon's writings about French colonial rule in Algeria and the Algerian War of Independence and Said's writings about the politics of place in the Palestinian struggle: Fanon 1967 [1959], and Said 1995 [1978], 2000).

Postcolonial studies offer critical perspectives on colonialism and its effects in the world today. Although the terms 'colonialism' and 'imperialism' are often used in similar ways, there are significant differences between them. Young contrasts the spatiality of power implied by these terms, writing that '[c]olonialism functioned as an activity on the periphery, economically driven; from the home government's perspective, it was at times hard to control. Imperialism, on the other hand, operated from the centre as a policy of state, driven by the grandiose projects of power' (16–17). While imperialism should be understood as a concept, colonialism should be understood largely as a *practice* (Young 2001), often involving settlement, trade and administration. As Said puts it, colonialism is 'almost always a consequence of imperialism' and represents a tangible manifestation of imperial power through 'the implanting of settlements on a distant territory' (1993, 9). Colonialism thus represents the imposition of political control through conquest and territorial expansion over people and places located at a distance from the imperial power. In recent years research across a wide range of disciplines has explored the cultural dynamics of colonialism, the intersections of colonial power and knowledge, and the importance of colonial representations in producing not only imaginative geographies of 'Other' people and places but also of the 'self'. Alongside more political-economic studies of colonialism, cultural studies of colonialism investigate the ways in which colonial power was made effective, riven by internal contradictions, and resisted by colonised people. One important approach is known as 'colonial discourse analysis', which can be traced back to Said's influential work on Orientalism (Said 1995 [1978]). As Ania Loomba explains, 'Colonial discourse…is not just a fancy new term for colonialism; it indicates a new way of thinking in which cultural, intellectual, economic or political processes are seen to work together in the formation, perpetuation and dismantling of colonialism. It seeks to widen the scope of studies of colonialism by examining the intersection of ideas and institutions, knowledge and power' (Loomba 1998, 54).

The cultural dynamics of colonialism and the intersections of colonial knowledge and power have been important themes in postcolonial geographical work. Although postcolonial studies have always been inherently geographical, geographers have only recently – particularly over the last decade – begun to address their theoretical and substantive challenges. Jonathan Crush explains that the aims of a postcolonial geography are diverse in scope, and include (1994, 336–337)

> [t]he unveiling of geographical complicity in colonial dominion over space; the character of geographical representation in colonial discourse; the de-linking of local geographical enterprise from metropolitan theory and its totalising systems of representation; and the recovery of those hidden spaces occupied, and invested with their own meaning, by the colonial underclass.

In contrast to the important work by geographers in the 1970s that considered colonialism and imperialism as part of a broader Marxist analysis of the capitalist world economy (Blaut 1975; Hudson 1977), postcolonial geographical work, particularly since the 1990s, has often been influenced by post-structuralist analyses of culture, identity and power. Although there is a growing body of work that considers the postcolonial geographies of globalisation and development (Corbridge 1993a, 1993b; Crush, 1995; for an overview of such work, see McEwan 2002), most studies have focused on cultural and historical themes and have informed a range of critical and contextual histories of geography. Geographical work has explored the spatiality of colonial power and its forms of knowledge, the spatial politics of representation and the material effects of colonialism in different places and at different times. Although postcolonial geographical studies (unlike some literary analyses and some largely conceptual accounts) are notable for their contextual specificity rather than aspatial abstraction, these contexts themselves usually remain limited to European high imperialism in the nineteenth and early twentieth centuries. The geographies of pre-modern colonialisms and colonial power exercised from places beyond Europe remain largely unexplored (Jones and Phillips 2005).

In countries such as Britain, France and Germany, the emergence in the nineteenth century of geography as an academic discipline and geographical education in schools were both closely tied to the exercise of imperial and colonial power (Bell et al. 1995; Livingstone 1992; Godlewska and Smith 1994; Ploszajska 2000). One important focus of postcolonial geographies has been to analyse the intersections of colonial power and the production of geographical knowledge as part of a wider attempt to write more critical histories of geography (McEwan 1998; Barnett 1998; Driver 1992, 2001; Gregory 1994). Because colonialism was about more than just economic exploitation, Felix Driver has called for contextual histories of geography that examine not only 'the *culture* of imperialism' (1992) but also the culture of geographical research and education. By focusing on school textbooks, teaching and fieldwork, Teresa Ploszajska shows that geographical education in British schools in the nineteenth and early twentieth centuries was closely tied to a British imperial imagination (2000). In his study of imperial exploration and geographical knowledge, Driver argues that it is important to move beyond largely textual analyses to consider the embodied practices of fieldwork, travel and science and their implications in shaping an embodied discipline of geography (2001).

Often closely connected to critical histories of the discipline, other postcolonial geographies have explored the spatiality of colonial power in terms that are more more discursive than disciplinary. Such postcolonial geographical work has explored the material and imaginative spatiality of colonial power, the cultural geographies of colonialism and the spatial politics of identity and representation. These themes have been addressed in the following five main, intersecting, areas of research (and see Blunt and McEwan 2002 for a collection of essays that show the intersections of each of these themes).

1. Geographies of encounter, conquest, colonisation and settlement, including studies of indigeneity, imperial networks of knowledge and power, and geographies of home, nation and empire.

2. Geographies of colonial representation in both written and visual forms, including work on travel writing, fiction, diaries, photography, maps and exhibitions.

3. The production of space in colonial and postcolonial cities, in terms of urban form, order and regulation, the iconography of urban landscapes, and everyday experiences of urban life in relation to imperialism, multiculturalism and global cities.

4. The gendered, sexualised and racialised spaces of colonialism, colonial discourse and postcoloniality, including work on white women, imperial travel and imperial domesticity, masculinity and imperial adventure, and the racialised embodiment and regulation of imperial sexualities.

5. Geographies of migration, diaspora and transnationality, with reference to past and present movements of people, capital, commodities and cultures, and geographies of identity, home and belonging, both in place and over space.

Like feminist geographical research, postcolonial geographies have the potential to span the diverse range of subjects and approaches within human geography. Unlike research in many other disciplines, postcolonial geographies are often located on a threshold between the humanities and social sciences in terms of sources, methodologies and analyses.

The interdisciplinary stimulus of postcolonial theory has clearly revitalised the geographical study of colonialism. But what, if anything, distinguishes a postcolonial geography from a geography of colonialism? It seems to me that there are at least two main differences. First, while postcolonial studies are diverse and contested, they share a political commitment that is broadly anti-colonial and thus different from the very histories and geographies that have helped to constitute colonial discourse. Second, while postcolonial theories are wide-ranging, they revolve around the intersections of colonial power and knowledge, the cultural significance of colonialism and the internal contradictions of colonial power. In both cases, postcolonial geographies provide *critical* readings of colonial power, knowledge and the production of space, and their effects in shaping the present world. But, more than this, postcolonial geographies explore the spatiality of colonial power and knowledge in challenging ways and argue that the spatial constitution and articulation of colonial power should be a central focus of postcolonial critique. At the same time, the spatiality of postcolonial critique itself has been heralded as one way of overcoming the impasse of temporality whereby the 'post' of postcolonialism is understood in chronological rather than critical terms. Loomba, for example, suggests that spatial rather than temporal difference can help to represent postcoloniality in more effective ways. As she writes (1998, 6),

> Imperialism, colonialism and the differences between them are defined differently depending on their historical mutations. One useful way of distinguishing between them might be to not separate them in temporal but in spatial terms and to think of imperialism or neo-imperialism as the phenomenon that originates in the metropolis, the process which leads to domination or control. Its result, or what happens in the colonies as a consequence of imperial domination, is colonialism or neocolonialism.

Although Loomba recognises the spatial constitution of colonial power and the spatial critique of postcolonialism, this vision of a postcolonial geography re-inscribes a binary distinction between metropolis and colony that obscures internal colonialisms as well as the multidirectional flows and effects – and continued existence – of colonial power. Such flows and effects clearly continue to resonate, both in and between metropolitan powers and colonised places, in the present as well as in the past (see, for example, Gregory, 2004). These postcolonial connections are increasingly studied as both cultural and economic in their manifestations and implications, as shown by work on the critical limits of hybridity in theorising migration and investment from Hong Kong to Vancouver (Mitchell 1997); studies of transnational commodity cultures between, for example, India and Britain (Jackson et al. 2004); and in postcolonial critiques of urban regeneration in East London and Birmingham (Jacobs 1996; Henry et al. 2002). While it is clearly important to challenge a temporal binary between a colonial past and a postcolonial present (the temporal binary that underpins a chronological rather than a critical understanding of postcolonialism) it is also important to challenge a spatial binary between colonial centres and postcolonial margins. Post-colonial geographies have begun to disrupt such a dualistic understanding of space, by highlighting the production of colonial space through, for example, flows of capital, people and knowledge; the contested and embodied spatiality of homes, nations and empires; and the material and imaginative spaces of colonial power, anti-colonial resistance and decolonisation. Unlike Driver's claim that 'academic debates over postcolonialism are becoming increasingly sterile, especially when framed in terms of an essential antagonism between history and theory' (2001, 7), I would argue that postcolonial geographies will continue to challenge and critique understandings not only of colonialism but also of the need to decolonise geographical knowledge, for the foreseeable future.

KEY REFERENCES

Blunt, A. and McEwan, C. eds. 2002. *Postcolonial Geographies*. London, Continuum.

Castle, G. ed. 2001. *Postcolonial Discourses: An Anthology*. Oxford, Blackwell.

Clayton, D. 2003. Critical imperial and colonial geographies, in K. Anderson, M. Domosh, S. Pile and N. Thrift eds. *Handbook of Cultural Geography*. London, Sage, 531–557.

Gregory, D. 2004. *The Colonial Present*, Oxford, Blackwell.

Jacobs, J. 1996. *Edge of Empire: Postcolonialism and the City*. London, Routledge.

Young, R. 2001. *Postcolonialism: An Historical Introduction*. Oxford, Blackwell.

OTHER REFERENCES

Ashcroft, B., Griffiths, G. and Tiffin, H. eds. 1998. *Key Concepts in Post-colonial Studies*. London, Routledge.

Barnett, C. 1998. Impure and worldly geography: the Africanist discourse of the Royal Geographical Society, 1831–1873, *Transactions of the Institute of British Geographers*, 23: 239–252.

Bell, M., Butlin, R. and Heffernan, M. eds. 1995. *Geography and Imperialism, 1820–1940*. Manchester, Manchester University Press.

Bhabha, H. 2001. Unsatisfied: notes on vernacular cosmopolitanism, in G. Castle ed. *Postcolonial Discourses: An Anthology*. Oxford, Blackwell, 39–52.

Blaut, J. 1975. Imperialism: the Marxist theory and its evolution, *Antipode*, 7: 1–19.

Corbridge, S. 1993a. Colonialism, postcolonialism and the political geography of the Third World, in P. J. Taylor ed. *Political Geography of the Twentieth Century*. London, Bellhaven, 173–205.

Corbridge, S. 1993b. Marxisms, modernities, and moralities: development praxis and the claims of distant strangers, *Environment and Planning D: Society and Space*, 11: 449–472.

Crush, J. 1994. Post-colonialism, decolonization and geography, in A. Godlewska and N. Smith eds. *Geography and Empire*. Oxford, Blackwell, 333–350.

Crush, J. ed. 1995. *Power of Development*. London, Routledge.

Driver, F. 1992. Geography's empire: histories of geographical knowledge, *Environment and Planning D: Society and Space*, 10: 23–40.

Driver, F. 2001. *Geography Militant: Cultures of Exploration and Empire*. Oxford, Blackwell.

Fanon, F. 1967 (1959). *A Dying Colonialism*. New York, Grove.

Godlewska, A. and Smith, N. eds. 1994. *Geography and Empire*. Oxford, Blackwell.

Gregory, D. 1994. *Geographical Imaginations*. Oxford, Blackwell.

Henry, N., McEwan, C. and Pollard, J. 2002. Globalization from below: Birmingham – postcolonial workshop of the world?, *Area*, 34: 117–127.

Hudson, B. 1977. The new geography and the new imperialism, 1870–1918, *Antipode*, 9: 12–19.

Jackson, P., Crang, P. and Dwyer, C. eds. 2004. *Transnational Spaces*. London, Routledge.

Jones, R. and Phillips, R. 2005. Unsettling geographical horizons: exploring premodern and non-European imperialism, *Annals of the Association of American Geographers*, 95: 141–161.

Livingstone, D. 1992. *The Geographical Tradition: Episodes in the History of a Contested Enterprise*. Oxford, Blackwell.

Loomba, A. 1998. *Colonialism/Postcolonialism*. London, Routledge.

McEwan, C. 1998. Cutting power lines within the palace? Countering paternity and eurocentrism in the 'geographical tradition', *Transactions of the Institute of British Geographers*, 23: 371–384.

McEwan, C. 2002. Postcolonialism, in R. Potter and V. Desai eds. *The Arnold Companion to Development Studies*. London, Arnold, 127–131.

Mitchell, K. 1997. Different diasporas and the hype of hybridity, *Environment and Planning D: Society and Space*, 15: 533–553.

Ploszajska, T. 2000. Historiographies of geography and empire, in B. Graham and C. Nash eds. *Modern Historical Geographies*. Harlow, Prentice Hall, 121–145.

Said, E. 1993. *Culture and Imperialism*. New York, Alfred A. Knopf.

Said, E. 1995 (1978). *Orientalism*. London, Penguin.

Said, E. 2000. *The End of the Peace Process: Oslo and After*. London, Granta.

Sidaway, J. 2002. Postcolonial geographies: survey-exploration-review, in A. Blunt and C. McEwan eds. *Postcolonial Geographies*. London, Continuum.

— Diaspora —

Anne-Marie Fortier

Theoretical discourses about diaspora have noticeably proliferated in recent years, namely within postcolonial studies (Gilroy 1993, 2000; Clifford 1994; Hall 1990; Radhakrishnan 1996; Brah 1996; Dhaliwal 1994). Once used to describe exile and the forced dispersal of Jews or Armenians, 'diaspora' is now widely used to describe transnational networks of immigrants, refugees, guest workers and so on. Deployed from a transnational and intercultural perspective in opposition to ethnically absolute approaches to migration, the term converses with other terms, such as border, transculturation, creolisation, *mestizaje*, hybridity.

The renewed currency of theoretical discourses on 'diaspora', with their focus on displacement and transnational networks of connections, inserts itself within a wider shift of focus within contemporary Euro-American social sciences, where the spatial takes precedence over the temporal in understanding social change. However, when thinking of diaspora, we must bear in mind that the present circulation of the term in cultural theory derives from the historically specific experience of the 'black Atlantic' (Gilroy 1993) and of anti-Zionist critiques of the return to Israel (Marienstras 1975, 1989; Boyarin and Boyarin 1993). Within post-colonial studies and critical cultural theory diaspora has become an emblem of multilocality, 'post-nationality' and the non-linearity of *both* movement and time. Diaspora constitutes a rich heuristic device to think about questions of belonging, continuity and community in the context of dispersal and transnational networks of connection. In sum, diaspora signifies a site where 'new geographies of identity' (Lavie and Swedenburg 1996) are negotiated across multiple terrains of belonging.

Multilocality refers to the multiple sites of attachment of diasporic subjects, and opens up 'a historical and experiential rift between the locations of residence and the locations of belonging' (Gilroy 2000, 124). In this respect, diaspora may be viewed not only as decidedly *post*-national – as multilocal sites of connections within a transnational network exceed national borders – but also as radically *anti*-national. Indeed, the presence and experiences of diasporic subjects puts any normative notion of culture, identity and citizenship in question by their very location *outside* the time-space of the nation, in which the language of integration, assimilation and inclusion takes for granted a linear narrative of migration. Integral to such narratives is the construction of time-space in terms of dichotomous notions of 'host-society versus homeland, here versus there, home versus away, progress versus backward, freedom versus unfreedom, the time of the West versus the timelessness of the East' (Moallem 2000, 2). In contrast, diaspora focuses on the analysis of intercultural and transcultural processes and forms, produced through forced dispersal (Gilroy 2000, 123).

Diaspora is not about travel or nomadism. Central to its definition are 'push factors' – that is, forced migration or displacement (Gilroy 1994, 207; Clifford 1994). Slavery, pogroms, genocide, famine, political persecutions, wars may be sources of the dispersal of populations. Paired with the emphasis on push factors is the stress on conditions of settlement within countries of immigration, which involve the re-articulation of multiple locations, temporalities and identifications in the effort to create new terrains of belonging within the place of migration.

This poses the question of the place of 'space' in definitions of diaspora. The association of diaspora with forced dispersal holds the potential risk of assuming the primacy of an original placement. In other words, by establishing the defining moment of diaspora solely in its inception (the traumatic uprooting from geographically located origins), it is easy to reduce diaspora to its connection with a clearly bounded time-space: the nation-space of the 'homeland'. Indeed, relations with the homeland are, for many social theorists, crucial in ascertaining diasporas and diasporic subjects (Safran 1991; Cohen 1997; Conner 1986; Tölölyan 1996). Such accounts risk engulfing diasporic populations into culturally unified groupings by virtue of their presumed common ethnic, national and/or geographic origin, firmly located in 'the homeland'. Moreover, by emphasising the centrality of the homeland, such conceptions of diaspora suggest that the homeland is the key stabilising factor to the perceived debilitating dangers of dispersal. In doing so, they re-instate the determining power of the nation state as the preferred institutional means to terminate diaspora dispersal: the 'return to the homeland' – not so much in terms of an actual physical return as in terms of reducing diaspora to a single origin – brings diaspora to a halt.

In contrast, several social theorists find in the rhizome[i] a particularly appropriate metaphor for thinking against ideas of cultural homogeneity founded on principles of unified trajectory between two fixed locations (Gilroy 2000, 128–129; Kaplan 1996, 143; Fortier 2000). The rhizomorphous pattern of diasporic dispersal posits a distinctly multilocal mapping of 'homes', breaking the simple explanatory sequence between consciousness and location – whether the latter is defined in terms of 'where you're from' or 'where you're at'. Rather, it suggests a chaotic network of interconnected 'nodes' through which culture and identity 'are inevitably the products of several interlocking histories and cultures, belonging at the same time to several homes' (Hall 1993, 362). In this sense, diaspora is about 'dealing equally with roots and routes' (Gilroy 1993, 190), or, more accurately, about examining the *social dynamics of rootings and routings*. Against the assumed isomorphism of space, place and culture, on the one hand, and the reification of uprootedness as the paradigmatic figure of postmodern life on the other, the heuristic potential of diaspora raises the ways in which belonging may involve *both* attachment and movement.

What, then, connects populations dispersed and fragmented within this rhizomorphous network? How are diasporic identities constructed? Memory, rather than territory, is the principal ground of identity formation in diaspora cultures, where 'territory' is de-centred and exploded into multiple settings. The thread of continuity, then, is the result of what Gilroy, following Leroy Jones, calls the 'changing same'. The changing same propels those who agree that 'we are more or less what we used to be' in a conflict about whether it is the more or the less that should be privileged in the project of identity (Gilroy 1995, 26). The changing same seizes the ways in which the tension between having been, being and becoming is negotiated, conjugated or resolved. Though some collective recollections may be lived as enduring traditions, they result, rather, from the processing and reprocessing of cultural forms.

The changing same not only defeats the idea that the homeland is the constant and sole principle of collective mobilisation, it also questions linear conceptions of history, continuity and progress. The changing same is part of the communal project of recovery; of the 'rediscovery' of a past, of a place, a *grounding*, which, as Stuart Hall points out, is grasped through reconstruction (1991, 36). In this sense, the changing same needs to be reconnected to 'the lived experience of locality' (Brah 1996, 192). Though remembrance is the primary modality of diasporic identity formation, it is also tied to the creation of the identity of places. As psychologist Olivia Espin suggests, migrants tend to ruminate on the relationship between geographical location and life's events, thus giving 'place' a special significance as a result of its association with events in their life course (1996, 82). The changing same, here, speaks of enduring identities, and attaches them – even on the surface, even momentarily – in local territory. In other words, it relates to the living 'memory of place' (Khan 1995, 95) without, however, reducing identity to that place. Memories, in diaspora, may be place-based, but they are not necessarily place-bound.

Hence, to speak of diasporic identity formation as a practice of *re-membering* places disturbs fixed notions of spatiality and territory, while it allows for considerations of memories as constituted by stationary 'moments', or intervals. Moreover, the root term 'member' connotes some kind of physical materiality that thickens the act of memory, gives it substance. The emphasis on remembering refers to the processes through which spaces of belonging – imagined and physical – are inhabited, in the literal sense of dwelling, in the sense of populating or 'membering' spaces with ghosts from the past, and in the sense of manufacturing subjects. Re-membering is not only about reprocessing elements of the past or of culture, or shaping/decorating our homes 'here' with objects that evoke places, people, or 'homes' elsewhere It is also about identifying 'members' who will fit in; norms of belonging are invariably deployed in practices of identity, thus arresting the flow of movement and migration with discursive injunctions of collective and individual selfhood.

The manufacturing of diasporic subjects is perhaps the issue that has been least examined in 'diaspora studies'. Notions of diaspora are often prone to myths of reproduction that rely on ideas of lineage and kinship. In this respect, the reproductive moment of diaspora is not left to chance (Gilroy 1994). Indeed, many diasporic cultural forms repeat nationalist biopolitics that posit the heterosexual, patriarchal family as the preferred institution capable of reproducing traditions and an original culture. In such cases, the indeterminacy of a dispersed and fragmented identity is solved by gendered encodings of culture, where definitions of authenticity are defined by ideas about family, fixed gender roles and generational responsibility: women as reproducers of absolute cultural difference, men as protectors of cultural integrity and allegiance, and generations as bearers of cultural continuity and change (Fortier 2000; Gray 2004). Recent developments in queer studies have attended to such conceptions of diaspora by queering ethnically defined diasporic formations. In the narrowest sense, 'queering the diaspora' (Puar 1998) forces a reconsideration of the heterosexist norms supporting definitions of ethnic diasporas. In the broadest sense, it argues for a critical methodology for evaluating ethnic-diasporic formations across multiple axes of difference and in their numerous local and global manifestations (Eng 1997, 39).

Hence the tendency to focus on ethnically specific populations in diaspora studies means that the new theoretical field based on 'diaspora' has not fully overcome some of the problems identified earlier with nationalist conceptions of culture, identity and belonging. Moreover, if diaspora is a heuristic device for the exploration of social processes of identity formation within multilocal and transcultural spaces of belonging, the question remains open as to how a culturally diverse 'community' can be diasporic, or imagined as such. Indeed, the presence of diasporic populations has forced 'the multicultural question' into debates about the future of the nation (Hall 2000), leading many Euro–American nations today to redefine themselves in terms of multiculturalism rather than monoculturalism. In the context of globalisation and the increased circulation of people, cultures and capital, contemporary nations have developed a 'diasporic horizon' – that is, a spatio-temporal horizon defined in terms of multilocality, diversity, dispersal and conflict. In this context, we might consider nations and other such spaces of inhabitants as 'diaspora spaces' (Brah 1996, 16), by way of exploring how – and by whom – the national 'home' comes to be imagined as diasporic and/or indigenous space. 'As such, the concept of diaspora space foregrounds the entanglement of genealogies of dispersion with those of "staying put"' (Brah 1996, 16). This would allow a further exploration of how formations of community, home and belonging could be better understood, as the outcome of differentiated histories of movement that were central to the colonial process are still lived and negotiated in the forming of diasporic as well as indigenous 'homes' (Hesse 2000).

NOTE

i The rhizome was introduced by Gilles Deleuze and Felix Guattari (1984) as a substitute for the single 'root-tree' version of philosophical thought, which they critically assessed as violently unitary, fixed and deep-seated. The rhizome serves to emphasise a more chaotic, multidirectional and mobile system of interconnected nodes. However, Deleuze and Guattari have been widely criticised for the Eurocentric and imperialistic inflections underpinning their theoretical discourse. Hence, the critics cited above insert the concept of rhizome within a theoretical project that seeks to bring questions of colonialism and neo-colonialism more to the foreground.

KEY REFERENCES

Boyarin, D. and Boyarin, J. 1993. Diaspora: generation and the ground of Jewish identity, *Critical Inquiry*, 19, 4: 693–725.

Brah, A. 1996. *Cartographies of Diaspora: Contesting Identities.* London and New York, Routledge.

Braziel, J. and Manny, A. eds. 2003. *Theorizing Diaspora: A Reader.* Oxford, Blackwell.

Clifford, J. 1994. Diasporas, *Cultural Anthropology*, 9, 3: 302–338.

Gilroy, P. 1993. *The Black Atlantic: Modernity and Double Consciousness.* London, Verso.

Gilroy, P. 2000. *Between Camps: Nations, Cultures and the Allure of Race.* London, Penguin.

Hall, S. 1990. Cultural identity and diaspora, in J. Rutherford ed. *Identity: Community, Culture, Difference.* London, Lawrence and Wishart, 222–237.

Marienstras, R. 1975. *Être un peuple en diaspora.* Paris, Maspero.

Marienstras, R. 1989. On the notion of diaspora, in G. Chaliand ed. *Minority Peoples in the Age of Nation States* (trans. by A. Berrett). London, Pluto, 119–125.

OTHER REFERENCES

Cohen, R. 1997. *Global Diasporas: An Introduction.* Seattle, University of Washington Press.

Conner, W. 1986. The impact of homelands upon diasporas, in G. Sheffer ed. *Modern Diasporas in International Politics.* New York, St. Martin's Press, 16–46.

Deleuze, G. and Guattari, F. 1984. *Anti-Oedipus: Capitalism and schizophrenia.* London, Athlone Press.

Dhaliwal, A. 1994. The traveling nation: India and its diaspora, *Socialist Review*, 24, 4: 1–11.

Eng, D. 1997. Out here and over there: queerness and diaspora in Asian American studies, *Social Text*, 15, 3–4: 31–52.

Espin, O. 1996. The immigrant experience in lesbian studies, in B. Zimmerman and T. McNaron eds. *The New Lesbian Studies: Into the Twenty-First Century.* New York, Feminist Press, 79–85.

Fortier, A-M. 2000. *Migrant Belongings: Memory, Space, Identity*. Oxford, Berg.

Gilroy, P. 1994. Diaspora, *Paragraph*, 17, 3: 207–212.

Gilroy, P. 1995. Roots and routes: black identity as an outernational project, in H.W. Harris, H.C. Blue and E. E. M. Griffith eds. *Racial and Ethnic Identity: Psychological Development and Creative Expression*. London and New York, Routledge, 15–30.

Gray, B. 2004. *Women and the Irish Diaspora*. London, Routledge.

Hall, S. 1991. Old and new identities, old and new ethnicities, in A.D. King ed. *Culture, Globalization and the World-system*. London, Macmillan, 19–39.

Hall, S. 1992. The question of cultural identity, in S. Hall, D. Held, T. McGrew eds. *Modernity and its Futures*. Milton Keynes and Cambridge, Open University Press and Polity, 274–316.

Hall, S. 1993. Culture, community, nation, *Cultural Studies*, 7, 3: 349–363.

Hall, S. 2000. Conclusion: the multicultural question, in B. Hesse ed. *Un/Settled Multiculturalisms: Diasporas, Entanglements, Transruptions*. London, Zed Books, 32–56.

Hesse, B. 2000. Introduction: un/settled multiculturalisms, in B. Hesse ed. *Un/Settled Multiculturalisms. Diasporas, Entanglements, Transruptions*. London, Zed Books, 1–30.

Kaplan, C. 1996. *Questions of Travel: Postmodern Discourses of Displacements*. Durham, NC and London, Duke University Press.

Khan, A. 1995. Homeland, motherland: authenticity, legitimacy, and ideologies of place among Muslims in Trinidad, in P. van der Veer ed. *Nation and Migration: The Politics of Space in the South Asian Diaspora*. Philadelphia, University of Philadelphia Press, 91–131.

Lavie, S. and Swedenburg, T. 1996. Between and among boundaries of culture: bridging text and lived experience in the third timespace, *Cultural Studies*, 10, 1: 154–179.

Moallem, M. 2000. *Genealogies of belonging in the Diaspora Space*. Paper presented at the European Network for Canadian Studies conference 'Recasting European and Canadian History: National Consciousness, Migration, Multicultural Lives', Bremen, 18–21 May.

Puar, J. 1998. Transnational sexualities: South Asian (trans)nation(alism)s and queer diasporas, in D. Eng and A. Hom eds. *Q & A: Queer in Asian America*. Philadelphia, Temple University Press, 405–421.

Radhakrishnan, R. 1996. *Diasporic Mediations: Between Home and Location*. Minneapolis and London, University of Minnesota Press.

Safran, W. 1991. Diasporas in modern societies: myths of homeland and return, *Diaspora*, 1, 1: 83–99.

Tölölyan, K. 1996. Rethinking diaspora(s): stateless power in the transnational moment, *Diaspora*, 5, 1: 3–34.

— Hybridity —

Katharyne Mitchell

'"Hybrid" is the nineteenth century's word. But it has become our own again.' Thus Robert Young (1995, 6) reminds us of the historical provenance of this popular contemporary concept, a term with excitingly transgressive prospects in cultural analysis, but heavily weighted with racial and biological connotations from the past. In recent years hybridity has reappeared as an important theoretical term in a number of different fields, including linguistics, cultural studies, literary criticism, postcolonial analysis and nature–society relations. While the term is employed slightly differently in each of these areas of thought, it also shares a number of characteristics across disciplines. The primary feature of hybridity is clearly the idea of integration and diffusion, of a thing that is derived from heterogeneous sources, and composed of incongruous elements. The organic hybrid bears the physical traces of these heterogeneous originating elements, yet emerges as a distinct entity, as a thing in its own right.

Common synonyms for hybridisation processes include words such as 'syncretism' and '*mestizaje*', but these terms tend to be circumscribed in particular ways; syncretism is generally linked with religious fusions, while *mestizaje* is commonly used in reference to racial mixtures. Similarly, 'grafting' has a distinctly biological connotation, while words such as 'creole' and 'pidgin' are primarily used to denote linguistic mixings. It is hybridity itself that has provided the broadest interpretive framework for the idea of a creative mixing process that has led to the formation of something distinctly new and different, but that contains within it the (often contradictory) traces of its progenitors.

Many cultural theorists working primarily with texts and discourse analysis herald the ways in which apparently hybrid subject positions can facilitate multivocal communications and the production of syncretic cultural forms. Owing to the manifest lack of an essentialised or fixed identity (through the derivation from heterogeneous sources and incongruous elements), the hybrid can stand as the perfect conduit for post-structuralist understandings of the advantages of pluralism, ambivalence and non-fixity. Because of its dialectical, neither/nor nature, hybridity is often celebrated as a process rather than a thing; its inherent resistance to fixed binaries causes it to remain in a perpetual state of flux, related to and yet not originating from or causing other moments, spaces or entities. For many cultural theorists, it is this ambivalent undecidability that has posited hybridity and hybrids as the perfect interlocutors of resistance to various kinds of essentialist and essentialising narratives.

The first major regeneration of hybridity as a useful theoretical concept was undertaken by Mikhail Bakhtin, in his discussion of the dialogic imagination. In an influential text, translated into English in the early 1980s, Bakhtin outlined a theory of linguistic hybridity in which he underlined the potential for language to be double-voiced and internally conflictual. He was concerned to show language's capacity to be 'two social languages within the limits of a single utterance', an utterance that, depending on the speaker's tone, voice, style and form of speech, might express differing positions, or hold oppositional or contradictory meanings (Bakhtin 1981, 358). Drawing examples from comic English novels of the nineteenth century, he emphasises, not just the capacity of language to be ambivalent and undecidable vis-à-vis the enunciatory meanings of a particular voice, but also how that voice might problematise the Other within the same speech act. Bakhtin writes (304–305),

> What we are calling a hybrid construction is an utterance that belongs, by its grammatical [syntactic] and compositional markers, to a single speaker, but that actually contains mixed within it two utterances, two speech manners, two styles, two 'languages', two semantic and axiological belief systems. We repeat, there is no formal – compositional and syntactic – boundary between these utterances, styles, languages, belief systems; the division of voices and languages takes place within the limits of a single syntactic whole, often within the limits of a single sentence. It frequently happens that even one and the same word will belong simultaneously to two languages, two belief systems that intersect in a hybrid construction – and consequently, the word has two contradictory meanings, two accents.

For Bakhtin, all contemporary languages are clearly the products of an evolutionary historical mixing of languages, but this type of historical mixing represents a form of unconscious or 'organic' hybridity, which is part of an inexorable and imperceptible process of amalgamation through time. He makes a sharp distinction between this form of unintentional hybridity and what he terms, 'intentional' hybridity, a conscious and highly political act that subverted and ironised through the division and separation of meaning. Bakhtin's focus on the internal tensions within language stemmed from this particular interest in conscious, intentional hybridity, for he recognised the subversive potential of a double-voicing within language. He writes, '[I]ntentional semantic hybrids are inevitably internally dialogic (as distinct from organic hybrids). Two points of view are not mixed, but set against each other dialogically' (360). Bakhtin perceived that it was this 'internally dialogic' doubleness of hybridity, its fusing of the unfusable, its ironic parodies and antagonisms, that were the very qualities that could undermine the legitimacy of the single authoritative voice. As Young (1995, 20) notes, it is this contestatory nature of the intentional hybrid, where the opposite or antithesis of the thing is contained within it and at the same time set against it, that provides the moment when 'one voice is able to unmask the other' and 'authoritative discourse is undone'.

Not surprisingly, the quality of resistance implicit in this undermining of the single voice of authority proved irresistible to a number of cultural and postcolonial theorists in the 1980s. One of the most interesting derivations arising from Bakhtin's linguistic analysis of hybridity was in the work of Homi Bhabha (1985, 1990), who transposed the concept of hybridity to the situation of colonialism. Like Bakhtin, Bhabha was interested in the subversive quality of the dialogic moment, which he applied to the concrete material relationships and narratives taking place between colonisers and colonised. Seeking to find a potential space of resistance that would counter the authority of colonial control, Bhabha seized on the potential of hybridity to create that space through linguistic ambivalence. Transposing the ideas of Bakhtin directly to the colonial case, he sought to show how the single-voiced authority of colonial discourse is 'undone' through the intentional hybridisation of language. As the colonial language becomes infused with the 'trace' of the language of the colonised, its doubleness infects its own systems of representation and control, effectively undermining the entire colonial edifice of power/knowledge.

Bhabha's work on cultural hybridity has been eagerly adopted by a number of cultural geographers, probably owing to his development of the concept of a 'third space'. The idea of third space takes the concept of hybridity to another level of resistance, positing an abstract 'displacing' space that intervenes in colonial systems of authority, a space inherently critical of essentialism and conceptualisations of original or originary culture, and thus effectively disrupting dominant and essentialising national narratives of space and time. For Bhabha, a critical component of these displacing spaces is ambivalence – the avoidance of completeness or closure, and the notion of a thing (or space) holding its opposite within it. Following Derrida's discussion of language, Bhabha looked at 'incomplete signification', or the places where connections in meaning are incomplete and ongoing (the signifier cannot connect exactly with the signified because of the 'irreducible excess of the syntactic over the semantic'), and related this to the spaces of the nation that are also incomplete or always already in process. In order to negotiate the meanings of cultural and political authority in the nation, Bhabha believed it necessary to examine the formation of the nation in the act of formation itself. The interrogation of the nation space in the act of its composition enables the alteration of its hegemonic narration. For Bhabha, these incomplete, processual spaces are the ambivalent, 'inbetween' spaces of the margins that allow for intervention and resistance in the narrative of the nation as authentic, whole and complete.

Several geographers have riffed off the idea of third space, including Edward Soja (1996, 5), who sought to open up a collective spatial imagination through a critical strategy of 'thirding-as-Othering'. Although Soja employed the term positively, many have also critiqued the concept on the basis that it relies on an abstraction away from the material social relationships and practices inherent in the actual production of space (Sparke 2005). Further, Bhabha's celebratory readings of the potential of a third space as a site of counter-authority and his metaphoric use of the language of space run the risk of an elision of regressive narratives coming 'from' the ambivalent margins as well as an appropriation of the concept itself for apolitical or reactionary political ends (Mitchell 1997). A final critique has been aimed at the hybridity discourse in general, deriding it as an overly intellectualised and meaningless idea fomented in a self-congratulatory way by a highly elite minority of diasporic 'third world' intellectuals, hopelessly removed from the everyday realities and material problems and interests of their own societies (Friedman 2000).

However, the concept of hybridity has not just appeared prominently in academic works of the late twentieth century but has also figured largely in literature, music and popular culture. In novels such as *The Satanic Verses*, *My Beautiful Laundrette* and *White Teeth*, Rushdie, Kureishi and Smith all explore the fragmented and dissonant identities of hybrid subjects as they negotiate the shifting terrain of a largely mobile and diasporic world. Drawing on icons of popular culture such as these, as well as on their own experiences as hybrid, diasporic subjects, both Stuart Hall and Paul Gilroy have explored the subject of hybridity through the lens of identity and subjectivity formation in the late modern era. Hall's (1990, 1992) contributions revolve primarily around the notion of hegemony and the necessity of forming alliances across difference. Borrowing from theorists as disparate as Gramsci, Derrida and Lacan, yet remaining intensely committed to a strong political opposition to Thatcherism and the ideology of neo-liberalism in general, Hall has argued not just for a recognition of multiplicity and ambivalence in identity formation but also for the need to forge counter-hegemonies regardless of differences. As one of the 'great contemporary prophets of hybridity' (Werbner 2000, 13), Hall has been tireless in his call for a pragmatic, hybrid, limited, yet committed campaign against the ravages and dislocations caused by free-market capitalism in the last several decades.

Like Hall, Gilroy's work on hybridity (1993) focuses on questions of identity, looking in particular at the subjectivity formation of black, diasporic subjects in the context of movement back and forth across the Atlantic. In this work he articulates the concept of 'double consciousness', wherein the interruptive, cultural voices and practices from the margins both disrupt narratives of modernity and race and create a double consciousness, or split subject, for the actors involved in the movement. In a different geographical setting, Gloria Anzaldúa (1987) and Nestor Canclini (1995) also examine the interlinked processes of cultural hybridisation and modernity that occur in cross-border, transnational movements such as these. They, along with a growing number of cultural geographers, have explored the cultural effects of a 'globalised' hybridisation, not just on the nation or on the formation of individual or collective identities, but also on the physical landscape, on architecture, music, language, local handicraft production, folkore and all the other cultural products and practices stemming from cross-fertilising, cross-border processes.

The concept of hybridity has also staged a comeback outside the cultural arena. In the sub-field of economic geography, Gibson-Graham (1996) has suggested that the concept of hybridity might usefully be employed with respect to the economy. Noting that academic representations of capitalism tend to construct a monolithic and all-powerful system, with a seemingly predetermined teleology, they argue that this discursive representation, in and of itself, reifies capitalism and adds to its strength and authority. They advocate, instead, a research and analytical agenda foregrounding economic hybridity – a discursive mode of representation that pays attention to the many fissures, gaps and counter-logics within capitalism, as well as to the many non-capitalist and semi-capitalist economic forms existing apart from or in creative tension with capitalism itself (see also Yang 2000 and Blim 1996).

Another key arena in which the concept of hybridity has blossomed is in nature–society relations. Environmental geographers such as Neil Smith (1996), Erik Swyngedouw (1999) and Cindi Katz (1998), have probed the boundaries of the nature/society split, calling in general for greater theoretical integration, and arguing against conceptual frameworks that tend to separate and purify things into discrete categories. Drawing extensively on the works of Donna Haraway (1991) and Bruno Latour (1993), who were concerned to show the numerous shapes and forms taken by hybrids of all varieties, including those combining subjects and objects or people and things, environmental geographers insist on the fundamental and dialectical interconnections between things natural and things social, the inseparability of society and nature and the ongoing and inexorable production of socio-nature as process.

Hybridity has been an importaant concept for theorising the beneficial, generally transgressive effects of mixtures of all kinds. In literary criticism and postcolonial studies it has served as a potent concept of resistance to fixed and discrete theoretical concepts, as well as to essentialising narratives of nation and race. In other areas it has also prefigured as a trenchant critique of modernist binaries and normative assumptions based on age-old notions of separation and linearity. If theorised as a process, and grounded in actual material relations and contexts, hybridity is apt to remain an important and useful theoretical concept, a potential space within which transformation can, and does, occur.

KEY REFERENCES

Bakhtin, M. 1981. *The Dialogic Imagination* (trans. by C. Emerson and M. Holquist). Austin, University of Texas Press.

Bhabha, H. ed. 1990. *Nation and Narration*. London, Routledge.

Gilroy, P. 1993. *The Black Atlantic: Modernity and Double Consciousness*. Cambridge, MA, Harvard University Press.

Hall, S. 1992. New ethnicities, in J. Donald and A. Rattansi eds. *'Race', Culture and Difference*. London, Sage, 252–259.

Young, R. 1995. *Colonial Desire: Hybridity in Theory, Culture and Race*. London, Routledge.

OTHER REFERENCES

Anzaldúa, G. 1987. *Borderlands/La Frontera*. San Francisco, Spinster/ Aunt Lute Press.

Bhabha, H. 1985. Signs taken for wonders: questions of ambivalence and authority under a tree outside Delhi, May 1817, *Critical Inquiry*, 12, 1: 144–165.

Blim, M. 1996. Cultures and the problems of capitalisms, *Critique of Anthropology*, 16: 1, 79–93.

Canclini, N. 1995. *Hybrid Cultures: Strategies for Entering and Leaving Modernity* (trans. by C. Chiappari and S. Lopez). Minneapolis, University of Minnesota Press.

Friedman, J. 2000. Global crises, the struggle for cultural identity and intellectual porkbarrelling: cosmopolitans versus locals, ethnics and nationals in an era of de-hegemonization, in P. Werbner and T. Modood eds. *Debating Cultural Hybridity: Multi-cultural Identities and the Politics of Anti-racism*. London, Zed Books, 70–89.

Gibson-Graham, J. K., 1996. *The End of Capitalism (As We Knew It): A Feminist Critique of Political Economy*. London, Blackwell.

Hall, S. 1990. Cultural identity and diaspora, in J. Rutherford ed. *Identity: Community, Culture Difference*. London, Lawrence and Wishart, 222–237.

Haraway, D. 1991. *Simians, Cyborgs and Women: The reinvention of nature*. New York, Routledge.

Latour, B. 1993. *We Have Never Been Modern* (trans. by C. Porter). Cambridge, Mass, Harvard University Press.

Katz, C. 1998. Whose nature, whose culture? Private productions of space and the preservation of nature, in B. Braun and N. Castree eds. *Remaking Reality: Nature at the End of the Millennium*. London, Routledge, 40–63.

Mitchell, K. 1997. Different diasporas and the hype of hybridity, *Environment and Planning D: Society and Space*, 15: 533–553.

Smith, N. 1996. The production of nature, in G. Robertson, M. Mash, L. Tickner, J. Bird, B. Curtis and T. Putnam eds. *FutureNatural: Nature, Science, Culture*. London, Routledge, 35–54.

Soja, E. 1996. *Thirdspace: Journeys to Los Angeles and Other Real-and-Imagined Places*. Cambridge, Blackwell.

Sparke, M. 2005. *In the Space of Theory: Postfoundational geographies of the nation-state*. Minneapolis, University of Minnesota Press.

Swyngedouw, E. 1999. Modernity and hybridity: nature, regeneracionismo, and the production of the Spanish waterscape, 1890–1930, *Annals of the Association of American Geographers*, 89, 3: 443–465.

Werbner, P. 2000. Introduction: the dialectics of cultural hybridity, in P. Werbner and T. Modood eds. *Debating Cultural Hybridity: Multicultural Identities and the Politics of Anti-racism*. London, Zed Books, 1–26.

Yang, M. M. 2000. Putting capitalism in its place, *Current Anthropology*, 41, 4: 477–494.

— Nature/Culture —

Steve Hinchliffe

Geographers have long been concerned with the divisions and relations between natures and cultures. Often working at the crossing points between these two realms, geographers have taken a lead in unsettling the divide between what is called nature and what is called culture. If cultural geography has succeeded in destabilising any sense that a pure, unadulterated nature exists, then we are left with something of a problem. Does this mean that there is no Other to culture? Is everything cultural? Is there nothing left to nature? The answer to all of these questions is 'yes', and 'no'. 'Yes', in the sense that there is no recourse to an absolute, unconditional, universal nature (whether it is a first or second nature, see Whatmore 1999) of laws and properties. 'No', in the sense that culture cannot be an all-consuming framework that is unaffected by the workings of sociable humans and non-humans, who act in ways that may well be left-field, out of the park or creative. We are used to the sense that cultures are indeterminate, in process, and as much the effects of actions as their causes (Mitchell 1995). One of the aims of this essay is to afford the same compliment to what we have been used to calling 'nature'. I will pursue this aim through one story, which comes from an engagement with laboratory sciences, before drawing some broader observations.

NATURE OR CULTURE?

Scrapie is a disease of sheep that has been endemic in some places for over 200 years. It is classified as a transmissible spongiform encephalopathy, a classification it shares with bovine spongiform encephalopathy (BSE) and the human Creutzfeldt Jakob Disease (CJD). These classifications have been made largely on the basis of visible symptoms, as, over the course of the last century, very little was known about the causes of the disease (other than, as the classification name suggests, it can pass or be transmitted from animal to animal). Over the course of the twentieth century people looked in vain for a bacterium, for hereditary causes, for a gene that makes hosts susceptible, and – what seemed the most likely of agents – a scrapie virus (Keyes 1999a, 1999b). Looking for a virus involves a whole suite of stories, practices, technologies, animals and people. One word to describe this would be an assemblage, the assemblage of virology. Assemblage is a term taken from Deleuze and Guattari (1988) and shares something with the Foucauldian term discourse that is used widely in cultural geography (Foucault 1970). However, assemblage has the advantage of being slightly less about disciplining behaviours and activities and more to do with enabling others to emerge through practice (Law 2004). When engaging with culture-natures, assemblage has the advantage of allowing all parties, be they scientific reports, microbes or people, to potentially change the course of events. Compared to some versions of discourse, it is less limiting both of what can act and what can be known. The end result of this remarkably successful assemblage is very often a virus – a discrete, replicating bundle of nucleic acid that can be moved or can move from one host organism to another, and manage to carry on its business of replicating and possibly, depending upon issues of organism suitability (or non-suitability), causing the host difficulties or disease.

A question at this point, for those interested in nature/culture, is: does this end result (the virus) exist before virology (see Latour 1999)? If nature is a pre-existing and bounded space, then the answer would have to be 'yes'. In the language of exploration, viruses are *discovered*. But, if the virus is solely the product of the assemblage of virology, then our answer would be 'no'. Viruses are *invented* as a means to explain disease. Yet another, perhaps more satisfactory, answer would be that discovery and invention are merely means of allocating special properties to either one of nature or culture. And, therefore, another way of looking at this is to suggest that, as scientists started to interact with viruses, not only did science change but viruses also changed. We're used to this idea in cultural geography. *Our* identities, we're reminded, are relational, and not simply the product of our inner make-up (Pile and Thrift 1995). Discovery rarely leaves the discoverers and the discovered unaltered by the experience (Driver 2001). This compliment should also be paid to non-humans, including animals (see Wolch and Emel 1998 and Philo and Wilbert 2000), microbes (Latour 1999) and machines (Hinchliffe 1996 and Bingham 1996). In this sense, the poles of nature and culture are inadequate to our understanding of the history of science and the historicity of microbes (Latour 1999, 146). This is difficult to express in abstract language, so, in order to understand this activity of microbe assemblages, we can carry on with the scrapie story.

In the scrapie example, things did not quite work out as well as virologists might have hoped. As materials with higher and higher concentrations of infectivity were isolated, a process that would, in the discipline of virology, lead to 'pure' virus, something was missing. Contrary to the discursive set-up, the blueprint for replication, nucleic acid, was seemingly absent from the laboratory-produced infective material. Without this, it was difficult to imagine (within the framework of virology) how the microbe could manage to carry the instructions necessary to produce the effects of an encephalopathy from one organism to another. There are two issues that I want to pull out of this story of a badly behaved experimental object.

First, the object that materialised was not as expected. The scientists were *not in control* of their experimental system. But, just as this led some to continue the search for the elusive virus or some other nucleic-acid-carrying entity, others started to listen, feel and work out procedures for interacting with these materials in ways that exceeded the discursive frame. Indeed, it was the ability to listen to the vagueness of the epistemic thing (Rheinberger 1997), or the putative object of inquiry, that was a condition of possibility for new knowledge. The scientists weren't falsifying or corroborating; rather, they were tinkering, interacting with apparatus and materialities of all kinds, writing and thinking... Another way of saying this is that the experiments were objective – but not in the sense of discovering, without the hindrance of ideology of culture, the real make-up of nature. Rather, those scientists that managed the experiments so that a different materiality could be engaged were being objective in the sense that they allowed the infectious materials to object to the stories that were being told about them (see Latour 2001a). The culture of virology was important, but not simply because it framed the experiments; it was important because it too was changing as a result of a whole series of actions and interactions performed by the scientists, the apparatus and – not least – the infective materials. Virology (culture) would never be the same again.

Second, it should not be presumed that, because the research was objective (allowing the experimental objects to object to the stories that were being told about them), we can appeal to a single, natural object in order to explain the experimental trajectory. While it is true to say that the experimental objects were not *anything* (they were not hapless, shapeless materials, or even fashion victims waiting for the virologist to give them any old form), I don't want to give the impression that these infective materials were natural objects (already formed and the same wherever or whenever they went). In other words, while it would be wrong to say that this infective material was culturally constructed, it would also be wrong to say that they were *a-social* – particularly if the term 'social' is understood as an ability to associate. Indeed, if we understand natures as *sociable*, then their importance to the experimental system – and, as it turns out their less welcome sociability across species boundaries and through an industrial-agricultural system – becomes easier to imagine. Just as virology would never be the same again, so it is with these non-viral infective microbes. *Their* history was also changing as they interacted with feed manufacturers, cows, cats, people, politicians, ministries, zoos, burger franchises, trading partnerships and so on (see Hinchliffe 2001). Perhaps it is also worth pointing out that these histories had already been written in an experiment that was bigger than the ones going on in the laboratories (see Latour 2001b). The collective experiment called, variously, the agricultural-industrial food production system had already helped to provide the conditions of possibility for different histories for these microbes – and there can be little doubt that they returned the favour, in the sense that the food system too might never be the same again (something that genetically modified organisms have found out to their cost).

Finally, as these new infective agents took shape in laboratories and in our food system, nature would never be the same again. It was now possible to talk about information transfer (disease transmission) in the absence of nucleic acid (DNA or RNA). In short, established theories of biological agency were starting to change (Keyes 1999b).

If, so far, we have said that our example of a disease is reducible neither to a culture nor to a nature, then what are we saying about cultures and natures? The first thing to say is that they no longer inhabit different spheres or regions (Braun and Castree 1998). Their histories and geographies are more entangled, meaning that as culture changes so too does nature, and as natures change so too do cultures. Second, this interrelationship is far from being one that we could describe as determined one way or the other. Culture does not determine nature (virology did not shape the scrapie agent), but neither does nature determine culture (the scrapie agent did not shape science). So, cultures and natures are probably not usefully thought of, in this instance, as subsets of one another. Nor does it make sense to say that nature is underdetermined by culture, or vice versa. For to do so would, as Bruno Latour has reminded us, repeat a tendency to allocate between what humans say and what the rest of the world does (Latour 2001a).

If we can't understand the laboratory material as either one of culture or one of nature, then another possibility is to imagine that it's a product and participant in a lively network. Rather than assuming that one element in all the elements that have been brought together in this laboratory is more important than all the others (and then allocating natural or cultural properties to that element), we could focus upon the relations and interactions that make up the infective material, the scientists, the reports, the funding and so on. This topology and approach would be familiar to those who have used actor network theory (ANT) to refute the analytical moves of conventional social science (see, for example, Callon and Law 1995, and, for this approach applied to wildlife, see Whatmore and Thorne 1998). Rather than allocating properties to a defined space (be that the space of the microbe or the space of virology), the task is to trace the production of relations, the assembling of empires that are irreducible to component pieces (and thereby irreducible to culture or nature).

It is worth ending by reinforcing a point made at the outset. We are used in cultural geography to talking of multiple cultures, that they are in process and indeterminate. In politics this often translates into a sensitivity to diversity, to different points of view, to contest and even to conflicts (Mouffe 2000). Extending the same compliment to natures is a fraught, if vital, process; fraught because we are used to nature (in the singular) being the bedrock that unites all these cultures (Latour 2001b). The unification can be in the form of an appeal to shared aspects of our nature ('We're all, at the end of the day human beings'). It can be an appeal to a shared reliance on natural capital (as in the third way, consensus politics of Anthony Giddens [1998] – see Featherstone 2001). Or nature can form the external arbiter on cultural affairs ('Nature knows best' – an ethic that inhabits much environmentalist thinking). If nature is unshackled from this foundational mooring then, politically, a few old certainties might well be lost. But multi-naturalism is vital if we are to avoid the short-cutting of due political process that accompanies appeals to a-social nature (Latour 2004). The nature of no culture cannot, Latour argues, 'be used to renew politics, since it is the oldest means devised to block politics' (Latour 2001b, 6). Appeals to a universal bedrock of Nature is a common problem for cultural politics. This is well known to geographers who have investigated the cultures and natures of totalitarian and even conservative regimes (Matless 1999), the cultures and natures of race and gender (Rose 1993; Buckingham-Hatfield 2000) and even the cultures and natures of the 'new enclosures movement' that is international nature conservation (see Escobar 1995 and Zimmerer 2000). Each reveals a singular nature to be a highly questionable, anti-democratic component in struggles to devise better ways of living. A huge challenge remains for cultural geography to demonstrate the sociability of natures without reducing humans and non-humans, living and non-living, to cultural followers of fashion.

KEY REFERENCES

Braun, B. and Castree, N. eds. 1998. *Remaking Reality: Nature at the Millennium*. London, Routledge.

Latour, B. 1999. *Pandora's hope: Essays on the reality of science studies*. Cambridge, Mass., Harvard University Press.

Latour, B. 2004. *Politics of Nature: How to bring the sciences into democracy*. Cambridge, Mass., Harvard University Press.

Whatmore, S. 2002. *Hybrid Geographies*. London, Sage.

OTHER REFERENCES

Bingham, N. 1996. Object-ions: from technological determinism towards geographies of relations, *Environment and Planning D: Society and Space*, 14: 635–658.

Buckingham-Hatfield, S. 2000. *Gender and the Environment*. New York, Routledge.

Callon, M. and Law, J. 1995. Agency and the Hybrid Collectif, *The South Atlantic Quarterly*, 94: 481–507.

Deleuze, G. and Guattari, F. 1998. *A Thousand Plateaus: Capitalism and Schizophrenia*. London, Athlone.

Driver, F. 2001. *Geography Militant: Cultures of Exploration and Empire.* Oxford, Blackwell.

Escobar, A. 1995. *Encountering Development: The Making and the Unmaking of the Third World*. Princeton, NJ, Princeton University Press.

Featherstone, D. 2001. *Spatiality, Political Identities and the Environmentalism of the Poor*. Unpublished Ph.D. thesis. Milton Keynes, Open University.

Foucault, M. 1970. *The Order of Things: An Archaeology of the Human Sciences.* London, Tavistock.

Giddens, A. 1998. *The Third Way: The Renewal of Social Democracy*. Cambridge, Polity.

Hinchliffe, S. 1996. Technology, power and space – the means and ends of geographies of technology, *Environment and Planning D: Society and Space*, 14: 659–682.

Hinchliffe, S. 2001. Indeterminacy in-decisions: science, politics and policy in the BSE crisis, *Transactions of the Institute of British Geographers*, 26, 2: 182–204.

Keyes, M.A. 1999a. The prion challenge to the 'Central Dogma' of Molecular Biology, 1965–1991, (part I) Prelude to prions, *Studies in the History and Philosophy of Biology and Biomedical Sciences*, 30, 1: 1–19.

Keyes, M.A. 1999b. The prion challenge to the 'Central Dogma' of Molecular Biology, 1965–1991 (part II) The problem with prions, *Studies in the History and Philosophy of Biology and Biomedical Sciences*, 30, 2: 181–218.

Latour, B. 2001a. *Good and Bad Science: The Stengers – Desprest Falsification Principle*. www.ensmp.fr/~latour/Articles/77-BERG.html.

Latour, B. 2001b. *What Rules of Method for the New Socio-scientific Experiments?* Paper presented at the Darmstadt Colloquium, 30 March (Mimeo available from the author at www.ensmp.fr/~latour/artpop/P-95%20Darmstadt.html.).

Law, J. 2004. *After Method: Mess in social science research.* London, Routledge.

Matless, D. 1999. *Landscape and Englishness.* London, Reaktion.

Mitchell, D. 1995. There's no such thing as culture: towards a reconceptualisation of the idea of culture in geography, *Transactions of the Institute of British Geographers*, 20: 102–116.

Mouffe, C. 2000. *The Democratic Paradox*. London, Verso.

Philo, C. and Wilbert, C. eds. 2000. *Animal Spaces, Beastly Places: New Geographies of Human–Animal Relations*. London, Routledge.

Pile, S. and Thrift, N. eds. 1995. *Mapping the Subject.* London, Routledge.

Rheinberger, H. J. 1997. *Towards a History of Epistemic Things: Synthesizing Proteins in the Test Tube.* Stanford, Stanford University Press.

Rose, G. 1993. *Feminism and Geography: The Limits of Geographical Knowledge*. Cambridge, Polity.

Whatmore, S. 1999. Hybrid geographies: rethinking the human in human geography, in D. Massey, J. Allen and P. Sarre eds. *Human Geography Today.* Cambridge, Polity, 22–40.

Whatmore, S. and Thorne, L. 1998. Wild(er)ness: reconfiguring the geographies of wildlife, *Transactions of the Institute of British Geographers*, 23, 4: 435–454.

Wolch, J. and Emel, J. eds. (1998). *Animal Geographies*. London, Verso.

Zimmerer, K. S. 2000. The reworking of conservation geographies: nonequilibrium landscapes and nature-society hybrids, *Annals of the Association of American Geographers*, 90, 2: 356–369.

— Socio-technical —

Nick Bingham

> [T]he social order is not a social order at all. Rather it is a *sociotechnical order*. What appears to be social is partly technical. What we usually call technical is partly social. In practice nothing is purely technical. Neither is anything purely social. And the same may be said for the economic, the political, the scientific, and the rest.
>
> J. Law, *A Sociology of Monsters*, p. 10 (emphasis in the original)

Compared to the titles of some of the other entries in this book, 'socio-technical' will not perhaps be especially familiar. A significant reason for this is that the concept is an awkward one, at least in its relation to cultural geography, its criticality oriented as much towards the field itself as to any object of study to which it may be applied. It is this awkwardness – in the form of three (linked) uncomfortable reminders that the notion provides us with – that I want to explore in this short essay as a way of presenting the opportunities and challenges that the socio-technical poses for past, present and future cultural geographies.

FIRST REMINDER

The first uncomfortable reminder that the concept 'socio-technical' provides us with as cultural geographers is that we have not always given material things the attention that they deserve. Or at least that, during the 'cultural turn' of the late 1980s and the 1990s, such was the (understandable) urge not to repeat the one-dimensional treatment of objects that had too often characterised the approaches from which that move was meant to offer an escape, that the pendulum swung to the other extreme. And so, even on those occasions when technologies, organisms, commodities and other non-humans were clearly involved in what was under investigation (work on the landscape, consumption, and the media spring to mind), there was a tendency – with honourable exceptions – to make sense of such matters using only the same the symbolic, textual and psychical registers as were being employed to analyse more classical interpersonal questions.

Certainly, frustration at the lack of available means of granting non-humans much of an independent or excessive existence contributed towards the taking of a detour by some in the discipline off what was rapidly becoming the beaten track of cultural geography. In search of tools better suited to the problematics with which they were concerned, the change in direction turned out to be a happy one, in that it led to an ongoing and productive encounter with the body of work best known as 'science and technology studies' (STS; see Jasanoff et al. 1995 for a comprehensive review of STS, and Biagioli 1999 for an excellent introductory reader). One of the first fruits of this engagement was the translation of the concept and the implications of the 'socio-technical' into the geographical literature. At once a deceptively simple (see the quote from sociologist John Law [1991] that opens this piece) and formidably multi-layered notion (see Latour 1999a, chap. 6, for a typically virtuoso cataloguing), the idea of 'technology and society as an intimately interconnected, heterogeneous ensemble of technical, social, political and economic elements' (Bijker 1995, 249) emerged from the interface of what historian of technology Wiebe Bijker identifies as three overlapping streams of work within STS: the 'systems approach', represented by the work of Thomas Hughes; the 'social construction of technology' approach, represented by that of Trevor Pinch and Bijker himself; and the 'actor-network' approach, represented by the work of Michel Callon, along with the aforementioned Bruno Latour and John Law. It has been the version of the socio-technical associated with the last of these three that has had by far the deepest and most lasting influence within geography, with publications by (among others) Bingham (1996), Steve Hinchliffe (1996), Jonathan Murdoch (1997), Nigel Thrift (1996) and Sarah Whatmore and Lorraine Thorne (1997) all serving as early illustrations of its utility within a variety of contexts.

SECOND REMINDER

It is in this and subsequent work that we find the second uncomfortable reminder offered by the concept of the socio-technical to us as cultural geographers. And that is that it is necessary to guard against the cultural turn becoming merely a U-turn that leads us to make the same mistakes, except in reverse, committed by those who came before (and then finally up the same blind alley). A very brief example should help to make both the dangers of this prospect and the chances that the socio-technical offers to avoid them a little clearer.

No two innovations can have received more attention in the years immediately preceding and following the turn of the twenty-first century than the internet and genetically modified (GM) food. With profoundly significant consequences, both have been widely represented in popular, intellectual and political arenas as the latest manifestations of what I have referred to elsewhere as 'frontier technologies'

(Bingham et al. 1999). Underpinning that representation has been the still depressingly ubiquitous discursive scaffold of technological determinism, according to which an unproblematic and stable distinction can be drawn between technology, on the one hand, and society on the other, with the former further assumed to 'impact' on the latter, causing various effects (see Fischer 1994 for a more nuanced discussion). Unsurprisingly, given the now almost ritual rejection within contemporary social science of technological determinism in all its manifestations, such actions have been met with disapproval from many critical corners of the academy as well as from elsewhere. Maybe more surprising, however, is the fact that finding alternative ways in which to effectively articulate changes associated with the internet and GM food (and thus challenge the booster rhetoric) has proved difficult, lending credence to what Keith Grint and Steve Woolgar have identified (1995) as some significant 'failures of nerve' in recent analyses of technology.

Most often, what this has meant is that the major response to technological determinism in these cases has taken the form of a shift away from accounts premised on the objects in question being the outcome of some kind of internal capacities or dynamics towards others in which they are seen as the expressions of the social conditions of their production. Hence, the internet starts to be described not as the end point of a technical teleology of communication devices but, rather, as the outcome of (say) masculine fantasies of disembodiment. Similarly, GM food becomes less the culmination of techniques of agricultural breeding and more the (say) latest stage in the capitalist domination of nature.

From the point of view of a socio-technically attuned geography, such a reaction to the problem of technological determinism is inadequate in at least two ways. Inadequate firstly because, in appealing to social rather than technical factors as an explanatory bottom line, all that has really changed is the order of the elements of the equation. Whereas before it was the technical objects that were strong and the social elements weak, now the situation is reversed. The fundamental fact of the assumed division between the technical and the social, however, remains unchallenged. As Madeline Akrich puts it, the 'traps' of technological determinism and social reductionism are 'symmetrical' (1993). And inadequate secondly because a purely social explanation is as caught up as a purely technical explanation within the impoverished spatio-temporal imagination of what Latour calls 'the Modern Constitution' (1993). As philosopher Peter Osborne has argued (1995), modernity is characterised by a particular 'politics of time' – that is to say, a particular way of conceiving the relationship between 'past', 'present' and 'future' that can be summarised in the phrase 'permanent transition'. According to Latour, such a dependence on the idea of 'radical revolution' (1993) is the only solution that the moderns have imagined to explain their endless production of things. For them, then, the march of time is signalled by a succession of 'frontier technologies', or what historical sociologist Claude Fischer calls 'emblems of modernity' (1994), of which the internet and GM food are just contemporary examples. Within this frame it becomes almost impossible to assess the implications of these and other innovations with any more subtlety than is offered by the 'two great resources' of the moderns: 'progress' and 'decadence' (Latour, 1993). In other words, technologies are assumed to leave their mark always and everywhere the same, and the only choice we have is to decide whether that is a very good or a very bad thing.

Faced with such mirror-image histories of determinism, what the concept of the socio-technical offers us by way of contrast is a chance to begin again 'in the midst of things' (Haraway 1992; Deleuze 1995; Bingham et al. 2001) before the purifications take place of which technology and society are the outcomes. Here, the internet becomes less an-other world and more an example of anthropologists of science and technology Leigh Star and Karen Ruhleder's reformulation of 'infrastructure' (1996): the more or less durable outcome of objects embedded within 'communities of practice' (Wenger 1998). Or, perhaps, the latest form of what philosopher Michel Serres terms 'message-bearing systems' (1995), requiring at least as much effort and entanglement as ever in an effort to exclude the noise inherent in all such assemblages (Bingham 1999). Here, as well, GM food becomes less a 'miracle food' or 'technical fix' and more a particularly visible example of the 'hot situations' (Callon 1998) or 'collective experiments' (Latour 1999b) that are increasingly multiplying the connections between diverse people, non-humans and places. Or, perhaps again, as a hybrid or rhizomatic topology (Whatmore 2002) in which all manner of lively knowledges and beings are folded together, rendering the distinction between the intimate and the distant a very blurred one.

In either case, what is most notable in comparison to the modernist accounts is how the question 'What is (the) new?' is supplemented with 'Where is (the) new?', and thus an imagery of an innovation 'falling from the sky' is exchanged for that of something 'finding its place' alongside and in relation to other things, techniques and procedures that already exist (Mol 1993). Replacement becomes addition. For with this gestalt shift from histories of determinism to geographies of open and could-be-otherwise futures comes the necessity of treating technologies as being as much shaped by 'contestation and dissensus' as anything else, and thus fully political (Barry 2001, 7). And with this talk of politics we come to the third uncomfortable reminder that the concept 'socio-technical' provides us with as cultural geographers…

THIRD REMINDER

…and that is that, if we wish to take things seriously, we have to be prepared to put ourselves and our theories 'at risk' (Stengers 1997). For being willing to accept not just that technical is always already partially social (the easier move) but also that the social is always already partially technical (and, moreover, always has been; see Dobres 2000, Ingold 2000 and Lemonnier 1993) entails some pretty radical alterations in how we think and do cultural politics. Just as feminism has taught us that (formally) including women in the polity involves and requires not simply an expansion but a transformation of that polity, so the same applies for objects.

In other words, if we want to give objects their due (or, better, their due process: Latour 1999a), our politics have to become as impure as our world and thus a 'cosmopolitics', to use a notion recently revived and recast by philosopher of science Isabelle Stengers (1997; see also Latour 1999a). What this implies, among other things is, as literary critic William Paulson has convincingly argued (2001, 98), is that the task of inventing new 'forms of relations' between humans is inseparable from (and, indeed, in some sense at least dependent upon) inventing new 'types of encounter (and conviviality)' with other (non-human) Others (and vice versa). It is precisely this imperative that has seen those working with the concept both inside and outside geography move beyond the mere fact of socio-technicality in the direction – whether by a focus on 'modalities' (Stassart and Whatmore 2003), 'conduct' (Hinchliffe 2001), 'styles' (Bingham in preparation) or 'regimes' of 'delegation' (Latour 1996) and 'justification' (Boltanski and Thévenot 1991) – of exploring the better and worse ways in which non-humans have been, are or could be socialised into the collectives of peoples and things of which the world is comprised.

There are signs at the time of writing that the detour on which the socio-technical became geographical may be coming to an end, in the sense that the concerns of those who made it are becoming more widely shared elsewhere within and around cultural geography (to pick one stream, see Jackson 1999, Du Gay and Pryke 2001 and the special issue of *Economy and Society* in 2002 on 'the technological economy'). Whether that means that we have heeded our uncomfortable reminders and learnt our lessons is as yet unclear, but, either way, the final question that the concept 'socio-technical' leaves us with is whether we are collectively critical enough of ourselves to explore the possibility that to go forward we might have to make (with apologies to Latour 1999c) one more turn after the cultural turn.

KEY REFERENCES

Latour, B. 1993. *We Have Never Been Modern*. London, Harvester Wheatsheaf.

Law, J. ed. 1991. *A Sociology of Monsters*. Oxford, Blackwell.

Stengers, I. 2000. *The Invention of Modern Science*. Minneapolis, University of Minnesota Press.

OTHER REFERENCES

Akrich, M. 1993. A gazogene in Costa Rica, in P. Lemonnier ed. *Technological Choices: Transformation in Material Cultures since the Neolithic*. London, Routledge, 289–337.

Barry, A. 2001. *Political Machines: Governing a Technological Society*. London, Athlone.

Biagioli, M. ed. 1999. *The Science Studies Reader*. London, Routledge.

Bijker, W. 1995. Sociohistorical technology studies, in S. Jasanoff, G. Markle, J. Petersen and T. Pinch eds. *Handbook of Science and Technology Studies*. Sage, London, 229–256.

Bingham, N. 1996. Object-ions: from technological determinism towards geographies of relations, *Environment and Planning D: Society and Space*, 14, 6: 635–657.

Bingham, N. 1999. Unthinkable complexity: cyberspace otherwise, in M. Crang, P. Crang and J. May eds. *Virtual Geographies.* London, Routledge, 244–260.

Bingham, N. in preparation. Taking things slowly: Lessons from the GM controversy, for a special issue of *Economy and Society* on 'Reconstituting natures'.

Bingham, N., Valentine, G. and Holloway, S. 1999. Where do you want to go tomorrow: connecting children and the internet, *Environment and Planning D: Society and Space*, 17, 6: 655–672.

Bingham, N., Valentine, G. and Holloway, S. 2001. Life around the screen: re-framing young people's use of the internet, in N. Watson and S. Cunningham-Burley eds. *Reframing Bodies.* London, Palgrave Macmillan, 228–243.

Boltanski, L. and Thévenot, L. 1991. *De la justification: les economies de grandeur.* Paris, Gallimard.

Callon, M. ed. 1998. *The Laws of the Markets.* Oxford, Blackwell.

Deleuze, G. 1995. *Negotiations.* New York, Columbia University Press.

Dobres, M.A. 2000. *Technology and Social Agency.* Oxford, Blackwell.

Du Gay, P. and Pryke, M. eds. 2001. *Cultural Economy.* London, Sage.

Fischer, C. 1994. *America Calling: A Social History of the Telephone to 1940.* Berkeley, University of California Press.

Grint, K. and Woolgar, S. 1995. On some failures of nerve in constructivist and feminist analyses of technology, in R. Gill and K. Grint eds. *The Gender Technology Relation: Contemporary Theory and Research.* London, Taylor and Francis, 48–76.

Haraway, D. 1992. The promises of monsters: a regenerative politics for inappropriate/d Others, in L. Grossberg, C. Nelson and P. Treichler eds. *Cultural Studies.* London, Routledge, 295–337.

Hinchliffe, S. 1996. Technology, power and space – the means and ends of geographies of technology, *Environment and Planning D: Society and Space*, 14, 6: 659–682.

Hinchliffe, S. 2001. Indeterminancy in-decisions: science, politics, and policy in the BSE Crisis, *Transactions of the Institute of British Geographers*, 26, 2: 182–204.

Ingold, T. 2000. *The Perception of the Environment: Essays in Livelihood, Dwelling and Skill.* London, Routledge.

Jackson, P. 1999. Commodity cultures: the traffic in things, *Transactions of the Institute of British Geographers*, 24, 2: 95–108.

Jasanoff, S., Markle, G., Petersen, J. and Pinch, T. eds. 1995. *The Handbook of Science and Technology Studies.* London, Sage.

Latour, B. 1996. Social theory and the study of computerised work sites, in W. Orlikowski, G. Walsham, M. Jones and J. DeGross eds. *Information Technology and Changes in Organisational Work.* London, Chapman & Hall, 295–307.

Latour, B. 1999a. *Pandora's Hope: Essays on the Reality of Science Studies.* Cambridge, MA, Harvard University Press.

Latour, B. 1999b. Ein Ding ist ein thing – a philosophical platform for a Left (European) Party, *Soundings*, 12: 12–25.

Latour, B. 1999c. One more turn after the social turn…, in M. Biagioli ed. *The Social Studies Reader.* London, Routledge, 276–289.

Lemonnier, P. ed. 1993. *Technological Choices: Transformation in Material Cultures since the Neolithic.* London, Routledge.

Mol, A. 1993. What is new? Doppler and its Others: an empirical philosophy of investigations, in I. Löwy ed. *Medicine and Change: Historical and Sociological Studies of Medical Innovation.* Paris, Les Editions INSERM, 107–125.

Murdoch, J. 1997. Towards a geography of heterogeneous associations, *Progress in Human Geography*, 21, 3: 321–337.

Osborne, P. 1995. *The Politics of Time: Modernity and Avant-Garde.* London, Verso.

Paulson, W. 2001. *Literary Culture in a World Transformed: A Future for the Humanities.* Ithaca, Cornell University Press.

Serres, M. 1995. *Angels: A Modern Myth.* Paris, Flammarion.

Star, S. L. and Ruhleder, K. 1996. Steps towards an ecology of infrastructure: design and access for large information spaces, *Information Systems Research*, 7, 1: 111–134.

Stassart, P. and Whatmore, S. 2003. Metabolising risk: food scares and the un/re-making of Belgian beef, *Environment and Planning A*, 35, 3: 449–462.

Stengers, I. 1997. *Power and Invention*. Minneapolis, University of Minnesota Press.

Thrift, N. 1996. New urban eras and old Technological fears: reconfiguring the goodwill of electronic things, *Urban Studies*, 33, 8: 1463–1493.

Wenger, E. 1998. *Communities of Practice: Learning, Meaning, and Identity.* Cambridge, Cambridge University Press.

Whatmore, S. 2002. *Hybrid Geographies.* London, Sage.

Whatmore, S. and Thorne, L. 1997. Nourishing networks: alternative geographies of food, in D. Goodman and M. Watts eds. *Globalizing Food.* London, Routledge, 287–304.

— Cyborg Cultures —

Judith Tsouvalis

Imagine a world where the conceptual boundaries between entities/'things' or processes that you have come to perceive and treat as separate and distinct no longer make sense. A world where various parts of your body can be replaced by prostheses, artificial implants and animal organs to improve or prolong your life, raising the question: are you human, machine or animal? A world where your pet can be cloned to relieve your grief at its loss and plants genetically modified to fit your ideals of beauty, if not of taste. In this world, robots can help reduce your workload, and information about you circulates through the electronic networks and machines of banks and insurance and marketing companies, influencing and monitoring your lifestyle. You might frequent an internet chat room and assume a different identity and sexuality, keeping your 'true self' hidden for ever in the digital maze. For many of us, this world is already a reality; a world where 'common-sense' divisions between categories and concepts such as 'nature' and 'culture', 'human' and 'machine', 'she' and 'he' no longer make much sense. The things and processes they encompass and delineate have begun to mingle and merge. They have begun to proliferate at such rapid rates and into such unstable forms and temporal constellations and alliances as to defy the fixity that the boundaries of earlier meaning-making processes imposed on them. This is the world of the *cyborg*, 'a creature of social reality as well as a creature of fiction', as Donna Haraway (1994) described it in her influential 'manifesto for cyborgs in the mid-1980s'; a creature whose one defining characteristic is that it cannot be defined. Cyborgs elude and transgress boundaries; they destabilise meanings and taken-for-granted views of the world. They are, perpetually, on the move, and busily reconfigure the world as we know it, including our conceptions of it and of ourselves. For Haraway, by the late twentieth century we had all become 'chimeras, theorized and fabricated hybrids of machine and organism'. In other words, we had all become 'cyborgs' (Haraway 1994, 83; Haraway 1991). But how did we get here?

To understand how cyborg realities, fantasies and metaphors have come about, it is necessary to consider the social processes, dreams and nightmares that have given rise to both their actual and discursive production in the Western world. First, concerning their actual production, it is worth noting that the term 'cyborg' is itself a hybrid: the result of a fusion of the terms 'cybernetic' and 'organism' (a 'hybrid' can be defined as 'anything derived from heterogeneous sources or composed of elements of different or incongruous kinds' (Hables Gray 1995, 275). Cybernetics was founded in 1947 by the US mathematician Norbert Wiener, and initially it was concerned with the study of using feedback mechanisms in control systems to produce automatic processes. Gradually it developed into the science of systems and their self-organisation, -regulation and -reproduction, and the development in laboratories of inanimate objects that behaved like living systems. Such 'objects' nowadays include, among others, artificial limbs, heart pacemakers and auditory brainstem implants, as well as robots with sensors programmed to take decisions, robot toys and fully automated factory systems with decision-making machines that operate up to managerial level. The term 'cyborg' was coined in 1960 by Manfred E. Clynes and Nathan S. Kline from the Dynamic Simulation Laboratory at Rockland State Hospital in New York. Clynes and Kline were investigating how to enhance the bodily functions of human beings so as to enable them to adjust to space travel and extraterrestrial environments (Hables Gray 1995, 29–33). At the same time, psycho-pharmacology research on neural-chemical implants and telemetric measuring were also carried out at Rockland States Hospital. These areas of research were closely linked to the Cold War pursuit of the 1950s and 1960s, such as CIA-sponsored behavioural control research (Hables Gray 1995, xvi). Since then, real-world cyborgs have increased and multiplied at an ever-faster rate in the folds of the science and technology networks spun by late capitalism, transgressing many conceptual boundaries hitherto taken for granted: between uniqueness and replication (e.g. the cloning of organisms); randomness and predictability (e.g. foetal gender selection); animal and human (e.g. transgenic organ transplants); public and private (e.g. the patenting of DNA sequences); and life and death (e.g. post-mortem fertilisation) (Pepperell and Punt 2000, 82).

Yet cyborg fictions, our second concern, are far older than the twentieth-century creatures of social reality just described. They predate the space age, the Cold War and the digital era by nearly two centuries, and initially reflected the Romantic response to the possibilities and dangers posed by the scientific and technological discoveries and innovations made during the Industrial Revolution. Then, as now, they questioned the ruthless, supposedly modern and progressive, pursuits of human beings to gain power and domination over 'nature'. In Mary Shelley's *Frankenstein*, a novel published in 1818, we find what could be described as the first fictional cyborg – a being brought to live through the re-animation and electrification of previously deceased body parts. Portrayed as a 'monster' that turns against its creator, who, in the ghastly realisation of what he has done, abandons it to its fate, Frankenstein today stands as a metaphor for morally questionable scientific pursuits; it is commonly used to describe genetically modified organisms, especially food crops (also known as 'Frankenstein crops/foods'), and the detrimental effects they might have on their environment. In Fritz Lang's 1926 movie *Metropolis*, robotics enter the scene, and we see here the origins of the urban, industrial (and, also, first female) cyborg. Perhaps the most widely known twentieth-century fictitious cyborg belonging to this genre is the cyborg warrior Terminator, played by Arnold Schwarzenegger in *Terminator I* (1984) and *Terminator II* (1991). *Terminator II* is particularly noteworthy for its 'advanced' cyborg model, which the older cyborg version, Schwarzenegger, has to fight. Called a 'shape shifter', this cyborg can take on the physical characteristics of whoever or whatever it comes into contact with – be it organic or inorganic. It is a cyborg that is nearly indestructible (although Schwarzenegger does, of course, in the true fashion of the classical hero, manage to 'terminate' him/her/it in the end). Cyborgs have appeared in many other forms and guises in science fiction novels, movies and video games over the twentieth century (for a comprehensive overview Hables Gray 1995, 473–477), and have become fetishes of strength, sexuality and immortality, as well as immorality (as the products of irresponsible science). In a way a thoroughly modernist creation, cyborg fictions reflect a critical, one might even say postmodern, engagement with modernist Utopias and Enlightenment ideals and their associated conceptual systems.

Our third and central theme here are the ways in which the ontological and epistemological challenges posed by cyborgs – real or imagined – have been met by academia. The widespread introduction of the cyborg *metaphor* into geography, anthropology, political theory, cultural studies, sociology (of science) and philosophy owes much to Haraway's manifesto for cyborgs mentioned earlier (Haraway 1994). Writing from a socialist feminist perspective, Haraway uses the cyborg as a metaphor to highlight the arbitrariness of the divisions conceptually imposed between entities and processes she perceives as interrelated in complex ways. In other words, cyborgs for her stand for boundary transgression. In her cyborg manifesto, she describes three such boundary transgressions as particularly crucial: first, that between human and animal; second, that between animal/human (organism) and machine; and, third, that between the physical and the non-physical. The challenge posed by the cyborg metaphor to orthodox ontologies and epistemologies offers, for Haraway, a political strategy to undermine dominant (Western) philosophical and cultural constructions of 'the' world. In her article, gender constructions are the central focus. She also points out that, while actual cyborgs might still go largely unnoticed in today's society, they are produced in increasing numbers by vast techno-scientific networks that are powered by capital flows that look for a profit, if not, literally, for a kill (most cyborg technology is military in origin and employed for military ends, such as during the Gulf Wars). For Haraway, cyborgs thus challenge various traditions of Western science and politics; 'the tradition of racist, male-dominant capitalism; the tradition of progress; the tradition of the appropriation of nature as a resource for the productions of culture; the tradition of reproduction of the self from the reflections of the other' (1994, 83).

Just as real-world cyborgs continue to proliferate unabatedly within circuits of capital, science and technology, so do cyborg metaphors in various academic debates.

In geography, it has perhaps been used most creatively to destabilise the taken-for-granted dualism between 'nature' and 'culture'/'society' (Demeritt 1994; 2001). This dualism, which underpins the division of geography into 'physical' and 'human' geography, is increasingly questioned by geographers keen to find ways of doing justice to the complex interrelationships between them. Thus urban geographers have used the cyborg metaphor to argue against the common-sense notion of cities as unnatural (or as non-Nature) (e.g. Harvey 1996; Swyngedouw 1996; Kaika and Swyngedouw 2000; Gandy 2002).

The cyborg metaphor – and, related to it, that of the hybrid (Whatmore 1999) – has highlighted the fact that 'nature' and 'culture' are social constructs, built on the assumption of an ontologically pure state. It has also raised questions about the dualisms' ideological effects, such as the cross-conceptual linkages commonly made between 'nature', the 'natural' and the 'normal', and the 'unnatural', 'abnormal' and 'artificial'. The realisation that entities, processes, discourses and ideas cannot be understood unless considered in a relational fashion, and claims that we need a new language to describe these 'cyborg-realities', have become a central concern in geography (Harvey and Haraway 1995). As Erik Swyngedouw has put it (1999, 445), '[N]atural or ecological conditions and processes do not operate separately from social processes, and...the actually existing socionatural conditions are always the result of intricate transformations of pre-existing configurations that are themselves inherently natural and social.' One way in which this has been addressed has been through actor network theory (Castree and MacMillan 2001, 208–224, for a review).

Another area of geography where the cyborg metaphor has come to play a central role has been where questions of race, gender, sexuality and identity are of key importance. Blurring the boundaries of these concepts, the cyborg metaphor has challenged the taken-for-granted ways in which they are often regarded. It has also raised important questions about the politics that attempt to keep their meanings stable and unchanging. Hence, in what are sometimes referred to as 'geographies of subject formation', the cyborg metaphor (and, again, that of the 'hybrid') has provided an effective means for undermining and disrupting constructions of 'pure' and clearly bounded identities, including that of the 'self' and the 'Other'. As such, it is linked to wider discourses on subjectivity, including those on transnationalism and globalisation, and has been used in conjunction with other currently popular metaphors in geography, such as that of the nomad, that of third space and that of paradoxical space (Pile and Thrift 1995; Soja 1996). The cyborg metaphor has come to play an important role in identity politics, and has been taken up in many sub-fields of geography, including cultural geography, political geography and medical geography.

Similar questions and concerns as those outlined above have, in true cyborg fashion, found their way into many other academic disciplines. Their proliferation should be considered in relation to the wider shifts in thinking that came to play an important role in academic scholarship in the last few decades of the twentieth century: postmodernism, post-structuralism and postcolonialism. Cyborgologists now even talk of a post-human world (Hayles 1999). Such shifts in perception are no doubt due to material changes in our practices and surroundings, and, in spite of the positive impacts real-world cyborgs and cyborg metaphors have had on our thinking, it should perhaps not be forgotten that 'the cyborg issues specifically from the militarised, indeed permanently war-state based, industrial capitalism of World War 2 and the post World War 2 Cold War' (Harvey and Haraway 1995, 514).

KEY REFERENCES

Castree, N. and MacMillan, T. 2001. Dissolving dualisms: actor-networks and the reimagination of nature, in N. Castree and B. Braun eds. *Social Nature: Theory, Practice and Politics*. Oxford, Blackwell, 208–224.

Demeritt, D. 1994. The nature of metaphors in cultural geography and environmental history, *Progress in Human Geography*, 18: 163–185.

Hables Gray, C. ed. 1995. *The Cyborg Handbook*. London, Routledge.

Haraway, D. 1994. A manifesto for cyborgs: science, technology, and socialist feminism in the 1980s, in S. Seidman ed. *The Postmodern Turn: New Perspectives on Social Theory*. Cambridge, Cambridge University Press, 82–115.

Haraway D. and Harvey, D. 1995. Nature, politics and possibilities: a debate and discussion with David Harvey and Donna Haraway, *Environment and Planning D: Society and Space*, 13: 507–527.

Pile, S. and Thrift, N. eds. 1995. *Mapping the Subject: Geographies of Cultural Transformation*. London, Routledge.

Swyngedouw, E. 1996. The city as a hybrid: on the nature, society and cyborg urbanisation, *Capitalism, Nature, Socialism*, 7, 2: 65–80.

OTHER REFERENCES

Demeritt, D. 2001. Being constructive about nature, in N. Castree and B. Braun eds. *Social Nature: Theory, Practice and Politics*. Oxford, Blackwell, 22–40.

Gandy, M. 2002. *Concrete and Clay: Reworking Nature in New York City*. Cambridge, MA, MIT Press.

Haraway, D. 1991. *Simians, Cyborgs and Women: The Reinvention of Nature*. London, Free Association Books.

Harvey, D. 1996. *Justice, Nature and the Geography of Difference*. Oxford, Blackwell.

Hayles, N.K. 1999. *How We became Posthuman: Virtual Bodies in Cybernetics, Literature, and Informatics*. Chicago, University of Chicago Press.

Kaika, M. and Swyngedouw, E. 2000. Fetishising the modern city: the phantasmagoria of urban technological networks, *International Journal of Urban and Regional Research*, 24, 1: 120–138.

Pepperell, R. and Punt, M. 2000. *The Postdigital Membrane: Imagination, Technology and Desire*. Bristol, Intellect Books.

Soja, E. W. 1996. *Thirdspace*. Oxford, Blackwell.

Swyngedouw, E. 1999. Modernity and hybridity: nature, regeneracionismo, and the production of the Spanish waterscape, 1890–1930, *Annals of the Association of American Geographers*, 89, 3: 443–465.

Whatmore, S. 1999. Hybrid geographies, in D. Massey, J. Allen and P. Sarre eds. *Human Geography Today*. Cambridge, Polity, 22–40.

CONTRIBUTORS

Editors

David Atkinson: Senior Lecturer in Geography, University of Hull

Peter Jackson: Professor of Human Geography, University of Sheffield

David Sibley: Visiting Research Fellow, School of Geography, University of Leeds

Neil Washbourne: Senior Lecturer in Media Studies, Leeds Metropolitan University

Contributors

David Atkinson: Senior Lecturer in Geography, University of Hull

Nick Bingham: Lecturer in Human Geography, Open University

Alison Blunt: Reader in Geography, Queen Mary, University of London

Alastair Bonnett: Professor of Social Geography, University of Newcastle

Ian Cook: Senior Lecturer in Geography, University of Birmingham

Denis Cosgrove: Professor of Geography, University of California, Los Angeles

Mike Crang: Reader in Geography, University of Durham

Tim Cresswell: Professor of Human Geography, University of Wales, Aberystwyth

Sally Eden: Senior Lecturer in Geography, University of Hull

Steven Flusty: Assistant Professor in Geography, York University, Toronto

Anne-Marie Fortier: Senior Lecturer in Sociology, Lancaster University

Steve Hinchliffe: Senior Lecturer in Geography, Open University

Phil Hubbard: Reader in Urban Social Geography, University of Loughborough

Peter Jackson: Professor of Human Geography, University of Sheffield

Mark Johnson: Senior Lecturer in Social Anthropology, University of Hull

Andrew Jonas: Professor of Human Geography, University of Hull

Robyn Longhurst: Senior Lecturer in Geography, University of Waikato, New Zealand.

James Martin: Senior Lecturer in Politics, Goldsmiths College, University of London.

Don Mitchell: Professor of Geography, Syracuse University, New York State

Katharyne Mitchell: Professor of Geography and Simpson Professor in the Public Humanities, University of Washington

Darren O'Byrne: Senior Lecturer in Sociology and Human Rights, University of Surrey, Roehampton

Suzanne Reimer: Lecturer in Geography, University of Southampton

David Sibley: Visiting Research Fellow, School of Geography, University of Leeds

Ola Söderström: Professeur de Géographie, Université de Neuchâtel

Ulf Strohmayer: Professor of Human Geography, National University of Ireland, Galway

Gearóid Ó Tuathail/Gerard Toal: Professor of Government and International Affairs, Virginia Polytechnic Institute and State University

Judith Tsouvalis: Research Associate, School of Geography and the Environment, University of Oxford

Neil Washbourne: Senior Lecturer in Media Studies, Leeds Metropolitan University

Aidan While: Lecturer in Town and Regional Planning, University of Sheffield.

Robert Wilton: Assistant Professor in Geography, McMaster University, Hamilton, Canada

Index